808.8
Gr   Green, Jonathon
         Sweet nothings.

W9-AJQ-087

SWEET NOTHINGS

Love Quotes for Lovers & Other Fools

JONATHON GREEN

QUILL *New York* 1984

Acknowledgments

As ever, a number of people have been kind enough to offer their advice and aid in the compilation of my collection of quotations. At the risk of ingratitude, I shall ask them all to be satisfied with a blanket vote of thanks for their welcome additions to my files.

More specifically, I would like to thank those concerned with the technical side of *Sweet Nothings*. To wit: Susan Ford; Lucien and Gabriel Green; my agent, Leslie Gardner; my editors in London and New York, Colin Honnor and Kristina Lindbergh; my copy editor in New York, Bruce Giffords; and Sally Payne, who created order from three thousand file cards.

Copyright © 1984 by Jonathon Green

Grateful acknowledgment is made for permission to quote from the following:

A Sleep of Prisoners by Christopher Fry. Copyright 1951 by Christopher Fry. Reprinted by permission of Oxford University Press.

The Lady's Not for Burning by Christopher Fry. Copyright 1948 by Christopher Fry. Reprinted by permission of Oxford University Press.

"Symptoms of Love" by Robert Graves. Copyright © 1961 by Robert Graves. Reprinted by permission of A.P. Watt Ltd.

Library of Congress Catalog Card Number: 84-60210

ISBN: 0-688-03662-7 (pbk)

Printed in the United States of America

First Quill Edition

1 2 3 4 5 6 7 8 9 10

BOOK DESIGN BY MARIA EPES

Contents

Introduction

Sweet Nothings is a collection of some three thousand–odd quotations about love. Sexual love, that is, or at least the love between men and women, with occasional forays into homosexuality, but excluding love for children, animals, one's country, and a variety of similar abstracts that manage to claim some part of our affections.

Herein are gathered many old favorites as well as a selection of thoughts and deliberations on love that have yet to acquire the patina of centuries of popular use, but which stand pertinent nonetheless in the modern, less obviously romantic world. Ranking just after or, more optimistically, on a par with money, love obsesses much of the world and naturally the material upon which a compiler may draw is massive in its extent. No book of quotations should set itself up as the last word in definitive collections, and while I hope that the bulk of love quotes that everyone knows, half-knows, or vaguely remembers are represented here, I acknowledge that there may be errors and omissions, few of which I can honestly dismiss as deliberate. This is my ninth book of quotations and like its predecessors it remains unashamedly idiosyncratic. To this end, along with the chestnuts, there are many inclusions that stray beyond love's more familiar expressions, particularly when one approaches our own decade.

One point struck me forcibly as I compiled this book, and it will become glaringly obvious to anyone who reads it. Irrespective of one's personal stand on feminism, it is impossible to ignore that a grotesque percentage of these quotations are repetitively and actively hostile towards women. It is not simply the comments on marriage, a traditional battleground drawing views that spring barely altered from the less subtle sitcom stereotypes. Even the exponents of more affectionate views of love, its more romantic and positive facets, stand firm upon the clichés and truisms of centuries of steamroller masculine opinions. The old parade troops by, reviewed to one's regret even by the smoothest of tongues: the virgin and the whore, the mother, the castrator . . . Witty, of course, and I wouldn't have included them had I too not found them enjoyable, but there is something depressing and devastating about their endless continuity. I have attempted to redress the balance—and in particular would recommend the admirable Helen Rowland, an American who stands alongside her peers Dorothy Parker and Edna St. Vincent Millay. Indeed, even their bittersweet verses accept female weakness, while Rowland's acid defiance has no time for such resignation. Of late the feminists have joined the battle, but more in polemic than on love. I have found what I could, but there seems to be precious little space for wit, let alone a sense of humor or detachment, in a crusade. The material simply isn't there, and a catalog of masculine failings in no way makes up for their having already existed.

I have been collecting quotations, at first sporadically, but with an increasingly consuming obsession, for many years. This means, unfortunately, that their dating and attribution is nothing if not variable. Where possible I have included the full name, source and date of my originator and his or her quotation. More often, I fear, the reader must bear with a less immaculate reference, the result either of ignorance, forgetfulness or the condition of whatever scrap of paper I was using as a filing system at the time.

Love is . . . a many-splendored thing, a hole in the heart, sex with some meaning, a bitch. Like beauty, often its instigator, it's a very personal thing. The thirteen hundred or so speakers, writers, poets, singers, wits, and the rest whose words make up these pages put their opinions on offer. That it persists in making the world go round is hard for me, at least, to believe. That it lies, in all its varied and I trust appealing aspects, at the heart of this book, I cannot, of course, deny.

JONATHON GREEN

1. The Power and the Glory

Love is not to be reason'd down, or lost/In high ambition or a thirst of greatness;/'Tis second life, it grows into the soul/Warms every vein, and beats in every pulse.
Joseph Addison, Cato, 1713

Mysterious love, uncertain treasure,/Hast thou more of pain or pleasure . . ./Endless torments dwell about thee:/Yet who would live, and live without thee!
Joseph Addison, Rosamond

Our love is like the misty rain that falls softly—but floods the river.
African proverb

The only big difference in the game of love over the last few thousand years is that they've changed trumps from clubs to diamonds.
Anonymous

It's love, it's love that makes the world go round.
Anonymous, Chansons Nationals et Populaires de France, Vol. 2

Love is friendship set to music.
Anonymous, quoted in The Times of London, St. Valentine's Day messages, 1982

Love is, above all, the gift of oneself.
    Jean Anouilh, *Ardèle*, 1948

Love has the quality of informing almost everything—even one's work.
    Sylvia Ashton-Warner, *Myself*, 1967

Among those whom I like or admire, I can find no common denominator, but among those I love, I can: all of them make me laugh.
    W. H. Auden, *The Dyer's Hand*, 1962

The speaking in a perpetual hyperbole is comely in nothing but love.
    Francis Bacon

Nuptial love maketh mankind; friendly love perfecteth it; wanton love corrupteth and embaseth it.
    Francis Bacon, *Essays*, 1597

Ask not of me, love, what is love?/Ask what is good of God above—/Ask of the great sun what is light—/Ask what is darkness of the night—/Ask of sin what may be forgiven—/Ask what is happiness of Heaven—/Ask what is folly of the crowd—/Ask what is fashion of the shroud—/Ask what is sweetness of thy kiss—/Ask of thyself what beauty is.
    P. J. Bailey, *Festus: A Large Party and Entertainment*, 1839

The sweetest joy, the wildest woe is love.
    P. J. Bailey, *Festus: A Love and Garden*, 1839

In matters of love, there is nothing more persuasive than a courageous stupidity.
    Honoré de Balzac

Love is the poetry of the senses.
> Honoré de Balzac, *The Physiology of Marriage*, 1829

The crowning glory of loving and being loved is that the pair make no real progress; however far they have advanced into the enchanted land during the day they must start again from the frontier next morning.
> J. M. Barrie, *Tommy and Grizel*, 1900

If thou wilt ease thine heart/Of love and all its smart/ Then sleep, dear, sleep.
> Thomas Beddoes, *Death's Jest Book*, 1850

Love is the wine of existence.
> Henry Ward Beecher, *Proverbs from Plymouth Pulpit*, 1887

Love is more just than justice.
> Henry Ward Beecher, *Proverbs from Plymouth Pulpit*, 1887

Oh, what a dear ravishing thing is the beginning of an Amour!
> Aphra Behn, *The Emperor of the Moon*, 1687

When all of the remedies and all of the rhetorical armour has been dropped, the absence of love in our lives is what makes them seem raw and unfinished.
> Ingrid Bengis, *Combat in the Erogenous Zone*, 1973

Love is like mushrooms. One doesn't know if they belong to the good or bad sort until it is too late.
> Tristan Bernard

There is no fear in love, but perfect love casteth out fear.
> The Bible, I John

Better is a dinner of herbs where love is, than a stalled ox and hatred therewith.
The Bible, Proverbs

Many waters cannot quench love, neither can the floods drown it: if a man would give all the substance of his house for love, it would utterly be contemned.
The Bible, Song of Solomon

Never seek to tell thy love/Love that never told can be/For the gentle wind does move/Silently, invisibly.
William Blake, Never Seek to Tell Thy Love

GEORGE SEGAL: Love is a miracle. It's like a birthmark. You can't hide it.
Blume in Love, script: Paul Mazursky, 1973

Something there is that moves me to love and I/Do know I love, but know not how or why.
Alexander Brome, Love's Without Reason, 1661

Love and ambition (I have heard men say) admit no fellowship.
Richard Brome, Love-sick Court, 1659

If thou must love me, let it be for naught/Except for love's sake only.
Elizabeth Barrett Browning, Sonnets from the Portuguese, 1850

Take away love, and our earth is a tomb.
Robert Browning, Fra Lippo Lippi, 1863

O lyric Love, half angel and half bird/And all a wonder and a wild desire.
Robert Browning, The Ring and the Book, 1868–1869

Eternal love doth keep/In his complacent arms, the earth, the air, the deep.

William Cullen Bryant, *The Ages*, 1821

Love dies only when growth stops.

Pearl S. Buck, *To My Daughters with Love*, 1967

Love has no thought of self!/Love buys not with the ruthless usurer's gold/The loathsome prostitution of a hand/Without a heart! Love sacrifices all things/To bless the thing it loves!

Edward Bufwer-Lytton, *The Lady of Lyons*, 1838

To see her is to love her,/And love but her for ever;/For nature made her what she is,/And ne'er made sic anither!

Robert Burns, *O, Saw Ye Bonnie Lesley*, 1792

Passion is the element in which we live; without it we but vegetate.

Lord Byron

Friendship may often, and does, grow into love, but love never subsides into friendship.

Lord Byron

Love will find its way/Through paths where wolves would fear to prey.

Lord Byron, *The Giaour*, 1813

Friendship is Love without his wings!

Lord Byron, *Hours of Idleness*, 1807

A poet without love were a physical and metaphysical impossibility.

Thomas Carlyle, *Critical and Miscellaneous Essays*, 1840

Love is ever the beginning of Knowledge as fire is of light.
  Thomas Carlyle, Essays: Death of Goethe, 1840

Love is greater than illusion, and as strong as death.
  Alberto Casella, Death Takes a Holiday, 1955

Love is the word used to label the sexual excitement of the young, the habituation of the middle-aged and the mutual dependence of the old.
  John Ciardi

Love's the weightier business of mankind.
  Colley Cibber, She Would and She Would Not, 1702

The art of love? It's knowing how to join the temperament of a vampire to the discretion of an anemone.
  E. M. Cioran, Syllogismes de l'Amertume, 1952

ORSON WELLS: A toast, Jedediah—to love on my terms. Those are the only terms anybody ever knows, his own.
  Citizen Kane, script: Herman Mankiewicz, Orson Wells, 1941

All thoughts, all passions, all delights,/Whatever stirs this mortal frame,/All are ministers of Love,/And feed his sacred flame.
  Samuel Taylor Coleridge, Love, 1799

Friendship often ends in love, but love in friendship—never.
  Charles Caleb Colton, Lacon, 1825

To love a thing means wanting it too live.
  Confucius, Analects, 6th century B.C.

If there's delight in love, 'tis when I see/That heart which others bleed for, bleed for me.
William Congreve, The Way of the World, 1700

We are first aware of love when we realize we are dependent on someone else for our happiness.
Jilly Cooper, The British in Love, 1980

Love alone/is the true seed of every merit in you/and of all acts for which you must atone.
Dante, The Divine Comedy, c. 1300

What the world needs now is love, sweet love/It's the only thing that there's just too little of.
Hal David, What the World Needs Now Is Love, 1965

You need someone to love you while you're looking for someone to love.
Shelagh Delaney, A Taste of Honey, 1959

Love maketh a wit of a fool.
Charles Dibdin, The Quaker, 1777

Unable are the Loved to die/For Love Is Immortality.
Emily Dickinson

It has been said that love robs those who have it of their wit, and gives it to those who have none.
Denis Diderot, Paradoxe sur le Comédien, 1773–1778

Many are the names applied to friendship; but where youth and beauty enter in, there friendship is rightly called love and is held to be the fairest of the gods.
Dio Chrysostom, Third Discourse on Kingship, 1493

The gratification of the senses soon becomes a very small part of that profound and complicated sentiment which we call Love. Love, on the contrary, is an universal thirst for a communion, not merely of the senses, but of our whole nature, intellectual, imaginative and sensitive. He who finds his antitype, enjoys a love perfect and enduring; time cannot change it, distance cannot remove it; the sympathy is complete.

>Benjamin Disraeli, *Henrietta Temple*, 1837

We are all born for love; it is the principle of existence and its only end.

>Benjamin Disraeli, *Sibyl*, 1845

For love, all love of other sights controls/And makes one little room, an everywhere.

>John Donne, *The Good-Morrow*, in *Collected Works*, 1633

Love, all alike, no season knows, nor clime/Nor hours, days, months, which are the rags of time.

>John Donne, *The Sun Rising*, in *Collected Works*, 1633

Where there is no love there is no sense either.

>Feodor Dostoevski, *Notes from Underground*, 1864

With love one can live even without happiness.

>Feodor Dostoevski, *Notes from Underground*, 1864

Love is love's reward.

>John Dryden, *Palamon and Arcite*, 1700

Love is the only effective counter to death.

>Maureen Duffy, *Wounds*, 1969

Love, love, love. All th' wurruld is love. Soft an' sweet an'
sticky it covers th' globe.
    Finley Peter Dunne, Mr. Dooley on Making a Will, 1919

Seas have their source, and so have shallow springs;/And
love is love in beggars and kings.
    Edward Dyer, The Lowest Trees Have Tops, c. 1600

I ain't lookin' to compete with you/Beat or cheat or mis-
treat you/Simplify you, classify you/Deny, defy, or crucify you/All I really want to do/Is, baby, be friends with
you.
    Bob Dylan, All I Really Want to Do, 1964

BURT LANCASTER: And what is love? Love is the morning
and the evening star.
    Elmer Gantry, script: Richard Brooks, 1960

No love can be bound by oath or covenant to secure it
against a higher love.
    Ralph Waldo Emerson, Essays, 1841

In the last analysis, love is only the reflection of a man's
own worthiness from other men.
    Ralph Waldo Emerson, Essays, 1841

Give all to love;/Obey thy heart;/Friends, kindred,
days,/Estate, good fame,/Plans, credit, and the Muse—
/Nothing refuse.
    *Ralph Waldo Emerson, Give All to Love, in Collected Works,
1846*

Love is the bright foreigner, the foreign self.
    Ralph Waldo Emerson, Journals, 1849

Love is the great enemy of Christian morality. The virtue of pride, which was once the beauty of mankind, has given place to that fount of all ugliness, Christian humility. Love, as Rimbaud said, must be reinvented.
  Max Ernst, Max Ernst, 1967

Venus, thy eternal sway/All the race of men obey.
  Euripides, Austice, 5th century B.C.

Love must not touch the marrow of the soul./Our affections must be breakable chains that we/can cast them off or tighten them.
  Euripides, Hippolytus, 428 B.C.

'Tis love that makes me bold and resolute,/Love that can find a way where path there's none,/Of all the gods the most invincible.
  Euripides, Hippolytus, 428 B.C.

Oh love! oh love! whose shafts of fire/Invade the soul with sweet surprise,/Through the soft dews of young desire/Trembling in beauty's azure eyes!
  Euripides, Hippolytus, 428 B.C.

Love teaches letters to a man unlearn'd.
  Euripides, Stheneboea, 5th century B.C.

Love: a word properly applied to our delight in particular kinds of food; sometimes metaphorically spoken of the favourite objects of all our appetites.
  Henry Fielding

Love is the blossom where there blows/Every thing that lives or grows.
  Giles Fletcher, Christ's Victory, 1610

Love is life's end (an end, but never ending);/All joys, all sweets, all happiness, awarding;/Love is life's wealth (ne'er spent, but ever spending);/More rich by giving, taking by discarding;/Love's life's reward, rewarded in rewarding.

Phineas Fletcher, Britain's Ida, 1628

Love's tongue is in the eyes.

Phineas Fletcher, Piscatory Eclogues, 1771

If you would be loved, love and be lovable.

Benjamin Franklin, Poor Richard's Almanack, 1755

Belief in the existence of other human beings as such is love.

French philosopher

Love is not to be trifled with.

French proverb

Love makes the time pass. Time makes love pass.

French proverb

A combination of exclusive attachment and credulous obedience is in general among the characteristics of love.

Sigmund Freud, Complete Works, 1955

. . . the peculiar state of being in love, a state suggestive of neurotic compulsion, which is thus traceable to an impoverishment of the ego as regards libido in favor of the love-object.

Sigmund Freud, Complete Works, 1955

Even in its caprices the usage of language remains true to some kinds of reality. Thus it gives the name "love" to a great many kinds of emotional relationship which we too group together theoretically as love; but then again it feels a doubt whether this love is real, true, actual love, and so hints at a whole scale of possibilities within the range of the phenomena of love.

   Sigmund Freud, Complete Works, 1955

Love is derived from the capacity of the ego to satisfy some of its instinctual impulses auto-erotically by obtaining organ-pleasure. It is originally narcissistic, then passes over on to objects, which have been incorporated into the extended ego, and expresses the motor efforts of the ego towards these objects as sources of pleasure.

   Sigmund Freud, Complete Works, 1955

Being in love consists of a flowing-over of ego-libido onto the object. It has the power to remove repressions and reinstate perversions. It exalts the sexual object into a sexual ideal. Since, with the object type (or attachment type), being in love occurs in virtue of the fulfillment of infantile conditions for loving, we may say that whatever fulfills that condition is idealized.

   Sigmund Freud, Complete Works, 1955

Love is the art of freedom, never that of domination.

   Erich Fromm, The Art of Loving, 1956

Love is union with somebody, or something, outside oneself, under the condition of retaining the separateness and integrity of one's own self.

   Erich Fromm, The Sane Society, 1955

Try thinking of love, or something/Amor vincit insomnia.

   Christopher Fry, A Sleep of Prisoners, 1950

Love, the itch, and a cough cannot be hid.

   Thomas Fuller, Gnomologia, 1732

Love is imminent in nature, but not incarnate.
  Richard Garnett

Thou canst not pray to God without praying to Love, but
mayest pray to Love without praying to God.
  Richard Garnett, De Flagello Myrteo

To love is to admire with the heart; to admire is to love
with the mind.
  Théophile Gautier

For Love can beauties spy/In what seem faults to every
common eye.
  John Gay, Trivia, 1716

What we call love is the desire to awaken and to keep
awake in another's body, heart and mind, the responsibility of flattering, in our place, the self of which we are
not very sure.
  Paul Geraldy, L'Homme et L'Amour, 1951

It is the special quality of love not to be able to remain
stationary, to be obliged to increase under pain of diminishing.
  André Gide, The Counterfeiters, 1926

Love is a platform upon which all ranks meet.
  W. S. Gilbert, H.M.S. Pinafore, 1878

But to love is quite another thing: it is to will an object for
itself, to rejoice in its beauty and goodness for themselves,
and without respect to anything other than itself.
  *Etienne Gilson, The Spirit of Medieval Philosophy, Gifford Lec-
tures, 1931–1932*

Love is the irresistible desire to be desired irresistibly.
  Louis Ginsberg, 1968

Love does not dominate, it cultivates.
    Johann Wolfgang von Geothe, 1790

Love grants in a moment/What toil can hardly achieve in an age.
    Johann Wolfgang von Goethe, Torquato Tasso

Love is a universal migraine/A bright stain on the vision/Blotting out reason.
    Robert Graves, Collected Poems, 1961

Love is a lock that linketh noble minds,/Faith is the key that shuts the spring of love.
    Robert Greene, Alcida, 1617

Ah, what is love? It is a pretty thing,/As sweet unto a shepherd as a king,/And sweeter too,/For kings have cares that wait upon a crown,/And cares can make the sweetest love to frown.
    Robert Greene, The Shepherd's Wife's Song

Love is . . . the drug which makes sexuality palatable in popular mythology.
    Germaine Greer, The Female Eunuch, 1970

Every theory of love, from Plato down, teaches that each individual loves in the other sex what he lacks in himself.
    G. Stanley Hall

Knowledge is the parent of love; wisdom, love itself.
    J. C. and A. W. Hare, Guesses at Truth, 1827

Love is a transitive verb.
    Harry S. Haskins, Meditations in Wall Street

Love is that condition in which the happiness of another person is essential to your own.
  Robert A. Heinlein, *Stranger in a Strange Land*, 1961

Love and a red nose cannot be hid.
  Thomas Holcroft, *Duplicity*

Love is the true price of love.
  George Herbert, *Jacula Prudentum*, 1651

Love rules his kingdom without a sword.
  George Herbert, *Jacula Prudentum*, 1651

Love: a transitory derangement of all the five senses. The chemistry of attraction.
  Oliver Herford, John Clay, *Cupid's Cyclopedia*, 1910

Love is a circle that doth restless move/In the same sweet eternity of love.
  Robert Herrick, *Love, What It Is*, 1648

Love . . . is a telescope given us, just for once, by God, to reveal to us wonders and glories hidden indeed from the unaided eye, but none the less real and glorious for that.
  James Hinton

Love is a conflict between reflexes and reflections.
  Magnus Hirschfeld, *Sex in Human Relationships*, 1935

No love so true as love that dies untold.
  Oliver Wendell Holmes, Sr., *The Mysterious Illness*

The supreme happiness of life is the conviction that we are loved.
  Victor Hugo, *Les Misérables*, 1862

Love is the magician, the enchanter, that changes worthless things to joy, and makes right-royal kings and queens of common clay. It is the perfume of that wondrous flower, the heart, and without that sacred passion, that divine swoon, we are less than beasts: but with it, earth is heaven and we are gods.

R. G. Ingersoll, Works, 1930

It is no doubt very tolerable, finite or creaturely love to love one's own in another, to love another for his conformity to one's self: but nothing can be in more flagrant contrast with the creative Love, all whose tenderness ex vi termini must be reserved only for what intrinsically is most bitterly hostile and negative to itself.

Henry James, quoted in Collected Papers of Charles Sanders Peirce

Love is like the measles; we all have to go through it. Also like the measles we take it only once.

Jerome K. Jerome, The Idle Thoughts of an Idle Fellow, 1889

It is hard for the human soul not to love something, and our mind must of necessity be drawn to some kind of affection.

Saint Jerome, letter

Love's like the measles—all the worse when it comes late in life.

Douglas Jerrold, Wit and Opinions, 1859

Love is only one of many passions . . . and has no great influence on the sum of life.

Samuel Johnson, Works, 1761

We must not ridicule a passion which he who never felt never was happy, and he who laughs at never deserves to feel.
Samuel Johnson, *Miscellanies*

Love doesn't make the world go round. Love is what makes the ride worthwhile.
Franklin P. Jones

As selfishness and complaint pervert and cloud the mind, so love with its joy clears and sharpens the vision.
Helen Keller, *My Religion*, 1927

Love is a sport in which the hunter must contrive to have the quarry in pursuit.
Alphonse Kerr

People think love is an emotion. Love is good sense.
Ken Kesey

Love begins with love; friendship, however warm, cannot change to love, however mild.
Jean de La Bruyère

True love is the ripe fruit of a lifetime.
Alphonse de Lamartine, *Graziella*, 1862

Where love finds the soul he neglects the body, and only turns to it in his idleness as to an afterthought. Its best allurements are but the nuts and figs of the divine repast.
Walter Savage Landor, *Imaginary Conversations*, 1824–1829

Love has become a four letter word.
Fritz Lang

By the accident of fortune a man may rule the world for a time, but by virtue of love he may rule the world forever.
Lao Tze, *The Simple Way*, 6th century B.C.

What the bloom is on fruit, the charm of novelty is to love; it imparts a luster which is easily effaced and which never returns.
La Rochefoucauld, *Maxims*, 1665

It is with true love as it is with ghosts; everyone talks of it, but few have seen it.
La Rochefoucauld, *Maxims*, 1665

There is only one kind of love, but there are a thousand imitations.
La Rochefoucauld, *Maxims*, 1665

You must always be a-waggle with love.
D. H. Lawrence, *Bibbles*, 1932

Love should be practiced like Lent, secretly and dumbly.
Paris Leary, *A Controversy of Poets*, 1965

Waters are lost, and fires will die;/But love alone can fate defy.
Nathaniel Lee, *Theodosius*, 1680

Love doesn't just sit there, like a stone, it has to be made, like bread; remade all the time, made new.
Ursula K. LeGuin, *The Lathe of Heaven*, 1971

Love never dies of starvation, but often of indigestion.
Ninon de L'enclos, *L'Esprit des Autres*

And in the end the love you take/Is equal to the love you make.

John Lennon, Paul McCartney, The End

Love is a force . . . it is not a result, it is a cause. It is not a product, it produces. It is a power, like money or steam or electricity. It is valueless unless you can give something else by means of it.

Anne Morrow Lindbergh, Locked Rooms and Open Doors, 1974

People talk about love as though it were something you could give, like an armful of flowers.

Anne Morrow Lindbergh, Locked Rooms and Open Doors, 1974

There is no harvest for the heart alone/The seed of love must be/Eternally/Resown.

Anne Morrow Lindbergh, The Unicorn and Other Poems, 1956

O, there is nothing holier, in this life of ours, than the first consciousness of love,—the first fluttering of its silken wings.

Henry Wadsworth Longfellow, Hyperion, 1839

Love keeps the cold out better than a cloak./It serves for food and raiment.

Henry Wadsworth Longfellow, The Spanish Student, 1844

JENNIFER JONES: Oh Mark, we both know that even the fat, ugly people in this world believe that being in love makes them beautiful and justifies everything.

Love Is a Many-Splendored Thing, script: John Patrick, 1955

That love for one, from which there doth not spring/Wide love for all, is but a worthless thing.

James Russell Lowell, Sonnet 3, 1840

As love knoweth no laws, so it regardeth no conditions.
  John Lyly, *Euphues*, 1578

Th'important business of your life is love.
  George Lyttelton, *Advice to a Lady*, 1733

Delicacy is to love what grace is to beauty.
  Mme. de Maintenon, *Maximes*, c. 1700

The ecstasy of religion, the ecstasy of art and the ecstasy of love are the only things worth thinking about or experiencing.
  Don Marquis, *The Almost Perfect State*, 1927

Affection is created by habit, community of interests, convenience and the desire of companionship. It is a comfort rather than an exhilaration.
  W. Somerset Maugham, *The Summing Up*, 1938

We receive love—from our children as well as others—not in proportion to our demands or sacrifices or needs, but roughly in proportion to our own capacity to love.
  Rollo May, *Man's Search for Himself*, 1953

Love is the triumph of imagination over intelligence.
  H. L. Mencken

Duty does not have to be dull. Love can make it beautiful and fill it with life.
  Thomas Merton, *The Sign of Jonas*, 1953

Love is not all: it is not meat nor drink/Nor slumber nor a roof against the rain;/Nor yet a floating spar to men that sink.
  Edna St. Vincent Millay, *Fatal Interview*, 1931

He that would eat of love must eat it where it hangs.
> Edna St. Vincent Millay, *The Harp-Weaver and Other Poems*, 1923

Love refines/The thoughts, and heart enlarges, hath his seat/In reason, and is judicious, is the scale/By which to heavenly love thou mayest ascend.
> John Milton, *Paradise Lost*, 1667

Love is a fool who knows not what he is saying.
> Molière, *Le Dépit Amoureux*, 1656

Love, for too many men in our time, consists of sleeping with a seductive woman, one who is properly endowed with the right distribution of curves and conveniences and one upon whom a permanent lien has been acquired through the institution of marriage.
> Ashley Montagu, *The Natural Superiority of Women*, 1954

Love is nothing else but an insatiate thirst of enjoying a greedily desired object.
> Michel de Montaigne, *Essays*, 1588

One of the glories of society is to have created woman where Nature made a female, to have created a continuity of desire where Nature only thought of perpetuating the species; in fine, to have invented love.
> George Moore, *Impressions*, 1913

And the love that loves the love that loves the love that loves the love that loves to love the love that loves to love the love that loves.
> Van Morrison, *Madame George*

Love can't always do work. Sometimes it just has to look into the darkness.
> Iris Murdoch, *The Nice and the Good*, 1968

Love does not express itself on command; it cannot be called out like a dog to its master—merely because one thinks one needs to see it. Love is autonomous, it obeys only itself.
> Robert C. Murphy, *Psychotherapy Based on Human Longing*, 1960

To love, that's the point—what matters whom?/What does the bottle matter provided we can be drunk?
> Alfred de Musset, *Premières Poésies*, 1852

I find that love in its highest—in its most spiritual form is a passion so grossly out of proportion to the dimensions of life that it can only be defined, as Plato says, as "a desire for the eternal possession" of the beloved object—for his or her ever-growing perfection and bliss; while removal by death, if no reunion be looked for, at once reduces this life to an act of endurance alone.
> F.W.H. Myers, *Fragments of Inner Life*, 1904

The ivy clings to the first tree it meets. This, in a few words, is the story of love.
> Napoleon

Love is an emotion experienced by the many and enjoyed by the few.
> George Jean Nathan, *The Autobiography of an Attitude*, 1925

Love is the emotion that a woman feels always for a poodle dog and sometimes for a man.
> George Jean Nathan, *The Theater, the Drama, the Girls*, 1921

Love is more afraid of change than destruction.
> Friedrich Nietzsche, *Miscellaneous Maxims and Options*, 1879

GRETA GARBO: Why must you bring in wrong values? Love is a romantic designation for a most ordinary biological—or shall we say chemical—process. A lot of nonsense is talked and written about it.
> *Ninotchka*, script: Charles Brackett, Billy Wilder, Walter Reisch, 1939

[Love]: A game of secret, cunning stratagems in which only the fools who are fated to lose reveal their true aims or motives—even to themselves.
> Eugene O'Neill, *More Stately Mansions*, 1964

Youth's for an hour/Beauty's a flower/But love is the jewel that wins the world.
> Moira O'Neill, *Songs of the Glens of Antrim*, 1901

If you'd be loved, be worthy to be loved.
> Ovid, *The Art of Love*

Love is a naked child: do you think he has pockets for money?
> Ovid, *Loves*

Love is universal, and love is easy to merchandise.
> Warner Pagliara, *Esquire*, 1971

'Tis that delightsome transport we can feel/Which painters cannot paint, nor words reveal,/Nor any art we know of can conceal.
> Thomas Paine, *What Is Love?*

Love is not the dying moan of a distant violin—it's the triumphant twang of a bed spring.

    S. J. Perelman

TONY RANDALL: Love isn't an option, it's a chemical reaction. We've never even kissed—well, they didn't hit the moon with the first missile shot, either.

    Pillow Talk, script: *Stanley Shapiro, Maurice Richlin, 1959*

[Love is] the joy of the good, the wonder of the wise, the amazement of the gods; desired by those who have no part in him, and precious to those who have the better part in him.

    Plato, Symposium, c. 380 B.C.

Spice a dish with love and it pleases every palate.

    Plautus, Casina, 3rd century B.C.

Let Wealth, let Honour, wait the wedded dame,/August her deed, and sacred be her fame;/Before true passion all those views remove;/Fame, Wealth, and Honour! what are you to Love?

    Alexander Pope, Eloisa to Abelard, 1717

Love is purely a creation of the human imagination . . . the most important example of how the imagination continually outruns the creature it inhabits.

    Katherine Anne Porter, quoted in Contemporary Novelists, 1976

Love . . . is a projection of that maternal or paternal cannibalism which desires to hug what belongs to it, even unto death.

    John Cowper Powys, The Meaning of Culture

Love is space and time made directly perceptible to the heart.
Marcel Proust

. . . to love must and can only be an appendix to life, it must certainly not form its substance.
Nelly Ptaschkina, Diary, 1919

Love is not dumb. The heart speaks many ways.
Jean Racine, Britannicus, 1669

It is no longer a heat concealed in my blood, it is Venus herself grasping her prey.
Jean Racine, Phèdre, 1677

Yet what is Love, good shepherd, sain?/It is a sunshine mixed with rain.
Sir Walter Raleigh, Now What Is Love?, c. 1600

Love is the common denominator.
Alain Resnais, New York Herald Tribune, 1963

Love consists in this, that two solitudes protect and border and salute each other.
Rainer Maria Rilke, Letters to a Young Poet, 1904

To be loved means to be consumed. To love is to give light with inexhaustible oil. To be loved is to pass away, to love is to endure.
Rainer Maria Rilke, The Notebooks of Malte Laurids Brigge, 1910

Were it not for love,/Poor life would be a ship not worth the launching.
Edwin Arlington Robinson, Tristram, 1927

One makes mistakes, that is life. But it is never quite a mistake to have loved.
> Romain Rolland, *Summer*, 1923

The giving of love is an education in itself.
> Eleanor Roosevelt

Love is a mystery which, when solved, evaporates. The same holds for music.
> Ned Rorem, *Music from Inside Out*, 1967

Love is like a rose, the joy of all the earth . . ./Love is like a lovely rose, the world's delight.
> Christina Rossetti, *Hope*, in *Collected Poems*, 1882

Love is two minutes fifty-two seconds of squishing noises. It shows your mind isn't clicking right.
> Johnny Rotten (John Lydon)

Love is what you feel for a pussy cat or a dog. It doesn't apply to humans and if it does it just shows how low you are. It shows your intelligence isn't clicking.
> Johnny Rotten (John Lydon), 1977

What is love? Two souls and one flesh. Friendship? Two bodies and one soul.
> Joseph Roux, *Meditations of a Parish Priest*, 1886

Trust thou thy Love; if she be proud, is she not sweet?/ Trust thou thy Love: if she be mute, is she not pure?/Lay thou thy soul full in her hands, low at her feet;—/Fail, sun and breath!—Yet for thy peace she shall endure.
> John Ruskin, *Trust Thou Thy Love*, in *Selected Poems*, 1882

Love should be a tree whose roots are deep in the earth, but whose branches extend into heaven.
  Bertrand Russell, *Marriage and Morals*, 1929

Life has taught us that love does not consist in gazing at each other, but in looking outwards together in the same direction.
  Antoine de Saint-Exupéry, *Airman's Odyssey*, 1939

The invisible path of gravity liberates the stone. The invisible slope of love liberates man.
  Antoine de Saint-Exupéry, *Flight to Arras*, 1942

Love is an egotism of two.
  Antoine de Salle

True love's the gift which God has given/To man alone beneath the heaven . . ./It is the secret sympathy,/The silver link, the silken tie,/Which heart to heart, and mind to mind,/In body and in soul can bind.
  Sir Walter Scott, *The Lay of the Last Minstrel*, 1805

Love is the god of gods, and no god is greater than love.
  Johannes Secundus, *Basia*

Love means never having to say you're sorry.
  Erich Segal, *Love Story*, 1970

There's beggary in the love that can be reckoned.
  William Shakespeare, *Anthony and Cleopatra*, 1606–1607

But love, first learned in a lady's eyes,/Lives not alone immured in the brain,/But, with the motion of all elements,/Courses as swift as thought in every power,/And gives to every power a double power,/Above their functions and their offices./It adds a precious seeing to the eye;/A lover's eyes will gaze an eagle blind;/A lover's ears will hear the lowest sound,/When the suspicious head of theft is stopp'd:/Love's feeling is more soft and sensible/Than are the tender horns of cockled snails:/Love's tongue proves dainty Bacchus gross in taste,/For valour, is not love a Hercules? . . . And when Love speaks, the voice of all the gods/Makes heaven drowsy with the harmony./Never durst poet touch a pen to write/Until his ink were temper'd with Love's sighs.

    William Shakespeare, Love's Labour's Lost, 1595

Love looks not with the eyes but with the mind,/And therefore is wing'd Cupid painted blind.

    William Shakespeare, A Midsummer Night's Dream, 1595–1596

Love is not love/Which alters when it alteration finds,/Or bends with the remover to remove:/O, no! it is an ever-fixed mark,/That looks on tempests and is never shaken;/It is a star to every wandering bark,/Whose worth's unknown, although his height be taken./Love's not Time's fool, though rosy lips and cheeks/Within his bending sickle's compass come;/Love alters not with his brief hours and weeks,/But bears it out even to the edge of doom./If this be error and upon me proved,/I never writ, nor no man ever lov'd.

    William Shakespeare, Sonnet 116, 1593–1596

O! how this spring of love resembleth/The uncertain glory of an April's day.

    William Shakespeare, Two Gentlemen of Verona, 1594–1595

Love is a spirit all compact of fire.

    William Shakespeare, Venus and Adonis, 1593

Love is the salt of life.

    John Sheffield, Ode on Love, 1721

Familiar acts are beautiful through love.
Percy Bysshe Shelley, Prometheus Unbound, 1820

Love is but the discovery of ourselves in others, and the delight in the recognition.
Alexander Smith, Dreamthorp, 1863

The love of the famous, like all strong passions, is quite abstract. It's intensity can be measured mathematically and it is independent of persons.
Susan Sontag, The Benefactor, 1963

One word/Frees us of all the weight and pain of life:/ That word is love.
Sophocles, Oedipus at Colonus, 401 B.C.

Love: that self-love a deux.
Mme. de Staël

Love is nothing but the fear of mortal man at the thought of solitude.
Theodor Storm, Im Schloss

Is it not by love alone that we succeed in penetrating to the very essence of a being?
Igor Stravinsky, An Autobiography, 1936

Love in its essence is spiritual fire.
Emanuel Swedenborg, True Christian Religion, 1771

Love, as told by the seers of old,/Comes as a butterfly tipped with gold./Flutters and flies in sunlit skies,/ Weaving round hearts that were one time cold.
Algernon Charles Swinburne, Song, in Complete Works, 1904

Love's gift cannot be given/it waits to be accepted.
Rabindranath Tagore, Fireflies, 1928

Let the dead have the immortality of fame, but the living the immortality of love.
Rabindranath Tagore, Stray Birds, 1916

For love's humility is love's true pride.
Bayard Taylor, Poet's Journal, 1863

Love is the only gold.
Alfred, Lord Tennyson, Becket, 1884

Love is the master of the wisest. It is only fools who defy him.
William Thackeray, Miscellanies

It is best to love wisely, no doubt; but to love foolishly is better than not to be able to love at all.
William Thackeray, Pendennis, 1848

Love is a great thing, a great good in every wise; it alone maketh light every heavy thing and beareth evenly every uneven thing.
Thomas à Kempis, The Imitation of Christ, 1426

Why should we kill the best of passions, love?/It aids the hero, bids ambition rise/To nobler heights, inspires immortal deeds,/Even softens brutes, and adds a grace to virtue.
James Thomson, Sophonisba, 1730

There is no remedy for love but to love more.
Henry David Thoreau, Journal, 1839

Love is what you've been through with somebody.
James Thurber, *Life*, 1960

One cannot be strong without love./For love is not an irrelevant emotion; it is the blood of life, the power of re-union of the separated.
Paul Tillich, *The Eternal Now*, 1963

If so many men, so many minds, certainly so many hearts, so many kinds of love.
Leo Tolstoy, *Anna Karenina*, 1873–1876

Love is like those shabby hotels in which all the luxury is in the lobby.
Paul Jean Toulet, *Le Carnet de M. du Paur, Homme Public*, 1898

The absolute value of love makes life worth while, and so makes Man's strange and difficult situation acceptable. Love cannot save life from death; but it can fulfill life's purpose.
Arnold J. Toynbee, *Saturday Review*, 1969

You are as prone to love as the sun is to shine; it being the most delightful and natural employment of the Soul of Man: without which you are dark and miserable. For certainly he that delights not in Love makes vain the universe, and is of necessity to himself the greatest burden.
Thomas Traherne, *Centuries of Meditations*, 1908

Love is an act of endless forgiveness, a tender look which becomes a habit.
Peter Ustinov, *Christian Science Monitor*, 1958

For love is but the heart's immortal thirst/To be completely known and all forgiven.
Henry Van Dyke, *Love*, in *Collected Poems*, 1930

Men learned in the humanities are of the opinion that love is of four kinds, viz.

1. Love acquired by continual habit.
2. Love resulting from the imagination.
3. Love resulting from belief.
4. Love resulting from the perception of external objects.

 Vatsyayana, Kama Sutra

Love is a warm druggedness, a surrender of the will and mind to inchoate feelings of Togetherness. Thought is the enemy; any exercise of mind betrays Love. . . .
 Gore Vidal, Partisan Review, 1959

Love still is Nature's truth, and Death her lie.
 Theodore Watts-Dunton, The Coming of Love, 1897

The emotion, the ecstasy of love, we all want, but God spare us the responsibility.
 Jessamyn West, Love Is Not What You Think, 1959

Love is a human emotion that wisdom will never conquer.
 Percy White, Mr. Strudge

The love that no return doth crave/To knightly levels lifts the slave.
 John Greenleaf Whittier, The Henchman, 1888

Ah, better to love in the lowliest cot/Than pine in a palace alone.
 G. J. Whyte-Melville, Chastelar

It is love, and not German philosophy, that is the true explanation of this world, whatever may be the explanation of the next.

Oscar Wilde, *An Ideal Husband*, 1899

Love is an illusion.

Oscar Wilde, *The Picture of Dorian Gray*, 1891

Love is an energy which exists of itself. It is its own value.

Thornton Wilder, *Time*, 1958

Love is a talkative passion.

Bishop Wilson

Love . . . this fond imprisonment.

Thomas Wolfe, *You Can't Go Home Again*, 1947

PAULETTE GODDARD: Okay, sister, but my idea of love is that love isn't ashamed of nothing.

The Woman, script: Anita Loos, Jane Murfin, 1939

People who are sensible about love are incapable of it.

Douglas Yates

No woman ever loved her husband for his intellect or his admirable principles—or friend his friend—*love is the instinctive movement of personality.*

J. B. Yeats, *Letters to His Son, W. B. Yeats, and Others*, 1944

2. The Sorrow and the Pity

Yes, loving is a painful thrill,/And not to love more painful still;/But oh, it is the worst of pain,/To love and not be lov'd again.
  Anacreon, Odes, 6th century B.C.

Love's pleasure lasts but a moment; love's pain can last a lifetime.
  Anonymous French song

Oh, love is real enough, you will find it some day, but it has one archenemy—and that is life.
  Jean Anouilh, Ardèle, 1948

CAROLYN JONES: Just say you love me. You don't have to mean it.
  The Bachelor Party, script: Paddy Chayefsky, 1957

It is impossible to love and to be wise.
  Francis Bacon, Essays, 1625

To love without criticism is to be betrayed.
  Djuna Barnes, Nightwood, 1937

I say that the supreme and only pleasure in love lies in the certainty of doing evil.
  Charles Baudelaire

What is irritating about love is that it is a crime that requires an accomplice.
Charles Baudelaire

Love is the desire to prostitute oneself. There is, indeed, no exalted pleasure that cannot be related to prostitution.
Charles Baudelaire, Intimate Journals, 1887

Oh, love will make a dog howl in rhyme.
Francis Beaumont, John Fletcher, The Queen of Corinth, in Comedies and Tragedies, 1647

That desert of loneliness and recrimination that men call love.
Samuel Beckett, The New York Review of Books, 1971

Love, like Reputation, once fled, never returns more.
Aphra Behn, History of the Nun, 1689

Binding the hearts of gods and men,/Dishonest, wanton, and seducing she/Rules whom she will, both where and when.
Beroaldus, epigram

Love goes a-fishing with the rod Desire/Baiting his hook with Woman for delight./Attracted by the flesh the men-fish bite./He hauls them in and cooks them in his fire.
Bhartrihari, Love Goes A-fishing

Love, n: A temporary insanity curable by marriage or by the removal of the patient from the influences under which he incurred the disorder. This disease, like *caries* and many other ailments, is prevalent only among civilized races living under artificial conditions; barbarous nations breathing pure air and eating simple food enjoy immunity from its ravages. It is sometimes fatal, but more frequently to the physician than to the patient.

> Ambrose Bierce, *The Devil's Dictionary*, 1911

Love and sorrow twins were born/On a shining showery morn.

> Thomas Blacklock, *The Graham*, 1774

To fall in love is to create a religion that has a fallible god.

> Jorge Luis Borges, *Other Inquisitions*, 1952

Pity the selfishness of lovers; it is brief, a forlorn hope; it is impossible.

> Elizabeth Bowen, *The Death of the Heart*, 1938

Love is like fire. . . . Wounds of fire are hard to bear; harder still are those of love.

> Hjalmar Hjorth Boyesen, *Gunnar*, 1875

Thank God everything is quickly over—both love and grief.

> Bertolt Brecht, *Nannas Lied*

On the edge of the sea/A whale lay dying/And among its sighs it said/In love there is always pain.

> Gerald Brenan, *Thoughts in a Dry Season*, 1979

The first sigh of love is the last of wisdom.

> Antoine Bret, *École Amoureuse*, 1773

When first we met we did not guess/That love would prove so hard a master.

> Robert Bridges, *When First We Met We Did Not Guess*, 1912

Analysis kills love, as well as other things.

> John Brown, *Horae Subsecivoe*, 1858

Whoso loves/Believes the impossible.
Elizabeth Barrett Browning, Aurora Leigh, 1856

Such ever was love's way: to rise, it stoops.
Robert Browning, A Death in the Desert, 1863

Of course it's possible to love a human being if you don't
know them too well.
Charles Bukowski, Notes of a Dirty Old Man, 1969

Love is the business of the idle, but the idleness of the
busy.
Edward Bulwer-Lytton, Rienzi, 1835

Love indeed (I may not deny) first united provinces, built
cities, and by a perpetual generation makes and preserves
mankind; but if it rage it is no more love, but burning lust,
a disease, frenzy, madness, hell . . . It subverts kingdoms,
overthrows cities, towns, families: mars, corrupts, and
makes a massacre of men: thunder and lightning, wars,
fires, plagues, have not done that mischief to mankind, as
this burning lust, this brutish passion.
Robert Burton, The Anatomy of Melancholy, 1621

God is love, I daresay. But what a mischievous devil love
is.
Samuel Butler, Notebooks, 1912

When love's delirium haunts the glowing mind/Limping
Decorum lingers far behind.
Lord Byron, Answer to Some Elegant Verses Sent by a Friend

O love! what is it in this world of ours/Which makes it fatal to be loved? Ah, why/With cypress branches has thou wreathed thy bowers/And made they best interpreter a sigh!
> Lord Byron, *Don Juan*, 1819–1824

When love is not madness, it is not love.
> Pedro Calderón de la Barca, *El mayor monstruo los celos*, 1790

Love! the surviving gift of Heaven,/The choicest sweet of Paradise,/In life's else bitter cup distilled.
> Thomas Campbell, *Ode to the Memory of Burns*, in *Collected Works*, 1810

Give me more love or more disdain/The torrid or the frozen zone/Bring equal ease unto my pain/The temperate affords me none.
> Thomas Carew, *Mediocrity in Love Rejected*, in *Collected Poems*, 1870

PAUL NEWMAN: You don't know what love means. To you, it's just another four-letter word.
> *Cat on a Hot Tin Roof*, script: Richard Brooks, James Poe, 1958

Love, Arthur, is a poodle's chance of attaining the infinite, and personally I have my pride.
> Louis-Ferdinand Céline, *Journey to the End of the Night*, 1932

Love, in present day society, is just the exchange of two imaginary pictures, and the contact of one epidermis with another.
> Nicholas-Sébastien Chamfort, *Maximes et Pensées*, 1796

Love is like an epidemic—the more one is afraid, the more vulnerable to it one is.
> Nicholas-Sébastien Chamfort, *Maximes et Pensées*, 1796

A death for love's no death, but martyrdom.
George Chapman, *Revenge for Honour*, 1613

O love, all other pleasures/Are not worth thy pains.
Charleval, *Ballade*

Love is a thing aye full of busy dread.
Geoffrey Chaucer, *Troilus and Criseyde*, 1374

Love is either the shrinking remnant of something which
was once enormous; or else it is part of something which
will grow in the future into something enormous. But in
the present it does not satisfy. It gives much less than one
expects.
Anton Chekhov

It takes time and deeds, and this involves trust, it involves
making ourselves vulnerable to each other, to strip ourselves naked, to become sitting ducks for each other—and
if one of the ducks is shamming, then the sincere duck
will pay in pain—but the deceitful duck, I feel, will be the
loser.
Eldridge Cleaver, *Soul on Ice*, 1968

Love's despair is but Hope's pining ghost!
Samuel Taylor Coleridge, *The Visionary Hope*, in *Complete Poetic
Works*, 1828

What a recreation it is to be in love! It sets the heart aching so delicately, there's no taking a wink of sleep for the
pleasure of the pain.
George Colman the younger, *The Mountaineers*, 1794

Love is a spaniel that prefers even punishment from one
hand to caresses from another.
Charles Caleb Colton

Love, like death, a universal leveller of mankind.
William Congreve, *The Double Dealer*, 1694

Love's but a frailty of the mind/When 'tis not with ambition join'd.
Williu ˄ Congreve, *The Way of the World*, 1700

The truth of every passion wants some pretence to make it live.
Joseph Conrad, *Lord Jim*, 1900

How wise are they that are but fools in love!
Jo Cooke, *How a Man May Choose a Good Wife*, 1610

Love is a tyrant sparing none.
Pierre Corneille, *Le Cid*, 1636

When love is satisfied, all its charm is gone.
Pierre Corneille, *Don Juan*

They love too much that die for love.
Randall Cotgrave, *Dictionary: Mourir*, 1611

It is obviously quite difficult to be no longer loved when we are still in love, but it is incomparably more painful to be loved when we ourselves no longer love.
Georges Courteline, *La Philosophie de Georges Courteline*, 1917

A mighty pain to love it is/And 'tis a pain that pain to miss/But of all pains, the greatest pain/It is to love, but love in vain.
Abraham Cowley, *From Anacreon*, 1656

. . . love/a burnt match skating in a urinal.
Hart Crane, *The Bridge*, in *Collected Poems*, 1938

Love is a sickness full of woes/All remedies refusing/A plant that with most cutting grows/Most barren with best using/Why so?/More we enjoy it, more it dies/If not enjoy'd, it sighing cries/Hey ho.
Samuel Daniel, Hymen's Triumph, 1615

Love, who forgives no beloved for loving.
Dante

Ideal love is a lie put about by poets.
Alphonse Daudet, Tartarin sur les Alpes

Lovers derive their pleasures from their misfortunes.
Diogenes

Truly love can be called thrice a brigand: he is wakeful, reckless and strips us bare.
Diophanes of Myrina

Whoever loves, if he do not propose/The right true end of love, he's one that goes/To sea for nothing but to make him sick.
John Donne, Elegies, in Collected Works, 1633

Love is a growing or full constant light/And his first minute, after noon, is night.
John Donne, A Lecture upon the Shadow

That reason of all unreasonable actions.
John Dryden, The Assignation, 1672

And love's the noblest frailty of the mind.
John Dryden, The Indian Emperor, 1665

Pains of love be sweeter far/Than all other pleasures are.
John Dryden, Tyrannic Love, 1669

The pain of love is the pain of being alive. It's a perpetual wound.
>   Maureen Duffy, *Wounds*, 1969

Love Is Just a Four-Letter Word
>   Bob Dylan, *song title*

Love compels cruelty/To those who do not understand love.
>   T. S. Eliot, *The Family Reunion*, 1939

Ah Love! Could thou and I with fate conspire/To grasp this sorry scheme of things entire/Would not we shatter it to bits—and then/Re-mould it nearer to the Heart's Desire.
>   Edward FitzGerald, *The Rubáiyát of Omar Khayyám*, 1859

Pleasure of love lasts but a moment/Pain of love lasts a lifetime.
>   Jean Pierre Claris de Florian, *Celestine*, 1842

Love is the tyrant of the heart; it darkens/Reason, confounds discretion; deaf to counsel,/It runs a headlong course to desperate madness.
>   John Ford, *The Lover's Melancholy*, 1629

The heart errs like the head; its errors are not any the less fatal, and we have more trouble getting free of them because of their sweetness.
>   Anatole France, *Little Pierre*, 1918

Try to reason about love, and you will lose your reason.
>   French proverb

The credulity of love is the most fundamental source of authority.
Sigmund Freud

There is hardly any activity, any enterprise, which is started with such tremendous hopes and expectations, and yet which fails so regularly, as love.
Erich Fromm, The Art of Loving, 1956

It seems that it is madder never to abandon one's self than often to be infatuated; better to be wounded, a captive and a slave, than always to walk in armor.
Margaret Fuller, Summer on the Lakes, 1844

Love and pride stock Bedlam.
Thomas Fuller, Gnomologia, 1732

Even as love crowns you so shall he crucify you. Even as he is for your growth so is he for your pruning.
Khalil Gibran, The Prophet, 1923

A life without love, without the presence of the beloved, is nothing but a mere magic-lantern show. We draw out slide after slide, swiftly tiring of each, and pushing it back to make haste for the next.
Johann Wolfgang von Goethe, Elective Affinities, 1809

Friendship is a disinterested commerce between equals; love, an abject intercourse between tyrants and slaves.
Oliver Goldsmith, The Good-Natured Man, 1768

Love, love, love—all the wretched cant of it, masking egotism, lust, masochism, fantasy under a mythology of sentimental postures, a welter of self-induced miseries and joys, blinding and masking the essential personalities in the frozen gestures of courtship, in the kissing and the

dating and the desire, the compliments and the quarrels which vivify its barrenness.
Germaine Greer, The Female Eunuch, 1970

Love is a hole in the heart.
Ben Hecht, Winkelberg, 1950

If two people love each other there can be no happy end to it.
Ernest Hemingway

Love is something that hangs up behind the bathroom door and smells of Lysol.
Ernest Hemingway, To Have and Have Not, 1937

To be loved is very demoralizing.
Katharine Hepburn on ABC-TV, 1975

Love's a man of war,/And can shoot,/And can hit from far.
George Herbert, Discipline, 1633

Delusion: hope's dressmaker.
Oliver Herford, John Clay, Cupid's Cyclopedia, 1910

Love's of itself too sweet; the best of all/Is when love's honey has a dash of gall.
Robert Herrick, Another of Love, 1648

To love is to know the sacrifices which eternity exacts from life.
John Oliver Hobbes, School for Saints, 1896

Pity is love when grown into excess.
Sir Robert Howard, The Vestal Virgin, 1665

Love is an excuse for its own faults.
Italian proverb

The word "love" bridges for us those chasms of momentary indifference and boredom which gape from time to time between even the most ardent lovers.
Aldous Huxley, *The Olive Tree*, 1937

It must be love, it's a bitch.
Mick, Jagger, Keith Richards, *Bitch*

Self-love depressed, becomes self-loathing.
Sally Kempton, *Esquire*, 1970

Perfect love means to love the one through whom one became unhappy.
Sören Kierkegaard

. . . this strange, intoxicating distemper of love, which I have heard described as a disease . . . surely one affection above all others one would pray to be innoculated with.
John Knyreton, *Diary of a Surgeon in the Year 1750–51*

Love between the sexes is a sin in theology, a forbidden intercourse in jurisprudence, a mechanical insult in medicine, and a subject philosophy has no time for.
Karl Kraus

Love is a strange master. Happy is he who knows love and its wounds only by report.
Jean de La Fontaine, *Le Lion Amoureux*, 1668

I believe [love] doesn't exist, save as a word; a sort of wailing phoenix that is really the wind in the trees.
D. H. Lawrence, *Letters*

How alike are the groans of love to those of the dying.
Malcolm Lowry, *Under the Volcano*, 1947

No-one has ever loved anyone, the way everyone wants to be loved.
Mignon McLaughlin

Love is simple to understand if you haven't got a mind soft and full of holes. It's a crutch, that's all, and there isn't a one of us doesn't need a crutch.
Norman Mailer, *Barbary Shore*, 1951

He who loves the more is the inferior and must suffer.
Thomas Mann, *Death in Venice*, 1903

Love, the mild servant, makes a drunken master.
John Masefield, *The Widow in the Bye Street*, 1912

Love is not always blind and there are few things that cause greater wretchedness than to love with all your heart someone who you know is unworthy of love.
W. Somerset Maugham, *The Summing Up*, 1938

Love is only the dirty trick played on us to achieve continuation of the species.
W. Somerset Maugham, *A Writer's Notebook*, 1949

Human love is often but the encounter of two weaknesses.
François Mauriac, *Colin, Where Is Your Brother?*, 1962

Love is the mind's strong physic, and the pill/That leaves the heart sick and o'erturns the will.
Thomas Middleton, *Blurt*, 1602

Love is all in fire, and yet is ever freezing;/Love is much in winning, yet is more in losing:/Love is ever sick, and

yet is never dying;/Love is ever true and yet is ever lying;/Love does doat in liking, and is mad in loathing;/Love indeed is anything, yet indeed is nothing.
   Thomas Middleton, Blurt, 1602

This have I known always: Love is no more/Than the wide blossom which the wind assails,/Than the great tide that treads the shifting shore,/Strewing fresh wreckage gathered in the gales;/Pity me that the heart is slow to learn/What the swift mind beholds at every turn.
   Edna St. Vincent Millay, The Harp-Weaver and Other Poems, 1923

Love's grimaces bear a strong resemblance to the truth.
   Molière, La Malada Imaginaire, 1673

The only victory in love is flight.
   Napoleon, Maxims, 1804–1815

There is always some madness in love. But there is also always some reason in madness.
   Friedrich Nietzsche, Thus Spake Zarathustra, 1883–1891

Anxiety is love's greatest killer. It makes others feel as you might when a drowning man holds onto you. You want to save him, but you know he will strangle you with his panic.
   Anaïs Nin, Diaries, 1968

There are as many pangs in love as shells upon the shore.
   Ovid, The Art of Love

Hell's afloat in lover's tears.
   Dorothy Parker

Drink and dance and laugh and lie/Love, the reeling midnight through/For tomorrow we shall die!/(But, alas, we never do.)
> Dorothy Parker, *Death and Taxes*, 1931

Four be the things I'd be better without—/Love, curiosity, freckles and doubt.
> Dorothy Parker, *Enough Rope*, 1927

The moods of love are like the wind,/And none knows whence or why they rise.
> Coventry Patmore, *The Angel in the House*, 1854–1862

A broken hand works, but not a broken heart.
> Persian proverb

In love, it is the victim who looks most like a hero.
> Charles Plisnier, *False Passports*

It is a mistake to speak of a bad choice in love, since, as soon as a choice exists, it can only be bad.
> Marcel Proust

There can be no peace of mind in love, since the advantage one has secured is never anything but a fresh starting point for further desires.
> Marcel Proust, *Remembrance of Things Past: Within a Budding Grove*

Those whose suffering is due to love are, as we say of certain invalids, their own physicians.
> Marcel Proust, *Remembrance of Things Past: Within a Budding Grove*

A god could hardly love and be wise.
> Publilius Syrus, *Moral Sayings*, 1st century B.C.

Love, like a tear, rises in the eye and falls upon the breast.
Publilius Syrus, Moral Sayings, 1st century B.C.

To love is to allow abuse.
Pierre Reverdy, En Vrac, 1956

Love, our subject/we've trained it like ivy to our walls/ baked it like bread in our ovens/worn it like lead at our ankles.
Adrienne Rich

Human nature is so constructed that it gives affection most readily to those who seem least to demand it.
Bertrand Russell, The Conquest of Happiness, 1930

To fear love is to fear life, and those who fear life are already three parts dead.
Bertrand Russell, Marriage and Morals, 1929

Who promised love should be happiness? Nature may have some other end.
Mark Rutherford, Last Pages from a Journal, 1915

Every little girl knows about love. It is only her capacity to suffer because of it that increases.
Françoise Sagan, Daily Express, 1957

Love does not cause suffering: what causes it is the sense of ownership, which is love's opposite.
Antoine de Saint-Exupéry, The Wisdom of the Sands, 1948

Not to believe in love is a great sign of dullness. There are some people so indirect and lumbering that they think all real affection must rest on circumstantial evidence.
George Santayana, The Life of Reason, 1905–1906

Love, whether sexual, parental, or fraternal, is essentially sacrificial, and prompts a man to give his life for his friends.

George Santayana, The Life of Reason, 1905–1906

And love is loveliest when embalm'd in tears.

Sir Walter Scott, The Lady of the Lake, 1810

I wonder why love is so often equated with joy, when it is everything else as well—devastation, balm, obsession, granting and receiving excessive value, and losing it again. It is recognition, often, of what you are not, but might be. It sears and heals. It is beyond pity and above law. It can seem like truth.

Florida Scott-Maxwell, The Measure of My Days, 1972

Love is merely a madness; and, I tell you, deserves a dark house and a whip as madmen do: and the reason why they are not so punished and cured is that the lunacy is so ordinary that the whippers are in love too.

William Shakespeare

Cupid: his disgrace is to be called boy; but his glory is to subdue men.

William Shakespeare

PHEBE: Good shepherd, tell this youth what 'tis to love.
SILVIUS: It is to be all made of sighs and tears . . ./It is to be all made of faith and service . . ./It is to be all made of fantasy/All made of passion, and all made of wishes;/All adoration, duty and observance;/All humbleness, all patience, and impatience;/All purity, all trial, all obeisance.

William Shakespeare, As You Like It, 1598–1600

Love is a familiar; Love is a devil; there is no evil angel but Love.
William Shakespeare, Love's Labour's Lost, 1595

By heaven, I do love; and it hath taught me to rhyme, and to be melancholy.
William Shakespeare, Love's Labour's Lost, 1595

Ay me! For aught that I ever could read/Could ever hear by tale or history/The course of true love never did run smooth.
William Shakespeare, A Midsummer Night's Dream, 1595–1596

Love is a smoke raised with the fume of sighs;/Being purged, a fire sparkling in lovers' eyes;/Being vex'd, a sea nourish'd with lovers' tears:/What is it else? a madness most discreet,/A choking gall and a preserving sweet.
William Shakespeare, Romeo and Juliet, 1595

She never told her love,/But let concealment, like a worm i' the bud,/Feed on her damask cheek.
William Shakespeare, Twelfth Night, 1600

How wayward is this foolish love/That, like a testy babe, will scratch the nurse/And presently all humbled kiss the rod.
William Shakespeare, The Two Gentlemen of Verona, 1594–1595

Love's a mighty lord;/And hath so humbled me, as I confess/This is no woe to his correction,/Nor to his service no such joy on earth./Now no discourse, except it be of love;/Now can I break my fast, dine, sup, and sleep,/Upon the very naked name of love.
William Shakespeare, The Two Gentlemen of Verona, 1594–1595

Of honey and of gall in love there is store:/The honey is much, but the gall is more.
  Edmund Spenser, The Shepheardes Calender, 1579

Love is the *fart*/Of every heart/It pains a man when 'tis kept close/And others doth offend when 'tis let loose.
  Sir John Suckling

KATHARINE HEPBURN: The Venus flytrap—a devouring organism—aptly named for the goddess of love.
  Suddenly Last Summer, script: Gore Vidal, Tennessee Williams, 1959

Pain melted in tears and was pleasure;/Death tingled with blood and was life.
  Algernon Charles Swinburne, Masque of Queen Bersabe, in Complete Works, 1904

For though I know he loves me/Tonight my heart is sad/His kiss was not so wonderful/As all the dreams I had.
  Sara Teasdale, Collected Poems, 1911

O, beauty, are you not enough?/Why am I crying after love?
  Sara Teasdale, Rivers to the Sea, 1915

A mastiff dog/May love a puppy cur for no more reason/Than that the twain have been tied up together.
  Alfred, Lord Tennyson, Queen Mary, 1875

He that shuts Love out, in turn shall be/Shut out from Love, and on her threshold lie/Howling in the outer darkness.
  Alfred, Lord Tennyson, 1832

For you to ask advice on the rules of love is no better than to ask advice on rules of madness.
Terence, *The Eunuch*, 161 B.C.

There is no living in love without suffering.
Thomas à Kempis, *The Imitation of Christ*, 1426

Love is the child of illusion and the parent of disillusion; love is consolation in desolation; it is the sole medicine against death, for it is death's brother.
Miguel de Unamuno, *The Tragic Sense of Life*, 1921

Human nature being what it is, legend and literature are full to overflowing with tragic lovers—there's hardly a couple who don't end up horizontal, bloody and fruitless. . . . Why should that be? What is the point of suffering if you can't survive to enjoy the relief?
Peter Ustinov, *Romanoff and Juliet*, 1961

God created man, and finding him not sufficiently alone, gave him a companion to make him feel his solitude more.
Paul Valéry, *Tel Quel*, 1943

What they call love is nothing but yearning sorrow.
Walther von der Vogelweide

Everybody winds up kissing the wrong person goodnight.
Andy Warhol, *From A to B and Back Again*, 1975

Love is a sour delight, a sugar'd grief,/A living death, an ever-dying life;/A breach of Reason's law, a secret thief,/A sea of tears, an everlasting strife;/A bait for fools, a scourge of noble wits,/A deadly wound, a shot which ever hits.
Thomas Watson, *Passionate Century of Love*, 1582

[Love] is merely the exchange of two momentary desires and the contact of two skins.

Simone Weil, quoted in The Faber Book of Aphorisms

What a silly thing love is! It is not half as useful as logic, for it does not prove anything and it is always telling one things that are not going to happen, and making one believe things that are not true.

Oscar Wilde, The Nightingale and the Rose, 1888

The biggest of all differences in this world is between the ones that had or have pleasure in love and those that haven't and hadn't any pleasure in love, but just watched sick with envy.

Tennessee Williams, Sweet Bird of Youth, 1959

A pity beyond all telling/Is hid in the heart of love.

William Butler Yeats, The Pity of Love, 1895

The course of true love never did run smooth. Love is a hurdler. Love laughs at locksmiths (but it needs locks). Love will find a way (but it must be a rough and hilly one). Above all: secrecy is the nerve of love. Everyone who subscribes to these sayings and whose life conforms to their pattern has somewhere in him chosen to do so. The obstacles are not given; we raise them.

Wayland Young, Eros Denied, 1965

3. *The Eyes of Love*

The duration of passion is proportionate with the original resistance of the woman.
  Honoré de Balzac

Each moment of a happy lover's hour/Is worth an age of dull and common life.
  Aphra Behn, Younger Brother, 1696

Nobody in love has a sense of humour.
  S. N. Behrman, The Second Man, 1927

Who would give a law to lovers?/Love is unto itself a higher law.
  Boethius, The Consolation of Philosophy, 524

Passion in a lover's glorious/But in a husband is pronounced uxorious.
  Lord Byron, Don Juan, 1819–1824

When too much zeal doth fire devotion,/Love is not love, but superstition.
  Richard Corbet

I am two fools, I know/For loving, and for saying so/in whining Poetry.
  John Donne, The Triple Fool

Who writes love letters grows thin, who carries them fat.
Dutch proverb

Passion has as much conscience as a worm entering a luscious apple.
Paul Eldridge, Horns of Glass

All mankind love a lover.
Ralph Waldo Emerson, Essays, 1841–1847

The lover is made happier by his love than the object of his affection.
Ralph Waldo Emerson, Journals, 1832

Let no man think he is loved by any when he loves none.
Epictetus, Fragments, 100

He is not a lover who does not love forever.
Euripides, The Trojan Women, 5th century B.C.

Lovers who love truly do not write down their happiness.
Anatole France, The Crime of Sylvester Bonnard, 1881

In love there is always one who kisses and one who offers the cheek.
French proverb

To be loved is the best way of being useful.
French proverb

A person who loves has, so to speak, forfeited a part of his narcissism, and it can only be replaced by his being loved.
Sigmund Freud, Complete Works, 1955

It is easier to live through someone else than to become complete yourself.

Betty Friedan, *The Feminine Mystique,* 1963

It's an extra dividend when you like the girl you're in love with.

Clark Gable

We must resemble each other a little in order to understand each other. But we must be a little different to love each other.

Paul Geraldy, *L'Homme et L'Amour,* 1951

Or love me less, or love me more/And play not with my liberty:/Either take all, or all restore;/Bind me at least, or set me free.

Sidney Godolphin, in *Poems of Sydney Godolphin,* 1931

To be loved for what one is, is the greatest exception. The great majority love in another only what they lend him, their own selves, their version of him.

Johann Wolfgang von Goethe, *Wisdom and Experience*

When one loves somebody, everything is clear—where to go, what to do—it all takes care of itself and one doesn't have to ask anybody about anything.

Maxim Gorky, *The Zykovs,* 1914

Why is it better to love than be loved? It is surer.

Sacha Guitry

It is written in the code of love: he who strikes the blow is himself struck down.

Hadewijch

Perhaps a great love is never returned.

Dag Hammarskjöld, *Markings,* 1964

A lover without indiscretion is no lover at all.
  Thomas Hardy, *The Hand of Ethelberta*, 1876

Wisely a woman prefers to a lover a man who neglects her./This one may love her some day, some day the lover will not.
  John Hay, *Distichs*

How few of us know how to make love properly, and how very few, after making it, know how to keep it.
  Oliver Herford, John Clay, *Cupid's Cyclopedia*, 1910

Experience: an expensive tutor.
  Oliver Herford, John Clay, *Cupid's Cyclopedia*, 1910

I suppose there is nothing in lovers' letters, at least people say so; but there is a good deal of happiness in saying that nothing.
  George Birbeck Hill, *letter to his fiancée*, 19th century

Don't threaten me with love, baby. Let's just go walking in the rain.
  Billie Holiday

Love is sparingly soluble in the words of men, therefore they speak much of it; but one syllable of woman's speech can dissolve more of it than a man's heart can hold.
  Oliver Wendell Holmes, Sr., *The Autocrat of the Breakfast-Table*, 1857–1858

The love we give away is the only love we keep.
  Elbert Hubbard, *The Note Book*, 1927

Considered just as lovers, there's probably not much to choose between a tomcat and a prophet.
  Henrik Ibsen, *Peer Gynt*, 1867

I love you very much because with you I found a way to love myself again.
    Attila Jozsef

Though a man excels in everything, unless he has been a lover his life is lonely, and he may be likened to a jeweled cup which can contain no wine.
    Yoshida Kenko, The Harvest of Leisure, 1330–1335

Heaven grant us patience with a man in love!
    Rudyard Kipling

At the beginning of love and at its end the lovers are embarrassed to be left alone.
    Jean de La Bruyère

The head does not know how to play the part of the heart for long.
    La Rochefoucauld, Maxims, 1665

Passion often turns the cleverest men into idiots and makes the greatest blockheads clever.
    La Rochefoucauld, Maxims, 1665

It is difficult to love those whom we do not esteem, but it is no less difficult to love those whom we esteem much more than ourselves.
    La Rochefoucauld, Maxims, 1665

HERBERT MARSHALL: If you love a person, you can forgive anything.
    The Letter, script: *Howard Koch,* 1940

When love its utmost vigour does employ/Ev'n then, 'tis but a restless wandering joy:/Nor knows the lover, in that wild excess,/With hands or eyes, what first he would possess. . . .

> Lucretius, *De Rerum Natura IV*, 1st century B.C.

A man is privileged when his passion obliges him to betray his convictions to please the woman he loves.

> René Magritte, quoted in H. Torczyner, *Magritte: The True Art of Painting*, 1979

Who ever loved, that loved not at first sight?

> Christopher Marlowe, *Hero and Leander*, 1598

Usually passion wants to grab and yank.

> Catherine Marshall, *Christy*, 1967

A lover . . . tries to stand in well with the pet dog of the house.

> Molière

Lovers. Not a soft word, as people thought, but cruel and tearing.

> Alice Munro, *Something I've Been Meaning to Tell You*, 1974

We can only learn to love by loving.

> Iris Murdoch, *The Bell*, 1958

Discovering reciprocal love should really disenchant the lover as regards the beloved. "What! She is modest enough to love even you? Or stupid enough? Or . . ."

> Friedrich Nietzsche, *Beyond Good and Evil*, 1886

With the generosity of a great lord the happy lover smiles upon everything about him. But the great lord's generosity is always in moderation and involves no effort. It is

not a very expansive sort of generosity; actually it originates in disdain.
José Ortega y Gasset, 1946

He who says over-much "I love not" is in love.
Ovid

Value each lover according to the gifts he brings.
Ovid

Scratch a lover, and find a foe!
Dorothy Parker, *Enough Rope*, 1927

My soul is crushed, my spirit sore/I do not like me anymore/I cavil, quarrel, grumble, grouse/I ponder on the narrow house/I shudder at the thought of men/I'm due to fall in love again.
Dorothy Parker, *Enough Rope*, 1927

The heart has its reasons, which reason does not know.
Blaise Pascal, *Pensées*, 1670

'Tis never for their wisdom that one loves the wisest, or for their wit that one loves the wittiest; 'tis for benevolence and virtue and honest fondness one loves people.
Hester Lynch Piozzi, *letter to Fanny Burney*, 1781

Find me a reasonable lover, and I'll give you his weight in gold.
Plautus

To love is human; to be indulgent is human, too.
Plautus

The greatest love is a mother's; then comes a dog's; then comes a sweetheart's.
> *Polish proverb*

Ye gods! annihilate but space and time/And make two lovers happy.
> *Alexander Pope, The Art of Sinking in Poetry,* 1735

The man that loves and laughs must sure do well.
> *Alexander Pope, Imitations of Horace,* 1733

Be to her virtues very kind;/Be to her faults a little blind;/Let all her ways be unconfined;/And clap your padlock on her mind.
> *Matthew Prior, An English Padlock,* 1705

We are ordinarily so indifferent to people that when we have invested one of them with the possibility of giving us joy, or suffering, it seems as if he must belong to some other universe, he is imbued with poetry.
> *Marcel Proust*

Lovers know what they want, but not what they need.
> *Publilius Syrus, Moral Sayings,* 1st century B.C.

An angry lover tells himself many lies.
> *Publilius Syrus, Moral Sayings,* 1st century B.C.

Love eagerly believes everything it wants to.
> *Jean Racine, Mithridate,* 1673

Love me and the world is mine.
> *David Reed,* 1906

The man who wouldn't be a fool over the right woman doesn't deserve to have the right woman be a fool over him.

Reflections of a Bachelor

The people who are in dead earnest never make love, they just love.

Reflections of a Bachelor

The lover is a monotheist who knows that other people worship different gods but cannot himself imagine that there could be other gods.

Theodor Reik, *Of Love and Lust*, 1957

The man who has never made a fool of himself in love will never be wise in love.

Theodor Reik, *Of Love and Lust*, 1957

Although it is idiotic to fall in love at first sight, it is not an unpleasant occurrence to be fallen in love with at first sight.

Frank Richardson, *2835 Mayfair*, 1907

Only by oneself, apart, can one consummate this seemingly most shared experience that love is.

Rainer Maria Rilke, *Letters*, 1945

For one human being to love another; that is perhaps the most difficult of all our tasks, the ultimate, the last test and proof, the work for which all other work is but preparation.

Rainer Maria Rilke, *Letters to a Young Poet*, 1904

Those who are loved live poorly and in danger. Ah, that they might surmount themselves and become lovers. Around those who love is sheer security. No one casts suspicion on them any more, and they themselves are not in a position to betray themselves.

Rainer Maria Rilke, *The Notebooks of Malte Laurids Brigge*, 1910

Love decentralizes, truth universalizes: he who speaks addresses all mankind; he who loves incarnates all mankind in himself.

Eugen Rosenstock-Huessy

I do not always admire what I love, neither do I always love what I admire.

Joseph Roux, *Meditations of a Parish Priest*, 1886

We do not live in accordance with our mode of thinking, but we think in accordance with our mode of loving.

V. V. Rozinov

Love makes a subtle man out of a crude one, it gives eloquence to the mute, it gives courage to the cowardly and makes the idle quick and sharp.

Juan Ruiz, *El Amor*

Many people when they fall in love look for a little haven of refuge from the world, where they can be sure of being admired when they are not admirable, and praised when they are not praiseworthy.

Bertrand Russell, *The Conquest of Happiness*, 1930

. . . that pane of glass called passion . . . It may distort things at times, but it's wonderfully convenient.

Françoise Sagan, *A Certain Smile*, 1956

If you tame me, then we shall need each other. To me, you will be unique in all the world. To you, I shall be unique in all the world.
Antoine de Saint-Exupéry, The Little Prince, 1943

The lover knows much more about absolute good and universal beauty than any logician or theologian, unless the latter, too, be lovers in disguise.
George Santayana, The Life of Reason, 1905–1906

You've got to love something enough to kill it.
Martin Scorsese

She's deceiving, I believing/What can lovers wish for more.
Sir Charles Sedley

It was a lover and his lass/With a hey, and a ho, and a hey nonny no/That o'er the green cornfield did pass/In the spring time, the only pretty ring time/When the birds do sing, hey ding a ding ding/Sweet lovers love the spring.
William Shakespeare, As You Like It, 1598–1600

But love is blind, and lovers cannot see/The pretty follies that themselves commit.
William Shakespeare, Merchant of Venice, 1596

Base men being in love have then a nobility in their natures more than is native to them.
William Shakespeare, Othello, 1604–1605

They say all lovers swear more performance than they are able and yet reserve an ability that they never perform, vowing more than the perfection of ten and discharging less than the tenth part of one.
William Shakespeare, Troilus and Cressida, 1602

I may command where I adore.
  William Shakespeare, Twelfth Night, 1598–1600

If ever thou shalt love,/In the sweet pangs of it remember me;/For such as I am all true lovers are,/Unstaid and skittish in all motions else,/Save in the constant image of the creature/That is beloved.
  William Shakespeare, Twelfth Night, 1598–1600

They do not love that do not show their love.
  William Shakespeare, The Two Gentlemen of Verona, 1594–1595

They love indeed who quake to say they love.
  Sir Philip Sidney, Sonnets

In fact, all loves but one's own have an element of the tiresome.
  C. P. Snow, The New Men, 1954

INGRID BERGMAN: People "fall in love"—as they put it—because they respond to certain hair coloring, or vocal tones, or mannerisms that remind them of their parents.
  Spellbound, script: Ben Hecht, 1945

Such is the rule of modesty: a woman of feeling betrays her sentiments for her lover sooner by deed than by word.
  Stendhal

The impassioned man hasn't time to be witty.
  Stendhal

To be loved at first sight, a man should have at the same time something to respect and something to pity in his face.
  Stendhal, On Love, 1822

For Kings and lovers are alike in this/That their chief art in reign dissembling is.
  Sir John Suckling, Loving and Beloved, 1638

Love remains a secret even when spoken/for only a lover truly knows that he is loved.
  Rabindranath Tagore, Fireflies, 1928

The loving are the daring.
  Bayard Taylor, The Song of the Camp, in Complete Poems, 1856

Strephon kissed me in the spring/Robin in the fall/And Colin only looked at me/And never kissed at all/Strephon's kiss was lost in jest/Robin's lost in play/But the kiss in Colin's eyes/Haunts me night and day.
  Sara Teasdale, The Look

The anger of lovers renews their love.
  Terence, The Woman of Andros, 166 B.C.

We love being in love, that's the truth on't.
  William Thackeray

The Love-god inflames/more fiercely/those he sees are reluctant to surrender.
  Tibullus, Elegies, 1st century B.C.

To a philosopher there is nothing to equal the absurdity of a man in love.
  James Turner, Love Letters, 1970

With sincere lovers reason can do nothing against desire.
  Gui d'Uisel

He who cannot feel in his heart some sweet taste of love is quite dead; for what is the use of living without love, except to annoy people.
  Bernard de Ventadour

Who can deceive a lover?
  Vergil, Aeneid, 1st century B.C.

I can understand companionship. I can understand bought sex in the afternoon. I cannot understand the love affair.
  Gore Vidal, The Sunday Times of London, 1973

Love is much nicer to be in than an automobile accident, a tight girdle, a higher tax bracket or a holding pattern over Philadelphia.
  Judith Viorst, Redbook, 1975

"His love is violent but base"—a possible sentence, "His love is deep but base"—an impossible one.
  Simone Weil

It is difficult not to be unjust to what one loves.
  Oscar Wilde, The Critic as Artist, 1890

When you really want love you will find it waiting for you.
  Oscar Wilde, De Profundis, 1905

The maxim for any love affair is "Play and pray, but on the whole do not pray when you are playing and do not play when you are praying." We cannot yet manage such simultaneities.
  Charles Williams

No one in love is free—or wants to be.
  Tennessee Williams, Sweet Bird of Youth, 1959

Love that's soonest hot, is ever soonest cold.
George Wither, *Fidelia*, 1617

NORMA SHEARER: No pride at all! That's a luxury a woman in love can't afford.
The Women, script: Anita Loos, Jane Murfin, 1939

You must love him, ere to you/He will seem worthy of your love.
William Wordsworth, *A Poet's Epitaph*, 1799

4. *The Real Thing*

In fool's paradise there is room for many lovers.
Samuel Hopkins Adams, *Tenderloin*, 1959

Romance and work are great diversions to keep you from dealing with yourself.
Cher Bono Allman, *Playboy*, 1975

In real love you want the other person's good. In romantic love you want the other person.
Margaret Anderson, *The Fiery Fountains*, 1969

If two stand shoulder to shoulder against the gods,/ Happy together, the gods themselves are helpless/ Against them, while they stand so.
Maxwell Anderson, *Elizabeth the Queen*, 1930

Greensleeves was all my joy,/Greensleeves was my de-light/Greensleeves was my heart of gold,/And who but my Lady Greensleeves?

Anonymous, *A Handful of Pleasant Ditties*, 1584

Somewhere there waiteth in this world of ours/For one lone soul another lonely soul,/Each choosing each through all the weary hours./And meeting strangely at one sudden goal,/Then blend they, like green leaves with golden flowers,/Into one beautiful perfect whole;/And life's long night is ended, and the way/Lies open onward to eternal day.

Edwin Arnold, *Somewhere There Waiteth*, in *An Arnold Poetry Reader*, 1920

Only little boys and old men sneer at love.

Louis Auchincloss, *The Rector of Justin*, 1965

In love, one first deceives oneself, and then others—and that is what is called romance.

John Balderston, *Berkeley Square*, 1928

BARBARA STANWYCK: Yes, I love him. I love those hick shirts he wears with those boiled cuffs and the way he always has his vest buttoned wrong. He looks like a giraffe, and I love him. I love him because he's the kind of a guy who gets drunk on a glass of buttermilk, and I love the way he blushes right up to his ears. I love him because he doesn't know how to kiss—the jerk! I love him, Joe. That's what I'm trying to tell ya.

Ball of Fire, script: *Charles Brackett, Billy Wilder*, 1941

How many times do I love thee dear?/Tell me how many thoughts there be/In the atmosphere/Of a new fal'n year/Whose white and sable hours appear/The latest flakes of Eternity:/So many times do I love thee, dear.

Thomas Beddoes, *Torrismond*, 1890

. . . Whither thou goest, I will go; and where thou lodgest, I will lodge: thy people shall be my people, and thy God my God: Where thou diest, will I die, and there will I be buried: the Lord do so to me, and more also, if aught but death part thee and me.

The Bible, Ruth

Romance, n: Fiction that owes no allegiance to the God of Things As They Are.

Ambrose Bierce, The Devil's Dictionary, 1911

Love matches are made by people who are content, for a month of honey, to condemn themselves to a life of vinegar.

Countess of Blessington

Surabaya Johnny, why are you so cruel?/Surabaya Johnny, my God and I love you so/Surabaya Johnny, why am I so unhappy?/You have no heart, Johnny, and I love you so.

Bertolt Brecht, Surabaya Johnny

I thought that spring must last for ever more/For I was young, and loved, and it was May.

Vera Brittain, Poems, 1934

Day and night I find neither rest nor peace. If I sleep I am disturbed by tormenting dreams in which I see you, always severe, always grave, always incensed against me. Forgive me then, Monsieur, if I adopt the course of writing to you again. How can I endure life if I make no effort to ease its sufferings. . . .

Charlotte Brontë, letter to her Belgian professor

First time he kissed me, he but only kissed/The fingers of this hand wherewith I write/And ever since, it grew more clean and white.

    Elizabeth Barrett Browning, Sonnets from the Portuguese, 1850

How do I love thee? Let me count the ways/I love thee to the depth and breadth and height/My soul can reach, when feeling out of sight/For the ends of Being and ideal Grace.

    Elizabeth Barrett Browning, Sonnets from the Portuguese, 1850

My love is like a red red rose/That's newly sprung in June/Oh my love's like the melodie/That's sweetly played in tune.

    Robert Burns, My Love Is Like a Red Red Rose, 1803

Greta Garbo: Perhaps it's better if I live in your heart where the world can't see me. If I am dead, there'll be no stain on our love.

    Camille, script: Joe Atkins, Frances Marion, James Hilton, 1936

My sweetest Lesbia let us live and love/And though the sager sort our deeds reprove/Let us not weigh them. Heaven's great lamps do dive/Into their west and straight again revive/But soon as once set is our little light/Then must we sleep one ever-during night.

    Thomas Campion, A Book of Airs, 1610–1612

It is sad and wrong to be so dependent for the life of my life on any human being as I am on you; but I cannot by any force of logic cure myself at this date, when it has become second nature. If I have to lead another life in any of the planets, I shall take precious good care not to hang myself round any man's neck, either as a locket or a millstone.

    Jane Carlyle, quoted in Elizabeth Drew, The Literature of Gossip

HUMPHREY BOGART: Ilsa, I'm no good at being noble, but it doesn't take much to see that the problems of three little people don't amount to a hill of beans in this crazy world. Someday you'll understand that. Not now. Here's looking at you, kid.

Casablanca, script: Julius J. and Philip G. Epstein, Howard Koch, 1942

My Lord and Dear Husband, I commend me unto you. The hour of my death draweth fast on, and my case being such, the tender love I owe you forceth me, with a few words, to put you in remembrance of the health and safeguard of your soul, which you ought to prefer before all worldly matters, and before the care and tendering of your own body, for the which you have cast me into many miseries and yourself into many cares. For my part I do pardon you all, yea, I do wish and devoutly pray God that He will also pardon you. For the rest I commend unto you Mary, our daughter, beseeching you to be a good father unto her, as I heretofore desired. I entreat you also, on behalf of my maids, to give them marriage-portions, which is not much, they being but three. For all my other servants, I solicit a year's pay more than their due, lest they should be unprovided for. Lastly, do I vow, that mine eyes desire you above all things.

Catherine of Aragon, letter to Henry VIII, 1535

Maybe 'twould pain her to despise/A lover in this humble guise/I bear my lot;/I feel her presence in the air,/I know an angel has been there/And murmur not.

Chambers Journal: Reverence in Love, 1871

In life's great choral symphony, the keynote of the dominant melody is Love! Without the keynote there can be no music—there is dumbness where there should be sound—there is discord where there should be harmony. Love! the one vibrant tone to which the whole universe moves in tune—Love, the breath of God, the pulsation of His Being, the glory of His work, the fulfilment of His Eternal Joy.

Marie Corelli

With all they faults, I love thee still.

William Cowper, The Task, 1784

Daisy, Daisy, give me your answer, do!/I'm half crazy, all for the love of you!/It won't be a stylish marriage/I can't afford a carriage/But you'll look sweet upon the seat/Of a bicycle built for two.

Harry Dacre, Daisy Bell, 1892

CLIFTON WEBB: Love is not the exclusive province of adolescence, my dear. It's a heart ailment that strikes all age groups. Like my love for you. My love for you is the only malady I've contracted since the usual childhood diseases and it's incurable.

The Dark Corner, script: Jay Bratler, Bernard C. Shoenfeld, 1946

GROUCHO MARX: It's the old, old story: "Boy Meets Girl," Romeo and Juliet, Minneapolis and St. Paul.

A Day at the Races, script: Robert Pirosh, George Oppenheimer, George Seaton, 1937

Don't write!/I am sad and would just like to fade away/These beautiful summers without you are like love without a touch.

Marcelline Desbordes-Valmores, Les Séparés, in Poésies, 1820

I am mad with love. My passion is frenzy. The prospect of our immediate meeting overwhelms and entrances me. I pass my nights and days in scenes of strange and fascinating rapture. . . .

Benjamin Disraeli, letter to his fiancée, Mrs. Wyndham Lewis

Oh if thou carest not whom I love/Alas thou lovest not me.
John Donne

Come live with me and be my love/And we will some new pleasures prove/Of golden sands and crystal brooks /With silken lines and silver hooks.
John Donne, The Bait, in Collected Works, 1633

So well I love thee, as without thee I/Love Nothing. If I might chuse, I'd rather die/Than bee one day debarde they company.
Michael Drayton

This was not a young man making love to a girl. This was the meeting of twin souls. The light covering of flesh was so transmuted with ecstasy that earthly passion became a heavenly embrace of white, fiery flame.
Isadora Duncan, My Life

If not for you/Winter would have no spring/Couldn't hear the robin sing/I just wouldn't have a clue/Anyway it wouldn't ring true/If not for you.
Bob Dylan, If Not for You, 1970

I look down the tracks and see you coming—and out of every haze and mist your darling rumpled trousers are hurrying to me—Without you, dearest dearest I couldn't see or hear or feel or think—or live—I love you so and I'm never in all our lives going to let us be apart another night. It's like begging for mercy of a storm or killing Beauty or growing old, without you. I want to kiss you so—and in the back where your dear hair starts and your chest—I love you so—and I can't tell you how much—To think that I'll *die* without your knowing—Goofo, you've *got* to try [to] feel how much I do—how inanimate I am when you're gone—I can't even hate these damnable people—Nobody's got any right to live but us—and they're dirtying up our world and I can't hate them because I want you so—Come Quick—Come Quick to me—I could never do without you if you hated me and were covered with sores like a leper—if you ran away with another woman and starved me and beat me—I still would want you *I know*—Lover, Lover, Darling—Your Wife.

Zelda Fitzgerald, letter to F. Scott Fitzgerald, 1920

What a difference, my dear friend, between you and me! You find innumerable faults in me, whereas I see only one fault in you *(but perhaps it is the fault of my glasses)*. I mean this kind of avarice which leads you to seek a monopoly on all my affections, and not to allow me any for the agreeable ladies of your country. Do you imagine that it is impossible for my affection *(or my tenderness)* to be divided without being diminished? You deceive yourself, and you forget the playful manner with which you stopped me. You renounce and totally exclude all that might be of the flesh in our affection, allowing me only some kisses, civil and honest, such as you might grant your little cousins. What am I receiving that is so special as to prevent me from giving the same to her, without taking from what belongs to you? . . . The sweet sounds brought forth from the pianoforte by your clever hands can be enjoyed by twenty people simultaneously without diminishing at all the pleasure you so obligingly mean for me, and I could, with as little reason, demand from your affection that no other ears but mine be allowed to be charmed by those sweet sounds.

Benjamin Franklin, letter to Mme. Brillon, 1779

Two people coming together for the purpose of sexual satisfaction, in so far as they seek for solitude, are making a demonstration against the herd instinct, the group feeling.

The more they are in love, the more completely they suffice for each other.

Sigmund Freud, Complete Works, 1955

At the height of being in love, the boundary between ego and object threatens to melt away. Against all the evidence of his senses, a man who is in love declares that "I" and "you" are one, and is prepared to behave as if it were a fact.

Sigmund Freud, Complete Works, 1955

Romance, like alcohol, should be enjoyed, but must not be allowed to become necessary.

Edgar Z. Friedenberg, The Vanishing Adolescent, 1959

The moon is nothing/But a circumambulating aphrodisiac/Divinely subsidized to provoke the world/Into a rising birth-rate.

Christopher Fry, The Lady's Not for Burning, 1948

Romance is the glamour which turns the dust of everyday life into a golden haze.

Elinor Glyn, quoted in Rachel Anderson, The Purple Heart Throbs, 1974

There is a lady sweet and kind,/Was never face so pleased my mind;/I did but see her passing by,/And yet I love her till I die.

Barnabe Googe, There Is a Lady, 1563

Darlin Minkie ope youre makin steddy progress and beginnin ter think of oppin outer your nest and avin a short fly round. . . . Don't bovver to let loose eny muvverly large people on me I dont want to be muvvered just now if I do theres a chambermade wit'll take it on. . . . I could play at frowin you over—over the cliff I mean, but I woodn't do it

reely—and you cood play at bandonin me artlessly for buther—but you wouldn't do that neither.
    Kenneth Grahame, letter to his fiancée, Elspeth Thompson

Yes indeed, all peoples recognise romantic love, but they recognise it for what it is—temporary insanity—and try to pay as little attention to it as possible.
    John Greenaway, The Inevitable Americans

True Love: an old fashioned sentiment.
    Oliver Herford, John Clay, Cupid's Cyclopedia, 1910

Romance: *Once* upon a time. Seldom twice.
    Oliver Herford, John Clay, Cupid's Cyclopedia, 1910

Long, very long, have I left your last, dear letter—*read and read again*—without an answer. Take today my heartfelt thanks for it, though given in very few words. Henceforth, till we see each other face to face, you will hear little from me, and very seldom. Believe me, it is better so. It is the only right thing. It is a matter of conscience with me to end our correspondence, or at least to limit it. You yourself should have as little to do with me as possible. With your young life you have other aims to follow, other tasks to fulfil. And I—*I have told you so already*—can never be content with a mere exchange of letters. For me it is only half the thing; it is a false situation. Not to give myself wholly and unreservedly makes me unhappy. It is my nature. I cannot change it. You are so delicately subtle, so instinctively penetrating, that you will easily see what I mean. When we are together again, I shall be able to explain it more fully. Till then, and always, you will be in my thoughts. You will be so even more when we no longer have to stop at this wearisome halfway house of correspondence. *A thousand greetings.*
    Henrik Ibsen, letter to Emilie Bardach, 1890

Romance, like the rabbit at the dog track, is the elusive, fake, and never attained reward which, for the benefit and amusement of our masters, keeps us running and thinking in safe circles.

    Beverly Jones, *The Florida Paper on Women's Liberation*, 1970

Drink to me only with thine eyes/And I will pledge with mine/Or leave a kiss but in the cup/And I'll not look for wine.

    Ben Jonson, *The Forest*, 1616

It has just struck me. I came in at half past eleven. Since then I have been sitting in an easy chair like a fool. I could do nothing. I hear nothing but your voice. I am like a fool hearing you call me "Dear." I offended two men today by leaving them coolly. I wanted to hear your voice, not theirs. When I am with you I leave aside my contemptuous, suspicious nature. I wish I felt your head on my shoulder. I think I will go to bed. I have been a half-hour writing this thing. Will you write something to me? I hope you will. How am I to sign myself? I won't sign anything at all, because I don't know what to sign myself.

    James Joyce, *letter to Nora Barnacle*, 1904

Sweetest Fanny, You fear, sometimes, I do not love you so much as you wish? My dear Girl I love you ever and ever and without reserve. The more I have known you the more have I lov'd. In every way—even my jealousies have been agonies of Love, in the hottest fit I ever had I would have died for you. I have vex'd you too much. But for Love! Can I help it? You are always new. The last of your kisses was ever the sweetest; the last smile the brightest; the last movement the gracefullest. When you pass'd my window home yesterday, I was fill'd with as much admiration as if I had then seen you for the first time. You uttered a half complaint once that I only lov'd your

Beauty. Have I nothing else then to live in you but that? Do not I see a heart naturally furnish'd with wings imprison itself with me? No ill prospect has been able to turn your thoughts a moment from me. This perhaps should be as much a subject of sorrow as joy—but I will not talk of that. Even if you did not love me I could not help an entire devotion to you: how much more deeply then must I feel for you knowing you love me. My Mind has been the most discontented and restless one that ever was put into a body too small for it. I never felt my Mind repose upon anything with complete and undistracted enjoyment—upon no person but you. When you are in the room my thoughts never fly out of window; you always concentrate my whole senses. The anxiety shown about our Loves in your last note is an immense pleasure to me: however you must not suffer such speculations to molest you any more: nor will I any more believe you can have the least pique against me. Brown is gone out—but here is Mrs. Wyle—when she is gone I shall be awake for you.

John Keats, letter to Fanny Brawne, 1820

My love has made me selfish. I cannot exist without you. I am forgetful of everything but seeing you again—my life seems to stop there. I see no further. You have absorbed me. I have a sensation at the present moment as though I was dissolving—I should be exquisitely miserable without the hope of soon seeing you. My sweet Fanny, will your heart never change?

John Keats, letter to Fanny Brawne

I am you and you are me and what have we done to each other.

The Keeners' Manual

Sing the Lovers' Litany: "Love like ours can never die!"

Rudyard Kipling, The Lovers' Litany

I love a lassie, a bonnie, bonnie lassie,/She's as pure as the lily in the dell./She's as sweet as the heather,/The bonnie, bloomin' heather,/Mary, ma Scotch Blue-bell.

Harry Lauder, Gerald Grafton, I Love a Lassie

Two souls but with a single thought/Two hearts that beat as one.

Maria Lovell, Ingomar the Barbarian, 1854

My love for you tonight is so deep and tender that it seems to be outside myself as well. I am shut up fast like a little lake in the embrace of some big mountains, you would see me down below, deep and shining—and quite fathomless, my dear. You might drop your heart into me and you'd never hear it touch bottom. I love you—I love you—Goodnight. Oh Bogey, what it is to love like this!

Katherine Mansfield, letter to John Middleton Murry, 1918

Come live with me and be my Love,/And we will all the pleasures prove/That hills and valleys, dales and fields,/Or woods, or steepy mountain yields.

Christopher Marlowe, The Passionate Shepherd to His Love, 1599

I would/Love you ten years before the flood/And you should if you please refuse/Till the conversion of the Jews;/My vegetable love should grow/Vaster than empires and more slow.

Andrew Marvell, To His Coy Mistress, 1681

Where you used to be, there is a hole in the world, which I find myself constantly walking around in the daytime, and falling into at night. I miss you like hell.

Edna St. Vincent Millay, Letters

Some of the greatest love affairs I've known have involved one actor, unassisted.
    Wilson Mizner

For years I shall remember how you came down to Seaford House in your electric brougham. That vehicle is forever enshrined in my memory. You can never, and for this I pity you, you can never form any idea of the wonder it is to me to see you—to think you and to dream you.
    George Moore, letters to Lady Cunard, 1905

I wake filled with thoughts of you. Your portrait and the intoxicating evening which we spent yesterday have left my senses in turmoil. Sweet, incomparable Josephine, what a strange effect you have on my heart! Are you angry? Do I see you looking sad? Are you worried? . . . My soul aches with sorrow, and there can be no rest for your lover; but is there still more in store for me when, yielding to the profound feelings which overwhelm me, I draw from your lips, from your heart a love which consumes me with fire? Ah! It was last night that I fully realized how false an image of you your portrait gives! You are leaving at noon; I shall see you in three hours. Until then, mio dolce amor, a thousand kisses; but give me none in return, for they set my blood on fire.
    Napoleon, letter to Joséphine de Beauharnais, 1795

Romantic love is the privilege of emperors, kings, soldiers and artists; it is the butt of democrats, traveling salesmen, magazine poets and the writers of American novels.
    George Jean Nathan, Testament of a Critic, 1930

Another World Rachel let Sam kiss her, but rebuffed marriage idea. Jamie and Anne got chummy, but she's intent on winning Mac. . . .
Days of Our Lives Mickey caught Maggie and Evan in a clinch after Evan learnt Stuart died of a heart attack. Stefano denied any connection. . . .

The Doctors Barney balked at Luke's idea to modernize the Medicine Man and said Natalie used Luke. Greta said Katy made Lee Ann reject her. . . .

Edge of Night Spencer recognized the Black Widow who threatened Raven. Derek tried to forget Jinx by picking up other women. . . .

Guiding Light Jackie fought her hostility for Carrie and acted as her maid of honor. . . .

One Life to Live Karen agreed to a trip with Larry believing they would reconcile. Kate confronted Karen to reveal the baby switch. . . .

Ryan's Hope Jane gave Ox Roger's pearls. Ox agreed to a Dominican divorce, but feared the Mob would find and kill him. Yvonne abducted Faith. . . .

Texas Gretchen bound and gagged Ruby, then admitted killing Myles. Lurlene set off a fire alarm just as Gretchen was about to kill Ruby. . . .

The Young and Restless Sally told Greg about Chris and Snapper's separation. Chris assured Jack she's taking charge of her life. . . .

New York Daily News, Soap Opera Notes, 1982

Being a woman, you will say when you put this letter down "Well, he can't love me very much, as he would have made more fuss." Good God! More fuss! When my heart feels like a *peche Melba*.

Harold Nicolson, letter to Vita Sackville-West, 1919

The most ardent love is rather epigrammatic than lyrical.

Coventry Patmore, The Rod, The Root and The Flower, 1895

WILLIAM HOLDEN: Listen, baby, you're the only real thing I ever wanted. Ever. You're mine. I gotta claim what's mine, or I'll be nothing as long as I live. You love me. You know it. You love me. You love me. You love me.

Picnic, script: Daniel Taradash, 1955

Thou wast all that to me, love,/For which my soul did pine:/A green isle in the sea, love,/A fountain and a shrine.

Edgar Allan Poe, *To One in Paradise*, 1827

I love thee like pudding; if thou wert pie I'd eat thee.

John Ray, *English Proverbs*, 1678

I could easily kill my rival, but that would upset the Duchess too much.

Colonel Romanelli, who killed himself in Naples because the Duchess had left him, quoted by Stendhal in *The Edinburgh Review*

My heart is like a singing bird/Whose nest is in a watered shoot;/My heart is like an apple-tree/Whose boughs are bent with thickset fruit;/My heart is like a rainbow shell/That paddles in a halcyon sea;/My heart is gladder than all these/Because my love is come to me.

Christina Rossetti, *A Birthday*, in *Collected Poems*, 1882

Happy love has no history. Romance comes only into existence where love is fatal, frowned upon and doomed by life itself. What stirs lyrical poets to their finest flights is neither the delight of the senses nor the fruitful contentment of the settled couple; nor the satisfaction of love, but its *passion*. And passion means suffering. There we have the fundamental fact.

Dennis de Rougement, *Passion and Society*, 1956

Romance, that broken reed which leaves cruel splinters in the palm.

Berta Ruck, *Shopping for a Husband*, 1967

Alone, said I, dearest? Oh, we never part—/Forever, forever, thou'rt here in my heart;/Sleeping or waking, where'er I be,/I have but one thought, and that thought is of thee.
  John Ruskin, Remembrance, 1837

You are dearer to me than anybody ever has been or ever could be. If you died suddenly I should kill myself as soon as I had made provision for the boys. I really mean this. I could not live if I lost you. I do not think one could conceive of a love more exclusive, more tender, or more pure than I have for you. I think it is immortal, a thing which happens seldom. Darling, there are not many people who would write such a letter after sixteen years of marriage, yet who would be saying therein only one fiftieth of what they were feeling as they wrote it. It sometimes try to tell you the truth and then I find I have no words at my command which could possibly convey it to you.
  Vita Sackville-West, letter to Harold Nicholson, 1929

Doubt thou the stars are fire;/Doubt that the sun doth move;/Doubt truth to be a liar;/But never doubt I love.
  William Shakespeare, Hamlet, 1600

Give me my Romeo; and, when he shall die/Take him and cut him out in little stars,/And he will make the face of heaven so fine/That all the world will be in love with night/And pay no worship to the garish sun.
  William Shakespeare, Romeo and Juliet, 1594–1595

Shall I compare thee to a summer's day?/Thou art more lovely and more temperate. . . .
  William Shakespeare, Sonnet 18

Thy love is better than high birth to me,/Richer than wealth, prouder than garments' cost,/Of more delight than hawks or horses be.

William Shakespeare, sonnets

Didst thou but know the inly touch of love,/Thou wouldst as soon go kindle fire with snow,/As seek to quench the fire of love with words.

William Shakespeare, The Two Gentlemen of Verona, 1594–1595

True love in this differs from gold and clay,/That to divide is not to take away.

Percy Bysshe Shelley, Epipsychidion, 1821

"All I want is us to share the occasional candle-lit dinner and a bit of slap and tickle when your old man's away on business. No involvement. No strings. No complications." "Oh Myles, this is too wonderful." Relief flooded her entire being. Here at last was the casual fling she had always dreamt of.

Posy Simmonds, True Love, 1981

To Know, Know, Know You Is to Love, Love, Love You.

Phil Spector, song title, 1959

Ask nothing more of me, sweet/All I can give you I give/Heart of my heart were it more/More would be laid at your feet/Love that should help you to live/Song that should spur you to soar.

Algernon Charles Swinburne, The Oblation, in Collected Works, 1904

Bunnies can and will go to France. Yours affectionately, Jeremy. I miss you.

Jeremy Thorpe, letter to Norman Scott, 1961

POB Despite everything remember to go and hang yourself—
Shaggy and Cuddles

```
1. REM* 319 Loves 607
2. DATA 32.12.5.20.19.32
3. DATA 6,21,4,4,12,5,32,32
4. READ A
5. = Then Restore: X = N + 13
6. POKE 32768 + N, A:N = N + 1
GOTO4
```
The Times of London, St. Valentine's Day message, 1982

Jane do wop sh wa do wop sh boom do wop sh wa dop
wop shalangalanga I pine f'you x x x x x x x x x x x x x x
Hamster love you forever x x x x x x x x x x x x JWB
The Times of London, St. Valentine's Day message, 1982

A Character from a Chekhov short story and the Ha-Ha
sends in this crossword puzzle clue as a belated answer
to an advertisement in the Personal Columns of the Times
for 9th August 1975 and hopes for a response less hyp-
notic than before. With all these reasons at your feet I
kneel. GWK
The Times of London, St. Valentine's Day message, 1982

To Debbie Pookie Poople Pips from Petey Popsy Pooples—I
love you—be mine.
The Times of London, St. Valentine's Day message, 1982

The seamen on the wave, love,/When storm and tempest
rave, love,/Look to one star to save, love,/Thou art that
star to me!
John Tyler, To Julia Gardiner Tyler

Brevity may be the soul of wit, but not when someone's
saying "I love you."
Judith Viorst, Redbook, 1975

My own dear boy—Your sonnet is quite lovely and it is a marvel that those red roseleaf lips of yours should be made no less for the music of song than for the madness of kissing. Your slim gilt soul walks between passion and poetry. I know that Hyacinthus, whom Apollo loved so madly, was you in Greek days. Why are you alone in London, and when do you go to Salisbury? Do go there and cool your hands in the grey twilight of Gothic things, and come here whenever you like. It is a lovely place; it only lacks you, but go to Salisbury first. Always with undying love, Yours,

Oscar Wilde, letter to Lord Alfred Douglas, c. 1891

Half laughing god, half prattling, mischievous child.

P. G. Wodehouse, describing one "Bingo Little"

You Are the Sunshine of My Life

Stevie Wonder, song title

My sweet love how I long to see thee; think of me, wish for me, pray for me, pronounce my name when thou art alone, and upon thy pillow; and dream of me happily and sweetly.

William Wordsworth, letter to his wife, Mary

5. I Don't Believe You

Jealousy is that pain which a man feels from the apprehension that he is not equally beloved by the person whom he entirely loves.

Joseph Addison, The Spectator, 1711

A jealous ear hears all things.
Apocrypha, Wisdom of Solomon

Jealousy is nothing but the foolish child of pride.
Pierre de Beaumarchais, The Marriage of Figaro, 1784

Love is as strong as death, jealousy as cruel as the grave.
The Bible, Song of Solomon

Jealousy, n: The seamy side of love.
Ambrose Bierce, The Devil's Dictionary, 1911

Jealousy is no more than feeling alone against smiling enemies.
Elizabeth Bowen, The House in Paris, 1935

When one of the partners in a marriage reproaches the other for concealing things from him or even for lying, he has as a rule only himself to blame. He had allowed himself to become a person to whom it was not easy to confide or speak the truth.
Gerald Brenan, Thoughts in a Dry Season, 1979

Everything disturbs an absent lover.
Miguel de Cervantes, Don Quixote, 1605–1615

Jealousy is not at all low, but it catches us humbled and bowed down, at first sight.
Colette, Earthly Paradise, 1953

Of all the passions, jealousy is that which extracts the hardest service and pays the bitterest wages. Its service is to watch the success of our enemy; its wages, to be sure of it.
Charles Caleb Colton, Lacon, 1825

Jealousy's a proof of love/But 'tis a weak and unavailing medicine/It puts out the disease and makes it show/But it has no power to cure.
John Dryden, *All for Love*, 1678

It is not love that's blind, but jealousy.
Lawrence Durrell, *Justine*, 1957

Jealousy would be far less tortuous if we understood that love is a passion entirely unrelated to our merits.
Paul Eldridge, *Horns of Glass*

Jealousy—that dragon which slays love under the pretence of keeping it alive.
Havelock Ellis, *On Life and Sex*, 1937

At the gate where suspicion enters, love goes out.
English proverb

He that a white horse and a fair wife keepeth/For fear, for care, for jealousy scarce sleepeth.
John Florio

Possessiveness: Never be possessive. If a female friend lets on that she is going out with another man, be kind and understanding. If she says she would like to go out with all of the Dallas Cowboys, including the coaching staff, the same rule applies. Tell her "Kath, you just go right ahead and do what you think is right." Unless you actually care for her, in which case you must see to it that she has no male contact whatsoever.
Bruce Jay Friedman, *Esquire*, 1977

Symptoms of true love/Are leanness, jealousy/laggard dawns;/Are omens and nightmares/Listening for a knock/Waiting for a sign. . . .
Robert Graves, *Symptoms of Love*, 1961

Man is jealous because of his *amour-propre*; woman is jealous because of her lack of it.
    Germaine Greer, *The Female Eunuch*, 1970

Jealousy is the fear of losing the thing you love most. It's very normal. Suspicion is the thing that's abnormal.
    Jerry Hall, *Interview*, 1978

When I told my missis once I should never dream of being jealous of *her*, instead of up and thanking me for it, she spoilt the best frying pan we ever had.
    W. W. Jacobs, *Ship's Company*, 1911

Either you have a rival or you don't. If you have one, you must please in order to be preferred to him, and if you don't you must still please, in order to avoid having one.
    Pierre Choderlos de Laclos, *Les Liaisons Dangereuses*, 1782

Jealousy feeds upon suspicion, and it turns into fury, or it ends as soon as we pass from suspicion into certainty.
    La Rochefoucauld, *Maxims*, 1665

Jealousy is always born with love, but does not always die with it.
    La Rochefoucauld, *Maxims*, 1665

Jealousy is the greatest of all evils, and the one which arouses the least pity in the person who causes it.
    La Rochefoucauld, *Maxims*, 1665

When we are in love we often doubt that which we most believe.
    La Rochefoucauld, *Maxims*, 1665

Love that is fed by jealousy dies hard.
    Ovid, *Love's Cure*

For story and experience tell us/That man grows old and woman jealous.
    Matthew Prior

To jealousy, nothing is more frightful than laughter.
    Françoise Sagan, *La Chamade*, 1966

Jealousy is the great exaggerator.
    Friedrich von Schiller

Where love is great, the littlest doubts are fear;/When little fears grow great, great love grows there.
    William Shakespeare, *Hamlet*, 1600

Trifles light as air/Are to the jealous confirmations strong/As proofs of holy writ.
    William Shakespeare, *Othello*, 1604–1605

But jealous souls will not be answered so/They are not ever jealous for the cause/But jealous for they are jealous.
    William Shakespeare, *Othello*, 1604–1605

O! beware, my lord, of jealousy,/It is the green-eyed monster which doth mock/The meat it feeds on.
    William Shakespeare, *Othello*, 1604–1605

The success of any man with any woman is apt to displease even his best friends.
    Mme. de Staël, quoted in *The Book of Diversion*

It is not love that produces jealousy—it is selfishness.
    Justice Wallington, 1957

As gout in age from pox in youth proceeds/So, wenching past, then jealousy succeeds/The worst disease that love and wenching breeds.
William Wycherley, The Country Wife, 1672

I love to be envied, and would not marry a wife that I alone could love; loving alone is as dull as eating alone.
William Wycherley, The Country Wife, 1672

6. O Lucky Man

Men who cherish for women the highest respect are seldom popular with them.
Joseph Addison

Higgamous, hoggamous, woman's monogamous,/Hoggamous, higgamous, man is polygamous.
Anonymous

ELAINE STEWART: There are no great men, buster. There are only men.
The Bad and the Beautiful, script: Charles Schnee, 1952

Men are so made that they can resist sound argument, and yet yield to a glance.
Honoré de Balzac

Even if a man was delightful, no woman would marry him if she knew what he was like.
E. F. Benson, Paul, 1906

Male, n: A member of the unconsidered, or negligible sex. The male of the human race is commonly known, to the female, as Mere Man. The genus has two varieties: good providers and bad providers.

Ambrose Bierce, *The Devil's Dictionary*, 1911

Men would like to love themselves but they usually find that they cannot. That is because they have built an ideal image of themselves which puts their real self in the shade.

Gerald Brenan, *Thoughts in a Dry Season*, 1978

GOLDIE HAWN: A man who lies cannot love.

Cactus Flower, script: I.A.L. Diamond, 1969

Never love unless you can/Bear with all the faults of man!

Thomas Campion, *Advice to a Girl*, 1610–1612

To abuse a man is a lover-like thing and gives him rights.

Joyce Carey, *Herself Surprised*

Let no woman believe a man's oath, let none believe that a man's speeches can be trustworthy. They, while their mind desires something and longs eagerly to gain it, nothing fear to swear, nothing spare to promise; but as soon as the lust of their greedy mind is satisfied, they fear not then their words, they heed not their perjuries.

Catullus, *Odes*, 1st century B.C.

A woman knows how to keep quiet when she is in the right, whereas a man, when he is in the right, will keep on talking.

Malcolm de Chazal

Every man is to be had one way or another, and every woman almost any way.
Lord Chesterfield, *Letters to His Son*, 1750

The only really masterful noise a man ever makes in a house is the noise of his key, when he is still on the landing, fumbling for the lock.
Colette

Man was by Nature Woman's cully made:/We never are, but by ourselves, betrayed.
William Congreve, *The Old Bachelor*, 1693

O, I hate a lover that can dare to think he draws a moment's air, independent of the bounty of his mistress. There is not so impudent a thing in Nature as the saucy look of an assured man, confident of success.
William Congreve, *The Way of the World*, 1700

A man who has nothing to do with women is always incomplete.
Cyril Connolly, *The Unquiet Grave*, 1945

The last thing a woman will consent to discover in a man whom she loves or on whom she simply depends, is want of courage.
Joseph Conrad, *Victory*, 1915

What most men desire is a virgin who is a whore.
Edward Dahlberg, *Reasons of the Heart*, 1965

The average man is more interested in a woman who is interested in him than he is in a woman with beautiful legs.
Marlene Dietrich

Every man is made out of clay and daimon and no woman can nourish both.

Lawrence Durrell, *Justine*, 1957

If I was with a woman/I'd threaten to unload her/Every time she asked me to explain./If I was with a woman/She'd have to learn to cherish/The purity and depth of my disdain.

Ian Dury, *If I Was with a Woman*, 1979

A man has missed something if he has never woken up in an anonymous bed beside a face he'll never see again, and if he has never left a brothel at dawn feeling like jumping off a bridge into the river out of sheer physical disgust with life.

Gustave Flaubert

Find 'em, feel 'em, fuck 'em, and forget 'em!

The Four-F Club motto, 1950s

Would you be happier if a woman swore to you that she would love you always?

Anatole France

A man is already halfway in love with any woman who listens to him.

Brendan Francis

A person may love
1. According to the narcissistic type: a) what he himself is (i.e., himself), b) what he himself was, c) what he himself would like to be, d) someone who was once part of himself.
2. According to the anaclitic (attachment) type: a) the woman who feeds him, b) the man who protects him.

Sigmund Freud, *Complete Works*, 1955

The majority of men still dream of sex with a loving woman. Men love women at any price, love women even though, beginning in childhood, it is the female sex which makes the male feel guilty about what he desires most from them. . . . One of the reasons that men choose the masochistic role is that feeling they are wrong to want sex from women, they accept pain as the symbolic price they must pay. Humiliation is a kind of payment in advance for forbidden pleasure.

Nancy Friday, Men in Love, 1980

Macho does not prove mucho.

Zsa Zsa Gabor

The bachelor is a peacock, the engaged man a lion and the married man a jackass.

German proverb

The man who discovers a woman's weakness is like the huntsman in the heat of the day who finds a cool spring. He wallows in it.

Jean Giraudoux, Tiger at the Gates, 1935

Most men who rail against women are railing against one woman only.

Rémy de Gourmont

Let men tremble to win the hand of a woman, unless they win along with it the utmost passion of her heart!

Nathaniel Hawthorne, The Scarlet Letter, 1850

RICHARD CONTE: You like to get hurt. Always picking the wrong guy. It's a sickness with a lot of women. Always looking for a new way to get hurt by a new man. Get smart: there hasn't been a new man since Adam.

House of Strangers, script: Philip Yordan, 1949

A man who marries a woman to educate her falls victim to the same fallacy as the woman who marries a man to reform him.

 Elbert Hubbard, The Note Book, 1927

MAE WEST: It's not the men in my life, but the life in my men.

 I'm No Angel, script: Mae West, 1933

Men are always doomed to be duped, not so much by the arts of the [other] sex as by their own imaginations. They are always wooing goddesses and marrying mere mortals.

 Washington Irving, Bracebridge Hall, 1822

A gentleman who had been very unhappy in marriage, married immediately after his wife died: Johnson said, it was the triumph of hope over experience.

 Samuel Johnson, quoted in James Boswell, The Life of Samuel Johnson, 1791

It is commonly a weak man who marries for love.

 Samuel Johnson, quoted in James Boswell, The Life of Samuel Johnson, 1791

Marrying a man is like buying something you've been admiring for a long time in a shop window. You may love it when you get it home, but it doesn't always go with everything else in the house.

 Jean Kerr, The Snake Has All the Lines, 1960

Women speak because they wish to speak, whereas a man speaks only when driven to speech by something outside himself—like, for instance, he can't find any clean socks.

 Jean Kerr, The Snake Has All the Lines, 1960

Men are the reasons that women do not love one another.
Jean de La Bruyère, *Les Caractères, 1688*

The men that women marry/And why they marry them,
will always be/A marvel and a mystery to the world.
Henry Wadsworth Longfellow, *Michael Angelo, 1883*

The male sex still constitutes in many ways the most
obstinate vested interest one can find.
Lord Longford

Who loves not wine, women and song/Remains a fool his
whole life long.
Martin Luther

Women think of being a man as a gift. It is a duty. Even
making love can be a duty. A man has always got to get it
up and love isn't always enough.
Norman Mailer, *Nova, 1969*

Happy is the man with a wife to tell him what to do and a
secretary to do it.
Lord Mancroft, *The Observer, 1966*

Men are those creatures with two legs and eight hands.
Jayne Mansfield

A man marries to have a home, but also because he
doesn't want to be bothered with sex and all that sort of
thing.
W. Somerset Maugham, *The Circle, 1921*

Women want mediocre men, and men are working hard
to become as mediocre as possible.
Margaret Mead, 1958

The fundamental trouble with marriage is that it shakes a man's confidence in himself and so greatly diminishes his general competence and effectiveness. His habit of mind becomes that of a commander who has lost a decisive and a calamitous battle. He never quite trusts himself thereafter.

    H. L. Mencken, *Prejudices*, 1920

CLAUDE RAINS: You mustn't think too harshly of my secretaries. They were kind and understanding when I came to the office after a hard day at home.

    Mr. Skeffington, script: *Julius J. and Philip G. Epstein*, 1944

Marry a stupid woman—it will stop you looking stupid yourself.

    Molière, *L'École des Femmes*, 1662

Disguise our bondage as we will/'Tis woman, woman rules us still.

    Thomas Moore, *Sovereign Woman*, in *Works*, 1820

For me, a man I have loved becomes a kind of brother.

    Jeanne Moreau, *quoted in Oriana Fallaci, The Egotists*, 1963

There are two things no man will admit he can't do well: drive and make love.

    Stirling Moss, 1963

A man reserves his true and deepest love not for the species of woman in whose company he finds himself electrified and enkindled, but for that one in whose company he may feel tenderly drowsy.

    George Jean Nathan, *The Theater Book of the Year*, 1949–1950

Man is for woman always a means: the end is always the child.
Friedrich Nietzsche, Thus Spake Zarathustra

I wonder why men get serious at all. They have this delicate long thing hanging outside their bodies which goes up and down by its own will. If I were a man I would always be laughing at myself.
Yoko Ono, Grapefruit, 1970

The man she had was kind and clean/And well enough for everyday/But oh, dear friends/You should have seen/The one that got away.
Dorothy Parker, The Fisherwoman

Where's the man could ease a heart/Like a satin gown?
Dorothy Parker, The Satin Dress

The great truth is that women actually like men and men can never believe it.
Isabel Paterson, Ladies' Home Journal, 1944

GEORGE SANDERS: Adoring someone is certainly better than being adored. Being adored is a nuisance. You'll discover, Dorian, that women treat us just as humanity treats its gods: they worship us but keep bothering us to do something for them.
The Picture of Dorian Gray, script: Albert Lewin, 1945

A woman has got to love a bad man once or twice in her life to be thankful for a good one.
Marjorie Kinnan Rawlings

Shame is the feeling you have when you agree with the woman who loves you that you are the man she thinks you are.
  Carl Sandburg, Incidentals, 1950

O powerful love! that in some respects, makes a beast a man, in some other, a man a beast.
  William Shakespeare, The Merry Wives of Windsor, 1600

Woman's virtue is man's greatest invention.
  Cornelia Otis Skinner

I am glad I am not a man, for if I were I should be obliged to marry a woman.
  Mme. de Staël

In the Spring a young man's fancy lightly turns to thoughts of love.
  Alfred, Lord Tennyson, Locksley Hall, 1842

'Tis strange what a man may do, and a woman yet think him an angel.
  William Thackeray

"Success in the outside world breeds success in the inside world of sex," sermonizes Dr. Reuben. "Conversely, the more potent a man becomes in the bedroom, the more potent he is in business." Is God a super-salesman? You bet!—and get this—God eats it too!
  Gore Vidal, The New York Review of Books, 1970

What is a highbrow? It is a man who has found something more interesting than women.
  Edgar Wallace, interview, 1931

The real paradox is that the men who make, materially, the biggest sacrifices for their women should do the least for them ideally and romantically.

Edith Wharton, The Custom of the Country, 1913

The sexual revolution began with Man's discovering that he was not attractive to Woman, as such. The lion had a mane, the peacock his gorgeous plumage, but Man found himself in a three-button sack suit.

E. B. White

If we men married the women we deserve, we should have a very bad time of it.

Oscar Wilde, An Ideal Husband, 1899

The Ideal Man . . . he should always say much more than he means, and always mean much more than he says.

Oscar Wilde, A Woman of No Importance, 1894

A man who is much talked about is always attractive. One feels there must be something in him, after all.

Oscar Wilde, The Importance of Being Earnest, 1899

Hysteria is a natural phenomenon, the common denominator of the female nature. It's the big female weapon, and the test of a man is his ability to cope with it.

Tennessee Williams, The Night of the Iguana, 1961

Chumps always make the best husbands. When you marry, Sally, grab a chump. Tap his forehead first, and if it rings solid, don't hesitate. All the unhappy marriages come from the husband having brains. What good are brains to a man? They only unsettle him.

P. G. Wodehouse, The Adventures of Sally, 1922

Why are women so much more interesting to men than
men are to women?
    Virginia Woolf

7. Just Like a Woman

Women like silent men. They think they're listening.
    Marcel Achard, 1956

I should say that the majority of women (happily for society) are not very much troubled by sexual feeling of any
kind. . . . Love for her husband and a wish to gratify his
passion, and in some women the knowledge that they
would be deserted for courtesans if they did not waive
their own inclinations may induce the indifferent, the pas-
sionless to admit the embrace of their husbands.
    *Dr. William Acton, The Function and Disorders of the Reproduc-
    tive Organs, 1857*

A woman seldom asks advice before she has bought her
wedding clothes.
    Joseph Addison, The Spectator

Women are really much nicer than men/No wonder we
like them.
    Kingsley Amis, The Listener, 1978

A man who is honest with himself wants a woman to be
soft and feminine, careful of what she's saying and talk
like a man.
    Ann-Margret

All the privilege I claim for my own sex . . . is that of loving longest, when existence or when hope is gone.
Jane Austen, Persuasion, 1818

Next to being married, a girl likes to be crossed in love, a little now and then.
Jane Austen, Pride and Prejudice, 1813

Women—one half of the human race at least—care fifty times more for a marriage than for a ministry.
Walter Bagehot, The Monarchy, 1867

Anything may be expected and anything may be supposed of a woman in love.
Honoré de Balzac, The Physiology of Marriage, 1828

Next to the wound, what women make best is the bandage.
Jules Barbey d'Aurevilly

It's a sort of bloom on a woman. If you have it [charm] you don't need to have anything else; and if you don't have it, it doesn't much matter what else you have.
J. M. Barrie, What Every Woman Knows, 1908

Of all the paths that lead to a woman's love/Pity's the straightest.
Francis Beaumont, John Fletcher, The Knight of Malta, 1619

There is no other purgatory but a woman.
Francis Beaumont, John Fletcher, The Scornful Lady, 1610

The supreme happiness of the woman in love is to be recognized by the loved man as a part of himself; when he says "we," she is associated and identified with him, she shares his prestige and reigns with him over the rest of the world; she never tires of repeating even to excess, this delectable "we."

Simone de Beauvoir, *The Second Sex*, 1953

No woman is worth the loss of a night's sleep.

Sir Thomas Beecham, *Beecham Stories*, 1978

Is it really asking too much of a woman to expect her to bring up a husband and her children too?

Lillian Bell, *Ladies' Home Journal*, 1944

In this vain world, when men of intellect/Must soil their souls with service, to expect/A morsel at the worthless prince's gate/How could they ever hope to renovate/Their spirits?—were it not that fate supplies/The swinging girdles and lotus eyes—/Women, with swelling breasts that comfort soon/Wearing the beauty of the rising moon.

Bhartrihari, *In This Vain World*

Indiscretion, n: The guilt of women.

Ambrose Bierce, *The Devil's Dictionary*, 1911

Women in love are less ashamed than men. They have less to be ashamed of.

Ambrose Bierce, *The Devil's Dictionary*, 1911

A woman is like a dresser, some man always goin' through her drawers.

Blues song

All women are born so perverse/No man need boast their love possessing.

Robert Bridges, *All Woman Are Born So Perverse*

Most beautiful but dumb girls think they are smart and get away with it, because other people, on the whole, aren't much smarter.

Louise Brooks, quoted in Kenneth Tynan, *Show People*, 1980

Leave the lady, Willy, let the racket rip/She is going to fool you, you have lost your grip/Your brain is in a muddle, your heart is in a whirl/Come along with me, Willy, never mind the girl!

Gelett Burgess, *Willy and the Lady*

Alas! the love of women! it is known/To be a lovely and a fearful thing!

Lord Byron, *Don Juan*, 1819–1824

Man's love is of man's life a thing apart,/'Tis woman's whole existence.

Lord Byron, *Don Juan*, 1819–1824

In her first passion woman loves her lover,/In all the others all she loves is love.

Lord Byron, *Don Juan*, 1819–1824

The love of man? Exotic flower,/Broken, crushed, within an hour,/The love of woman? Storm-swept sea/Surging into eternity.

Ellen M. Carroll, *Man and Woman*, 1932

Women should be elusive, mysterious and chaste. And I think that every man's ideal—even though they pretend it isn't today—is to find the wonderful, charming, delightful girl who will surrender to them. . . . The girls today are so stupid . . . they forget . . . that every single young man has a mother who says nice girls don't.

Barbara Cartland, quoted in Rachel Anderson, *The Purple Heart Throbs*, 1974

Women's favors, M. de——used to say, are auction-room transactions, where neither feeling nor merit ever bid successfully.
Nicholas-Sébastien Chamfort

Women have, in general, but one object, which is their beauty, upon which scarce any flattery is too gross for them to swallow.
Lord Chesterfield, Letters, 1748

The man's desire is for the woman; but the woman's desire is rarely other than for the desire of the man.
Samuel Taylor Coleridge, Table Talk

Among all the forms of absurd courage, the courage of girls is outstanding. Otherwise there would be fewer marriages. . . .
Colette

If you cannot inspire a woman with love of you, fill her above the brim with love of herself—all that runs over will be yours.
Charles Caleb Colton, Lacon, 1825

Women are like tricks by slight of hand/Which, to admire, we should not understand.
William Congreve, Love for Love, 1695

Heav'n has no rage, like love to hatred turn'd/Nor Hell a fury, like a woman scorn'd.
William Congreve, The Mourning Bride, 1697

Some fall in love with women who are rich, aristocratic or stupid. I am attracted by those who mysteriously hold out a promise of the integrity which I have lost; unsubdued daughters of Isis, beautiful as night, tumultuous as the moon-stirred Atlantic.

Cyril Connolly, The Unquiet Grave, 1945

Rough Diamonds Are a Girl's Best Friend.

Jilly Cooper, Class, 1979

With every woman, to love a man is to feel that she must positively know just where he is going as soon as he is out of her sight.

Marion Crawford, Ladies' Home Journal, 1944

In my callow youth, I was badly scratched several times before I learned that if there is one thing no girl wants to be called it is wholesome.

Robertson Davies, The Table Talk of Samuel Marchbanks, 1951

Most women set out to try and change a man, and when they have changed him they do not like him.

Marlene Dietrich

Every woman should marry—and no man.

Benjamin Disraeli, Lothair, 1870

The most winning woman I ever knew was hanged for poisoning three little children for their insurance money.

Arthur Conan Doyle, The Sign of Four, 1890

Woman inspires us to great things, and prevents us from achieving them.

Alexandre Dumas

She takes just like a woman, yes she does/She makes love just like a woman, yes she does/And she aches just like a woman/but she breaks just like a little girl.

Bob Dylan, Just Like a Woman, 1966

You will start out standing/Proud to steal her anything she sees/But you will wind up peeking through her keyhole/Down upon your knees.

Bob Dylan, She Belongs to Me, 1965

I should like to know what is the proper function of women, if it is not to make reasons for husbands to stay at home, and still stronger reasons for bachelors to go out.

George Eliot

I'm not denyin' the women are foolish: God Almighty made 'em to match the men.

George Eliot, Adam Bede, 1859

All women know the value of love. But few will pay the price.

Beth Ellis, Blind Mouths, 1907

The girl with a future avoids the man with a past.

Evan Esar, The Humor of Humor, 1954

A woman, even when married to a cad/Ought to be deferential, not a squabbler.

Euripides, Andromache, c. 426 b.c.

When a woman behaves like a man, why doesn't she behave like a nice man?

Edith Evans, The Observer, 1956

Women are less interested in epidermal friction than in emotional vibrations.

Beatrice Faust, *Women, Sex and Pornography*, 1980

Behind every man with pull is a woman with push.

Robert Felix, 1965

Women are like elephants to me: I like to look at them, but I wouldn't want to own one.

W. C. Fields

In all your amours you should prefer old women to young ones . . . they have greater knowledge of the world.

Benjamin Franklin

Woman's basic fear is that she will lose love.

Sigmund Freud, *Civilization and Its Discontents*, 1930

Bitter indeed it is to be born a woman/It is difficult to imagine anything so low!/. . . No one sheds a tear when she is married off . . ./Her husband's love is as aloof as the Milky Way,/Yet she must follow him like a sunflower the sun./Their hearts are soon as far apart as fire and water/She is blamed for all and everything that may go wrong.

Fu Hsuan, *Yu-t'ai-hsin-yung*

Man may escape from rope and gun/Nay, some have out-liv'd the doctor's pill/Who takes a woman must be un-done/That basilisk is sure to kill./The fly that sips the treacle is lost in the sweets/So he that tastes woman, woman, woman/He that tastes woman, ruin meets.

John Gay, *The Beggar's Opera*, 1728

She who has never loved has never lived.

John Gay, *The Captives*, 1724

To win a woman in the first place one must please her, then undress her, and then somehow get her clothes back on her. Finally, so that she will allow you to leave her, you've got to annoy her.
> Jean Giraudoux, *Amphitryon 38*, 1929

Women are silver dishes into which we put golden apples.
> Johann Wolfgang von Goethe, quoted in P. Eckermann, *Conversations with Goethe*, 1828

She Stoops to Conquer
> Oliver Goldsmith, play title, 1773

Women and love always constitute the subject of conversation wherever there is a meeting of intellectual people socially brought together by eating and drinking.
> Edmond de Goncourt, *Journal*, 1887–1896

Of all the plagues with which the world is curst/Of every ill, a woman is the worst.
> George Granville, *The British Enchanters*, 1732

To be so beautiful, so alluring, that the man forgets all else and simply loves, that is what every woman wants and whoever denies it is in error, or wilfully lying.
> George Groddeck, *The Book of the It*, 1935

Here's to the love that lies in woman's eyes. And lies and lies and lies.
> Lewis C. Henry, *Toasts for All Occasions*

If men knew how women pass the time when they are alone, they'd never marry.
> O. Henry, *Memoirs of a Yellow Dog*

Adam's Rib: the original bone of contention.

Oliver Herford, John Clay, Cupid's Cyclopedia, 1910

Do not let any sweet-talking woman beguile thy good sense/with the fascination of her shape. It's your barn she's after.

Hesoid, Works and Days, c. 8th century B.C.

A woman would no doubt need a great deal of imagination to love a man for his virtue.

John Oliver Hobbes, The Sinner's Comedy, 1892

Man has his will—but woman has her way.

Oliver Wendell Holmes, Sr., The Autocrat of the Breakfast Table, 1857–1858

No woman ever falls in love with a man unless she had a better opinion of him than he deserves.

Edgar Watson Howe

One hair of a woman can draw more than a hundred pair of oxen.

James Howell, Familiar Letters, 1650

After a girl gits too big fer Santy Claus, she begins t'cast around for an easy mark.

Frank McKinney "Kin" Hubbard, Abe Martin's Primer

No matter how low their necks are cut, or how high their skirts get, we'll always have to take chances on their real disposition.

Kin Hubbard, The New York Times, 1953

The art of managing men has to be learned from birth. . . .
It depends, to some extent, on one's distribution of
curves, a developed instinct and a large degree of feline
cunning.
   Mary Hyde, *How to Manage Men*, 1955

CECIL PARKER: There is no sincerity like a woman telling
a lie.
   Indiscreet, script: Norman Krasna, 1958

A woman's whole life is a history of the affections.
   Washington Irving, *The Broken Heart*

She would have liked for instance . . . to marry; and nothing in general is more ridiculous, even when it has been
pathetic, than a woman who has tried and has not been
able.
   Henry James, *The Golden Bowl*, 1904

A woman is more responsive to a man's forgetfulness
than to his attentions.
   Jules Janin

A woman that's too soft and sweet is like a tapioca pudding—fine for them as likes it.
   Osa Johnson, *I Married Adventure*, 1940

Nature has given women so much power that the law has
very wisely given them little.
   Samuel Johnson

If I had no duties, and no reference to futurity, I would
spend my life driving briskly in a post-chaise with a pretty
woman.
   Samuel Johnson, quoted in James Boswell, *The Life of Samuel
   Johnson*, 1791

For women's tears are but the sweat of eyes.
Juvenal, Satires, c. 100

ROBERT ARMSTRONG: No, it wasn't the airplane. It was Beauty killed the Beast.
King Kong, script: James A Creelman, Ruth Rose, 1933

And a woman is only a woman, but a good cigar is a Smoke.
Rudyard Kipling, The Betrothed, 1899

When the Himalayan peasant meets the he-bear in his pride/He shouts to scare the monster, who will often turn aside/But the she-bear thus accosted rends the peasant tooth and nail/For the female of the species is more deadly than the male.
Rudyard Kipling, The Female of the Species

Take my word for it, the silliest woman can manage a clever man, but it needs a very clever woman to manage a fool.
Rudyard Kipling, Plain Tales from the Hills, 1888

A woman's guess is much more accurate than a man's certainty.
Rudyard Kipling, Plain Tales from the Hills, 1888

A woman occasionally is quite a serviceable substitute for masturbation. It takes an abundance of imagination, to be sure.
Karl Kraus

Women run to extremes—they are either better or worse than men.
Jean de La Bruyère, Les Caractères, 1688

Oh if thou lovest/And art a woman, hide thy love from him/Whom thou dost worship. Never let him know/ How dear he is.

Letitia Landon, *Despondency*, 1850

1. Lockjaw; 2. Hereditary obesity; 3. Shortness of breath; 4. Falling arches; 5. Mechanical engineering; 6. Draftsmanship; 7. Absolutely fireproof; 8. Day and night elevator service; 9. Laundry sent out before 8:30 A.M. will be returned the same day; 10. Please report to the management any incivility on part of employees.

Ring Lardner, *Specifications for the Ideal Woman*

I'm not sure if a mental relation with a woman doesn't make it impossible to love her. To know the mind of a woman is to end in hating her. Love means the pre-cognitive flow . . . it is the honest state before the apple.

D. H. Lawrence, *letter*, 1927

The real trouble about women is that they must always go on trying to adapt themselves to men's theories about women.

D. H. Lawrence

Being a woman is of special interest only to aspiring male transsexuals. To actual women, it is simply a good excuse not to play football.

Fran Lebowitz, *Metropolitan Life*, 1979

Why can't a woman be more like a man?

Alan Jay Lerner, *My Fair Lady*, 1956

. . . older woman, younger man! Popular wisdom claims that this particular class of love affair is the most poignant, tender, poetic, exquisite one there is, altogether the choicest on the menu.

Doris Lessing, *The Summer Before the Dark,* 1973

Love, that of every woman's heart/Will have the whole, and not a part,/That is to her, in Nature's plan,/More than ambition is to man,/Her light, her life, her very breath,/With no alternative but death.

Henry Wadsworth Longfellow, *The Golden Legend,* 1851

A woman is compromised the second she's born.

Clare Boothe Luce, *The Women,* 1937

Women are not men's equals in anything except responsibility. We are not their inferiors either, or even their superiors. We are quite simply a different race.

Phyllis McGinley, *The Province of the Heart,* 1959

A caress is better than a career.

Elisabeth Marbury, *interview on careers for women*

Anyone who says he can see through women is missing a lot.

Groucho Marx, *Quote and Unquote,* 1970

Don't say "And you know, you are the first," because he would pretend to believe it but only out of sheer courtesy. Say "Before I knew you, I didn't know what it was," because that men always believe.

Georges-Armand Masson

A woman will always sacrifice herself if you give her the opportunity. It is her favourite form of self-indulgence.

W. Somerset Maugham, *The Circle,* 1921

Women's hearts are like old china, none the worse for a break or two.
  W. Somerset Maugham, Lady Frederick, 1907

When women kiss it always reminds one of prize fighters shaking hands.
  H. L. Mencken

Love is based upon a view of women that is impossible to any man who has had any experience of them.
  H. L. Mencken, Prejudices, 1924

The allurement that women hold out to men is precisely the allurement that Cape Hatteras holds out to sailors: they are enormously dangerous and hence enormously fascinating.
  H. L. Mencken, The Smart Set, 1919

I expect that Woman will be the last thing civilised by Man.
  George Meredith, The Ordeal of Richard Feverel, 1859

Aren't women prudes if they don't and prostitutes if they do?
  Kate Millett, 1975

Treat a whore like a lady and a lady like a whore.
  Wilson Mizner

It goes far towards reconciling me to being a woman when I reflect I am thus in no danger of marrying one.
  Lady Mary Wortley Montagu

As soon as women belong to us, we no longer belong to them.
  Michel de Montaigne, Essays, 1588

Howe'er man rules in science and in art,/The sphere of woman's glories is the heart.

Thomas Moore, Epilogue to the Tragedy of Ina, in Works, 1820

Woman is: finally screwing and your groin and buttocks and thighs ache like hell and you're all wet and maybe bloody and it wasn't like a Hollywood movie at all but Jesus at least you're not a virgin any more but is this what it's all about? And meanwhile he's asking "Did you come?"

Robin Morgan, Sisterhood Is Powerful, 1970

The woman we love will always be in the right.

Alfred de Musset, Idylle, 1852

Joan is as good as my lady in the dark.

Duchess of Newcastle, Sociable Companions

A woman may very well form a friendship with a man, but for this to endure, it must be assisted by a little physical antipathy.

Friedrich Nietzsche

Two different things wanteth the true man: danger and diversion. Therefore wanteth he woman, as the most dangerous plaything.

Friedrich Nietzsche, Thus Spake Zarathustra, 1883–1891

If women didn't exist all the money in the world would have no meaning.

Aristotle Onassis

ED: Women are like banks, boy. Breaking and entering is a serious business.

Joe Orton, Entertaining Mr. Sloane, 1964

Destructive, damnable, deceitful woman!
    Thomas Otway, The Orphan, 1680

Oh woman! lovely woman! Nature made thee/To temper man: we had been brutes without you;/Angels are painted fair, to look like you.
    Thomas Otway, Venice Preserved, 1682

What is it that love does to a woman? Without it she only sleeps. With it alone she lives.
    Ouïda, Wisdom, Wit and Pathos, 1884

Whether a pretty woman grants or witholds her favors, she always likes to be asked for them.
    Ovid, The Art of Love

Most good women are hidden treasures who are only safe because nobody looks for them.
    Dorothy Parker

Ah wasteful woman, she who may/On her sweet self set her own price/Knowing man cannot choose but pay/How she has cheapened paradise.
    Coventry Patmore, The Angel in the House, 1856–1862

Woman gives herself as a prize to the weak and as a prop to the strong, and no man ever has what he should.
    Cesare Pavese

Woman . . . is a real devil, an enemy of peace, a source of provocation, a cause of disputes, from whom man must hold himself apart if he wishes to taste tranquility. . . . Let them marry, those who are attracted by the company of a wife, by nightly embraces, the screaming of children and the torment of insomnia. . . . As for us, if it is in our power, we will perpetuate our name through talent and not through marriage, through books and not through children, with the cooperation of virtue and not with that of a woman.

Petrarch, *Physic Against Fortune*, 14th century

GEORGE SANDERS: Women, as so many Frenchmen put it, inspire us with the desire to do masterpieces, and always prevent us from carrying them out.

The Picture of Dorian Gray, script: Albert Lewin, 1945

Boys don't make passes at female smart-asses.

Letty Cottin Pogrebin, 1972

The years that a woman subtracts from her age are not lost. They are added to other women's.

Diane de Poitiers

Every woman is at heart a rake.

Alexander Pope

Woman's at best a contradiction still.

Alexander Pope, *Moral Essays*, 1731–1735

There is not a woman in the world the possession of whom is as precious as that of the truth which she reveals to us by causing us to suffer.

Marcel Proust

A woman either loves or hates; there is no third course.

Publilius Syrus, *Moral Sayings*, 1st century B.C.

Married and unmarried women waste a lot of time feeling sorry for each other.
  Myrtle Reed, The Spinster Book, 1901

A woman whose dresses are made in Paris and whose marriage has been made in Heaven might be equally biased for and against free imports.
  Saki, The Unbearable Bassington, 1912

In their hearts women think that it is men's business to earn money and theirs to spend it.
  Arthur Schopenhauer, Parerga and Paralipomena, 1851

O Woman, in our hours of ease,/Uncertain, coy and hard to please,/And variable as the shade/By the light quivering aspen made;/When pain and anguish wring the brow/A ministering angel thou!
  Sir Walter Scott, Marmion, 1808

OPHELIA: 'Tis brief, my Lord.
HAMLET: As woman's love.
  William Shakespeare, Hamlet, 1600

When my love swears that she is made of truth/I do believe her, though I know she lies.
  William Shakespeare, Sonnet 138

The only way for a woman to provide for herself decently is for her to be good to some man that can afford to be good to her.
  George Bernard Shaw, Mrs. Warren's Profession, 1898

Here's to the maiden of bashful fifteen;/Here's to the widow of fifty;/Here's to the flaunting, extravagant queen;/And here's to the housewife that's thrifty./Let the toast pass—/Drink to the lass,/I'll warrant she'll prove an excuse for the glass.

Richard Brinsley Sheridan, *The School for Scandal*, 1777

To tell a woman what she may not do is to tell her what she can.

Spanish proverb

Love is the history of a woman's life; it is an episode in man's.

Mme. de Staël, *De l'Influence des Passions*, 1796

Man is the hunter; woman is his game:/The sleek and shining creatures of the chase,/We hunt them for the beauty of their skins;/They love us for it, and we ride them down.

Alfred, Lord Tennyson, *The Princess*, 1851

Women add zest to the unlicensed hours.

Allen D. Thomas

A constant woman—the greatest impossibility!

Tirso de Molina, *El amor y el amistad*, 1734

Women are well aware that what is commonly called sublime and poetical love depends not upon moral qualities, but on frequent meetings, and on the style in which the hair is done up, and on the color and cut of the dress.

Leo Tolstoy, *The Kreutzer Sonata*, 1890

A girl can't analyze marriage, and a woman . . . daren't.

Lady Troubridge, *The Millionaire*, 1907

In love women are professionals, men are amateurs.

François Truffaut, 1979

To be a woman is to have the same needs and longings as a man. We need love and we wish to give it. If only we could accept that there is no difference between us where human values are concerned. Whatever sex. Whatever life we have chosen to live.
    Liv Ullmann, Changing, 1976

It is possible that blondes also prefer gentlemen.
    Maimie Van Doren, Quote and Unquote, 1970

If women could be fair and yet not fond.
    Edward de Vere, Women's Changeableness

The female woman is one of the great institooshuns of which this land can boste.
    Artemus Ward, Artemus Ward, His Book, 1862

There's nothing sooner dry than a woman's tears.
    John Webster, The White Devil, 1608

From a wealth of living I have proved/I must be silent, if I would be loved.
    Anna Wickham, The Affinity, in Selected Poems, 1936

Women give to men the very gold of their lives. But they invariably want it back in small change.
    Oscar Wilde

I don't know that women are always rewarded for being charming. I think they are usually punished for it.
    Oscar Wilde, An Ideal Husband, 1899

All women become like their mothers. That is their tragedy. No man does. That's his.
    Oscar Wilde, The Importance of Being Earnest, 1899

The only way to behave to a woman is to make love to her, if she is pretty, and to someone else, if she is plain.
Oscar Wilde, The Importance of Being Earnest, 1899

The only way a woman can ever reform a man is by boring him so completely that he loses all possible interest in life.
Oscar Wilde, The Picture of Dorian Gray, 1891

The history of women is the history of the worst form of tyranny the world has ever seen. The tyranny of the weak over the strong; it is the only tyranny that lasts.
Oscar Wilde, A Woman of No Importance, 1894

Women—Sphinxes without secrets.
Oscar Wilde, A Woman of No Importance, 1894

Man, poor, awkward, reliable, necessary man, belongs to a sex that has been rational for millions and millions of years. He can't help himself. It is in his race. The History of Woman is very different. We have always been picturesque protests against the mere existence of common sense. We saw its dangers from the first.
Oscar Wilde, A Woman of No Importance, 1894

The gentler sex love blackmail. Show me a delicately nurtured female and I will show you a ruthless Napoleon of crime prepared without turning a hair to put the screws on some unfortunate male whose services she happens to be in need of. There ought to be a law. . . .
P. G. Wodehouse, Stiff Upper Lip, Jeeves, 1963

Women have served all these centuries as looking-glasses possessing the magic and delicious power of reflecting the figure of man at twice its natural size.
Virginia Woolf, A Room of One's Own, 1929

A creature not too bright or good/For human nature's daily food . . ./A perfect woman, nobly planned/To warn, to comfort and command. . . .
    William Wordsworth, letter to Mary Wordsworth

Why should women have more invention in love than men? It can only be, because they have more desires, more soliciting passions, more lust and more of the devil.
    William Wycherley, The Country Wife, 1672

Never give all the heart, for love/Will hardly seem worth thinking of/To passionate women if it seem/Certain, and they never dream/That it fades out from kiss to kiss. . . .
    William Butler Yeats, Never Give All the Heart, in Collected Poems, 1950

A beautiful woman who is pleasing to men is good only for frightening fish when she falls into the water.
    Zen proverb

8. Battle of the Sexes

Most married couples conduct themselves as if each party were afraid that the other one could see that it was the weaker.
    Alfred Adler, quoted in Count Hermann Keyserling, The Book of Marriage, 1926

There is one woman whom fate has destined for each of us. If we miss her, we are saved.

Anonymous, *The New York Times*, 1948

The woman whose life is of the head will strive to inspire her husband with indifference; the woman whose life is of the heart, with hatred; the passionate woman, with disgust.

Honoré de Balzac, *The Physiology of Marriage*, 1828

It is better to dwell in the corner of the housetop than with a brawling woman in a wide house.

The Bible, *Proverbs*

The more violent the love, the more violent the anger.

Burmese proverb

The man in arms 'gainst female charms,/Even he her willing slave is.

Robert Burns, *Lovely Davies*

Oh! too convincing—dangerously dear—/In woman's eye the unanswerable tear.

Lord Byron, *The Corsair*, 1814

A quarrel between man and wife is like cutting water with a sword.

Chinese proverb

Man and wife/Coupled together for sake of strife.

Charles Churchill, *The Rosciad*, 1761

There is more difference within the sexes than between them.

Ivy Compton-Burnett, *Mother and Son*, 1955

In the sex-war thoughtlessness is the weapon of the male, vindictiveness of the female.
Cyril Connolly, The Unquiet Grave, 1945

Never go to bed mad. Stay up and fight.
Phyllis Diller, Phyllis Diller's Housekeeping Hints, 1966

Just such disparity/As is 'twixt air and Angels' purity/'Twixt women's love and men's will ever be.
John Donne, Air and Angels, in Collected Works, 1633

Men live by forgetting—women live on memories.
T. S. Eliot, The Elder Statesman, 1958

It is a maxim that man and wife should never have it in their power to hang one another.
George Farquhar, The Beaux' Strategem, 1707

Most women have to ask themselves how a man could be so insensitive as to want to continue love-making when the baby is wailing or the telephone ringing; most men have wondered how a woman could be so easily diverted by such trivial interruptions.
Beatrice Faust, Women, Sex and Pornography, 1980

Men see coitus as the meat in the sandwich of foreplay and afterplay; women see it as the ice cream in a Bombe Alaska of intimate emotional exchange.
Beatrice Faust, Women, Sex and Pornography, 1980

When men and women die as poets sung/His heart's the last part moved, her last, the tongue.
Benjamin Franklin, Poor Richard's Almanack, 1732–1757

The music at a wedding procession always reminds me of the music of soldiers going into battle.
    Heinrich Heine

Love is a kind of war; hence those who fear,/No cowards must his royal ensigns bear.
    Robert Herrick, On Love, 1648

Breathes there a man with hide so tough/Who says two sexes aren't enough.
    Samuel Hoffenstein, The Two Sexes

"Boys will be boys"—"And even that wouldn't matter if we could prevent girls being girls."
    Anthony Hope, The Dolly Dialogues, 1894

Love has two evils—war, then peace.
    Horace, Satires, 1st century B.C.

To a man, the disappointment of love may occasion some bitter pangs: it wounds some feelings of tenderness—it blasts some prospects of felicity; but he is an active being— he may dissipate his thoughts in the whirl of varied occupation. . . . But woman's is comparatively a fixed, a secluded, and meditative life. . . . Her lot is to be wooed and won; and if unhappy in her love, her heart is like some fortress that has been captured, and sacked, and abandoned, and left desolate.
    Washington Irving, The Sketch Book, 1820

Feminine passion is to masculine as an epic is to an epigram.
    Karl Kraus

The first tiff in love, as the first misstep in friendship, is the only one we can turn to good use.
    Jean de La Bruyère

He is being devoured/by his dread of being devoured/ She is being devoured/By her desire to be devoured.
    R. D. Laing, Knots, 1970

All married couples should learn the art of battle as they should learn the art of making love. Good battle is objective and honest—never vicious and cruel. Good battle is healthy and constructive and brings to a marriage the principle of equal partnership.
    Ann Landers, Ann Landers Says That Truth Is Stranger . . ., 1968

A man defending husbands vs. wives or men vs. women has got about as much chance as a traffic policeman trying to stop a mad dog by blowing two whistles.
    Ring Lardner, Say It with Oil, 1923

It is hardly too much to say that most domestic tragedies are caused by the feminine intuition of men and the want of it in women.
    Ada Leverson

The First World War started because of a difference between Adam and Eve.
    Art Linkletter, A Child's Garden of Misinformation, 1963

The Japanese have a word for it. It's judo—the art of conquering by yielding. The Western equivalent of judo is "Yes, dear."
    J. P. McEvoy, Charlie Would Have Loved This

The libido of the tired housewife and her highly stressed executive husband seems to work in different ways. The man seems like to find escape from tension through sex, whereas the wife cannot enjoy sex until she escapes from her tension.

J. MacIntyre, *Australian Forum*, 1978

A woman can forgive a man for the harm he does her, but she can never forgive him for the sacrifices he makes on her account.

W. Somerset Maugham, *The Moon and Sixpence*, 1919

Men hate and fear women more than women hate and fear men. I think it is this rather than the male's superior strength that makes it possible for our civilization to be called "a man's world." It is not a contest of strength, it is a contest of hate.

Dr. Karl Menninger, *A Psychiatrist's World*, 1959

Tranquility in love is a disagreeable calm.

Molière, *Les Fourberies de Scapin*, 1671

Girls marry for "love." Boys marry because of a chronic irritation that causes them to gravitate in the direction of objects with certain curvilinear properties.

Ashley Montagu

A good marriage would be between a blind wife and a deaf husband.

Michel de Montaigne

Alas! how light a cause may move/Dissension between hearts that love!

Thomas Moore, *The Light of the Harem*, 1817

Man is lyrical, woman epic, marriage dramatic.
Novalis

Quarrels are the dowry which married folk bring to one another.
Ovid, The Art of Love

Love is a kind of warfare.
Ovid, The Art of Love

Woman wants monogamy/Man delights in novelty.
Dorothy Parker, Enough Rope, 1927

Even the wisest men make fools of themselves about women, and even the most foolish women are wise about men.
Theodor Reik, The Need to Be Loved, 1963

Love lessens woman's delicacy and increases man's.
Jean Paul Richter

Quarrels in France strengthen a love affair. In America they end it.
Ned Rorem, Paris Diary, 1966

When we want to read of the deeds that are done for love, whither do we turn? To the murder column.
George Bernard Shaw

It is a woman's business to get married as soon as possible, and a man's to keep unmarried as long as he can.
George Bernard Shaw, Man and Superman

I'm hungry for learnin'/Won't you answer me please/ Can a man and a woman live together in peace?
Paul Simon

Love is like war: you begin when you like and leave off when you can.
Spanish proverb

Men come of age at sixty, women at fifteen.
James Stephens, The Observer, 1944

Marriage is like life in this—that it is a field of battle, and not a bed of roses.
Robert Louis Stevenson, Virginibus Puerisque, 1881

Men and women differ in their sexual natures because throughout the immensely long hunting and gathering phase of human evolutionary history, the sexual desires and dispositions that were adaptive for either sex were for the other tickets to reproductive oblivion.
Donald Symons, The Evolution of Human Sexuality, 1980

Better to sit up all night than to go to bed with a dragon.
Jeremy Taylor, Holy Living and Dying, 1650

If I had had a pistol I would have shot him—either that or fallen at his feet. There is no middle way when one loves.
Lady Troubridge, The Millionaire, 1907

ALAN BATES: I was married for nine years. Eight of those years were very passionate. But . . . well, passion's a mild word for it, really. It's . . . well, it was more like war.
An Unmarried Woman, script: Paul Mazursky, 1978

From now on we are opposed, a man and a woman in love . . . the greatest, the most exhausting struggle in the world. Two moths racing for the flame—two cannibals devouring each other.
Peter Ustinov, Romanoff and Juliet, 1961

Just a little more loving and a lot less fighting and the world would be all right.

> Mae West, *Esquire*, 1968

When a woman marries again it is because she detested her first husband. When a man marries again, it is because he adored his first wife. Women try their luck, men risk theirs.

> Oscar Wilde, *The Picture of Dorian Gray*, 1891

Nothing spoils a romance so much as a sense of humour in the woman, or the want of it in the man.

> Oscar Wilde, *A Woman of No Importance*, 1893

The best part of married life is the fights—the rest is merely so-so.

> Thornton Wilder, *The Matchmaker*, 1957

He and Rosie had always been like a couple of turtle doves, but he knew only too well that when the conditions are right, a female turtle dove can express herself with a vigour which a Caribbean hurricane might envy.

> P. G. Wodehouse, *quoted in* R. Usborne, *A Wodehouse Companion*, 1981

9. *The Pleasure Principle*

My opinion is that taking the hard-working intellectual married man residing in London as the type, sexual congress had better not take place more frequently more than once in seven or ten days . . . in highly civilised communities the countinuance of a high degree of bodily and mental vigour is inconsistent with more than a *very moderate* indulgence in sexual intercourse.

Dr. William Acton, *The Function and Disorders of the Reproductive Organs*, 1857

I have to find a girl attractive or it's like trying to start a car without an ignition key.

Jonathan Aitken, *News of the World*, 1979

Is sex dirty? Only if it's done right.

Woody Allen, *Everything You Ever Wanted to Know About Sex*, 1972

Love is the answer, but while you are waiting for the answer, sex raises some pretty good questions.

Woody Allen, *New York Herald Tribune*, 1975

WOODY ALLEN: That was the most fun I've had without laughing.

Annie Hall, script: Woody Allen, Marshall Brickman, 1977

If it is not erotic, it is not interesting.

Fernando Arrabal

I was brought up to believe that it was insulting to sleep with your wife or any lady. A gentleman stays eagerly awake. He sleeps at his work.

Alan Ayckbourn, *The Norman Conquests*, 1975

It's not until sex has died out between a man and a woman that they can really love. And now I mean affection. Now I mean to be *fond of* (as one is fond of oneself)— to hope, to be disappointed, to live inside the other heart.

Enid Bagnold, *Autobiography*, 1969

Advice to long-married man on sex: Think of your mistress.

> Honoré de Balzac, *The Physiology of Marriage*, 1828

Sexuality is the lyricism of the masses.

> Charles Baudelaire, *Intimate Journals*, 1887

Drinking when we are not thirsty and making love at all seasons, madam: that is all there is to distinguish us from the other animals.

> Pierre de Beaumarchais, *The Barber of Seville*, 1775

Sex is like money—very nice to have but vulgar to talk about.

> Tonia Berg, 1971

For to be carnally minded is death.

> The Bible, Romans

The ability to make love frivolously is the chief characteristic which distinguishes human beings from the beasts.

> Heywood Broun, quoted in H. Teichman, *George S. Kaufman*, 1972

Man, we're all the same cats, we're all the same *schmuck*— Johnson, me, you, every *putz* has got that one chick, he's yelling like a real dum-dum: "Please touch it once. Touch it once, touch it once!"

> Lenny Bruce, quoted in J. Cohen, *The Essential Lenny Bruce*, 1966

Sex is interesting, but it's not totally important. I mean it's not even as important (physically) as excretion. A man can go seventy years without a piece of ass, but he can die in a week without a bowel movement.

> Charles Bukowski, *Notes of a Dirty Old Man*, 1969

Love is a way with some meaning; sex is meaning enough.
  Charles Bukowski, *Notes of a Dirty Old Man*, 1969

Thunder and lightning, wars, fires and plagues, have not done that mischief to mankind as this burning lust.
  Robert Burton, *Anatomy of Melancholy*, 1621

It doesn't matter what you do in the bedroom as long as you don't do it in the street and frighten the horses.
  Mrs. Patrick Campbell

Women in the street. The warm beast of desire that lies curled up in our loins and stretches itself with a fierce gentleness.
  Albert Camus, *Notebooks*, 1935–1942

Desire is a question to which no-one has the answer.
  Luis Cernuda, *No decia palabras*, in *Collected Poems*, 1971

The pleasure is momentary, the position ridiculous and the expense damnable.
  Lord Chesterfield (attrib.)

Sex ought to be a wholly satisfying link between two affectionate people from which they emerge unanxious, rewarded and ready for more.
  Alex Comfort, *The Joy of Sex*, 1972

There are only two guidelines in good sex: "Don't do anything you don't really enjoy" and "Find out your partner's needs and don't balk them if you can help it."
  Alex Comfort, *The Joy of Sex*, 1972

If our elaborate and dominating bodies are given to us to be denied at every turn, if our nature is always wrong and wicked, how ineffectual we are—like fishes not meant to swim.
> Cyril Connolly, *The Unquiet Grave*, 1945

Sex is only the liquid centre of the Newberry Fruit of friendship.
> Jilly Cooper, *SuperJilly*

Sex is the great amateur art. The professional, male or female, is frowned upon: he or she misses the whole point and spoils the show.
> David Cort, *Social Astonishments*, 1963

Sex is the last refuge of the miserable.
> Quentin Crisp, *The Naked Civil Servant*, 1968

Physiological expenditure is a superficial way of self-expression. People who incline towards physical love accomplish nothing at all.
> Salvador Dali, *Dairy of a Genius*, 1966

The act of sex, gratifying as it may be, is God's joke on humanity. It is man's last desperate stand at superintendancy.
> Bette Davis, *The Lonely Life*, 1962

Man and woman are two very evil-minded beasts.
> Denis Diderot, *Ceci N'est Pas un Conte*

Virtue is not photogenic.
> Kirk Douglas

Sex is about as important as a cheese sandwich. But a cheese sandwich, if you ain't got one to put in your belly, is extremely important.

Ian Dury

You come awake in a horny morning mood/And have a proper wriggle in the naughty naked nude/Roll against my body, get me where you want me/What happens next is private, it's also very rude.

Ian Dury, *Wake Up and Make Love with Me,* 1979

Your debutante knows what you need/But I know what you want.

Bob Dylan, *Stuck Inside of Mobile with the Memphis Blues Again,* 1966

If your life at night is good you think you have/Everything; but if in that quarter things go wrong/You will consider your best and truest interests/Most hateful.

Euripides, *Medea,* 431 B.C.

Sex may be a hallowing and renewing experience, but more often it will be distracting, coercive, playful, frivolous, discouraging, dutiful and even boring.

Leslie H. Farber, *The Ways of the Will*

Men . . . fail to notice that sex objects may perceive themselves as sex subjects.

Beatrice Faust, *Woman, Sex and Pornography,* 1980

The big difference between sex for money and sex for free is that sex for money usually costs a lot less.

Brendan Francis

The sexual instinct is undoubtedly the most powerful source of persisting increases of excitation (and consequently of neuroses). Such increases are distributed very unevenly over the nervous system. When they reach a considerable degree of intensity the train of ideas becomes disturbed and the relative value of the ideas is changed; and in orgasm thought is almost completely extinguished.

Sigmund Freud, Complete Works, 1955

. . . Apart from sick-nursing, no psychical factor is so well-calculated to produce reveries charged with affect as are the longings of a person in love. And over and above this the sexual orgasm itself . . . is closely akin to hypnoid states.

Sigmund Freud, Complete Works, 1955

The sexual behavior of a human being often *lays down the pattern* for all his other modes of reacting to life. If a man is energetic in winning the object of his love, we are confident that he will pursue his other aims with an equally unswerving energy; but if, for all sorts of reasons, he refrains from satisfying this strong sexual instincts, his behavior will be conciliatory and resigned . . . in other spheres of life as well.

Sigmund Freud, Complete Works, 1955

In one class of cases being in love is nothing more than object-cathexis on the part of the sexual instincts with a view to direct sexual satisfaction, a cathexis which expires, moreover, when this aim has been reached, this is what is called common, sensual love.

Sigmund Freud, Complete Works, 1955

The erotic has its reasons that reason does not know.

Nancy Friday, Men in Love, 1980

Erotic love begins with separateness, and ends in one-ness. Motherly love begins with oneness, and leads to sep-arateness.

Erich Fromm, *The Sane Society*, 1955

Sexual drive is the drug which sweeps us into passion and which we exaggerate to remove responsibility.

Jonathan Gathorne-Hardy, *Love, Sex, Marriage and Divorce*, 1981

LOUIS JOURDAN: The only people who make love all the time are liars.

Gigi, script: Alan Jay Lerner, 1958

From desire I plunge to its fulfillment, where I long once more for desire.

Johann Wolfgang von Goethe, *Faust*, 1770–1832

As in all other experiences, we always have the sexual ex-perience we deserve, depending on our loving kindness towards our self and others.

Thaddeus Golas, *The Lazy Man's Guide to Enlightenment*

Because of its secret nature, you should not talk or write about sex. You can have love talk with the person you're in love with—that's a different matter. But any talk of sex with others is anti-human.

Robert Graves, *Playboy*, 1970

Sex . . . can be summed up in three Ps: procreation, plea-sure and pride. From the long-range point of view, which we must always consider, procreation is by far the most important. . . . So female orgasm is simply a nervous cli-max to sex relations . . . and as such it is a comparative luxury from nature's point of view. It may be thought of as a sort of pleasurelike prize that comes with a box of ce-

real. It is all to the good if the prize is there, but the cereal is valuable and nourishing if it is not.
    Madeline Grey, *The Normal Woman*, 1967

Words have no language which can utter the secrets of love; and beyond the limits of expression is the expounding of desire.
    Shirazi Hafiz, *The Divan*, 1831

If men did not put their responsibilities above everything else, the bulk of love-making would not be done at night.
    Harry S. Haskins, *Meditations in Wall Street*, 1940

Don't forget, the penis is mightier than the sword.
    Screamin' Jay Hawkins

Always remember: after ten o'clock a man becomes a beast.
    Head of a women's college, *The Listener*, 1979

Sexual pleasure, rightly understood, is the most spiritual thing, sublimer, purer, more noble and ennobling than any prayer.
    James Hinton

Love making is radical, while marriage is conservative.
    Eric Hoffer

Oh! there's nothing in life like making love.
    Thomas Hood, *Miss Kilmansegg: Her Courtship*, 1841–1843

Chastity—the most unnatural of the sexual perversions.
    Aldous Huxley

Bed, as the Italian proverb succinctly puts it, is the poor man's opera.

Aldous Huxley, Heaven and Hell, 1956

The Kama Sutra is the Mrs. Beeton of sex.

Aldous Huxley, The Sunday Times of London, 1973

Wink, wink, nudge, nudge, say no more, know what I mean . . .

Eric Idle, Monty Python's Flying Circus, 1969

Acting is not very hard. The most important things are to be able to laugh and cry. If I have to cry, I think of my sex life. And if I have to laugh, well, I think of my sex life.

Glenda Jackson

If it were not for imagination, Sir, a man would be as happy in the arms of a chambermaid as of a Duchess.

Samuel Johnson, quoted in James Boswell, The Life of Samuel Johnson, 1791

. . . the Zipless Fuck. The zipless fuck was more than a fuck. It was a platonic ideal . . . the zipless fuck is absolutely pure. It is free of ulterior motives. There is no power game. The man is not "taking" and the woman is not "giving." No one is attempting to cuckold a husband or humiliate a wife. No one is trying to prove anything or get anything out of anyone. The zipless fuck is the purest thing there is. And it is rarer than the unicorn.

Erica Jong, Fear of Flying, 1973

It is hardly possible to estimate how many marriages fail to prosper or are actually ruined because the man lacks any inkling of the art of love.

Count Hermann Keyserling, The Book of Marriage

Outlets [orgasms] are as necessary as the tying off of an artery that has been cut, the provision of air for a suffocating man, or food for a starving man.

Alfred Kinsey, *Sexual Behavior in the Human Male*, 1948

Power is the great aphrodisiac.

Henry Kissinger, *The New York Times*, 1971

. . . a springlike enchantment! And don't think I'm talking about anything else but love in its strictly bodily sense. Even so, it is the domain of a chosen few.

Alexander Kuprin

I doubt that anything since DDT has been so overrated as sex, or with such catastrophic results . . . sex is vastly overrated, and most of us don't dare say so.

Irma Kurtz, 1974

The pleasure of making love increases the indifference felt towards the partner.

Claire Lardinois

That is really sex appeal: the communicating of a sense of beauty.

D. H. Lawrence, *Assorted Articles*

Whatever else can be said about sex, it cannot be called a dignified performance.

Helen Lawrenson, *Esquire*, 1977

Girls who put out are tramps. Girls who don't are ladies. This is, however, a rather archaic use of the word. Should one of you boys happen upon a girl who doesn't put out, do not jump to the conclusion that you have found a lady. What you have probably found is a lesbian.

Fran Lebowitz, *Metropolitan Life*, 1979

Lust is more abstract than logic; it seeks (hope triumphing over experience) for some purely sexual, hence purely imaginary, conjunction of an impossible maleness with an impossible femaleness.
C. S. Lewis, *The Allegory of Love*, 1936

What they call "heart" is located far lower than the fourth waistcoat button.
George Lichtenberg

Literature is mostly about sex and not much about having children and life is the other way round.
David Lodge, *The British Museum Is Falling Down*

Sex appeal is 50% what you've got and 50% what people think you've got.
Sophia Loren

Nature abhors a virgin—a frozen asset.
Clare Boothe Luce

Sex is not only a divine and beautiful activity; it's a murderous activity. People kill each other in bed. Some of the greatest crimes ever committed were committed in bed. And no weapons were used.
Norman Mailer, *Playboy*, 1968

The only way to resolve a situation with a girl is to jump on her and things will work out.
Lee Marvin, *Esquire*, 1970

The new lust gives the lecher the new thrill.
John Masefield, *Widow in the Bye Street*, 1912

Continental people have sex life; the English have hot-water bottles.
George Mikes, *How to Be an Alien*, 1946

It's not true that life is one damn thing after another—it's one damn thing over and over.
  Edna St. Vincent Millay

On the one hand nature . . . has attached to that desire the noblest, most useful and most pleasant of all her acts; while on the other she allows us to fell and vilify it as insolent and of ill repute, to blush for it and to command abstinence. Are we not brutes to call the act that makes us, brutish?
  Michel de Montaigne, Essay on Virgil, 1588

It must be admitted that we English have sex on the brain, which is a very unfortunate place to have it.
  Malcolm Muggeridge

If you aren't going all the way, why go at all?
  Joe Namath

Like hatred, sex must be articulated or, like hatred, it will produce a disturbing internal malaise.
  George Jean Nathan, Passing Judgments, 1935

Sex—the poor man's polo.
  Clifford Odets

Sex is a bad thing because it rumples the clothes.
  Jackie Onassis, attrib. by Gore Vidal in Peter York, Style Wars, 1980

Nine tenths of that which is attributed to sexuality is the work of our magnificent ability to imagine, which is no longer an instinct, but exactly the opposite—a creation.
  José Ortega y Gasset

For a woman to give herself to a man is no more wasteful than taking a light from a torch, or using water when it is needed. In fact, not to do so is a waste.

Ovid, The Art of Love

He said:/"Let us stay here/Now this place has emptied/And make gentle pornography with each other/ While the partygoers go out/And the dawn creeps in/Like a stranger" ... So they did/Right there among the woodbines and the Guinness stains/And later he caught a bus and she a train/And all there was between them then/was rain.

Brian Patten, Party Piece, 1967

The best contraceptive is a glass of cold water. Not before or after, but instead.

Pakistani delegate at an International Planned Parenthood Federation conference

To be satisfied, each of us must know what he or she wants. We can get our clothes or our meat off the rack, but sex should be custom-tailored to our order.

Katherine Perutz, Viva, 1976

There is no greater nor keener pleasure than that of bodily love—and none which is more irrational.

Plato, The Republic, c. 386 B.C.

Give me a willing nymph! 'tis all I care,/Extremely clean, and tolerably fair,/Her shape her own, whatever shape she have,/And just that white and red which nature gave.

Alexander Pope, A Sermon Against Adultery

These natural freedoms are but just/There's something generous in mere lust.
> *A Ramble in St. James's Park*, quoted in W. Young, *Eros Denied*, 1965

The difference is wide that the sheets will not decide.
> John Ray, *English proverbs*, 1670

The garter has hanged more men than the halter.
> *Reflections of a Bachelor*

The sexual drive is nothing but the motor memory of previously experienced pleasure.
> *Wilhelm Reich*

There is need of variety in sex, but not in love.
> *Theodor Reik, Of Love and Lust*, 1957

Sexuality throws no light upon love, but only through love can we learn to understand sexuality.
> *Eugen Rosenstock-Huessy*

Though Argus hundred eyes in watch doth keep,/Yet lust at length will lull them all asleep.
> *Francis Rous, Thule*, c. 1640

Civilised people cannot fully satisfy their sexual instinct without love.
> *Bertrand Russell, Marriage and Morals*, 1929

Any enjoyment is weakened when shared.
> *Marquis de Sade*

Sexual pleasure is, I agree, a passion to which all others are subordinate, but in which they all unite.

Marquis de Sade, Philosophy in the Bedroom, 1795

The full force of sexual desire is seldom known to a virtuous woman.

William Sanger, A History of Prostitution, 1859

Love comforteth like sunshine after rain,/But Lust's effect is tempest after sun;/Love's gentle spring doth always fresh remain,/Lust's winter comes ere summer half be done;/Love surfeits not, Lust like a glutton dies;/Love is all truth, Lust full of forged lies.

William Shakespeare, Venus and Adonis, 1593

The lusts and greeds of the Body scandalize the Soul; but it has to come to heel.

Logan Pearsall Smith, Afterthoughts, 1913

Experiences aren't pornographic, only image and representations are.

Susan Sontag, 1967

The only chaste woman is one who has not been asked.

Spanish proverb

"Sex," she says, "is a subject like any other subject. Every bit as interesting as agriculture."

Muriel Spark, The Hothouse by the East River, 1973

No man can be held throughout the day by what happens throughout the night.

Sally Stanford, The Lady of the House, 1966

Prudery is a form of avarice.

Stendhal

Chastity is a wealth that comes from the abundance of love.

> Rabindranath Tagore, *Stray Birds*, 1916

Sex, treated properly, can be one of the most gorgeous things in the world.

> Elizabeth Taylor

Eroticism is not the excess of pleasure but the pleasure of excess.

> Bernard Tschumi, *ZG*, 1982

The bodies of lovers are the forms of ineffable Desire,/Male and female serpents of the Holy Spirit/ Breathing out its essence in individual outline.

> W. J. Turner, *The Pursuit of Psyche*

The decline of incest as a marketable theme is probably due to today's inadequate middle-class housing. In large Victorian houses with many rooms and heavy doors, the occupants could be mysterious and exciting to one another in a way that those who live in rackety developments could never hope to be.

> Gore Vidal, *The New York Review of Books*, 1966

Sex is. There is nothing more to be done about it. Sex builds no roads, writes no novels and sex certainly gives no meaning to anything in life but itself.

> Gore Vidal, *Norman Mailer's Self-Advertisements*, 1960

The sexual act burns away the self-image, at least for the moment, and confronts one with the self; it measures our capacities for feeling and perceiving, for affection, courage, hard work and joy—and exposes our pettiness, apathy, cowardice and selfishness. I believe that Freud was right in reverse: it is not so much the sexual experience that forms the character, *it is the character that forms the sexual experience.*

Stephen Vizinczey, *In Praise of Older Women*, 1966

Fantasy love is much better than reality love. Never doing it is very exciting. The most exciting attractions are between two opposites that never meet.

Andy Warhol, *From A to B and Back Again*, 1975

Sex is an emotion in motion.

Mae West

Usually the men who spend the most time talking about sex never get around to doing it—and if they should be ready, their prospective partner is probably bored and long gone.

Mae West, *Mae West on Sex, Health and ESP*, 1975

In real life, women are always trying to mix something up with sex—religion, or babies, or hard cash; it is only men who long for sex separated out, without rings or strings.

Katharine Whitehorn, *The Observer*, 1964

A man who moralises is usually a hypocrite, and a woman who moralises is invariably plain.

Oscar Wilde, *Lady Windermere's Fan*, 1893

You come out of a woman and you spend the rest of your life trying to get back in.

Heathcote Williams, *The Speakers*, 1964

There are two kinds of sex, classical and baroque. Classical sex is romantic, profound, serious, emotional, moral, mysterious, spontaneous, abandoned, focussed on a particular person and stereotypically feminine. Baroque sex is pop, playful, funny, experimental, conscious, deliberate, amoral, anonymous, focussed on sensation for sensation's sake, and stereotypically masculine. The classical mentality taken to an extreme is sentimental and finally puritanical; the baroque mentality taken to an extreme is pornographic and finally obscene. Ideally a sexual relationship ought to create a satisfying tension between the two modes. . . .

Ellen Willis, *Classic and Baroque Sex in Everyday Life*, 1979

It is certainly very hard to write about sex in English without making it sound unattractive. *Come* is a horrible word to apply to something ecstatic.

Edmund Wilson, *The Thirties*, 1980

Platonic love is love from the neck up.

Thyra Samter Winslow, 1952

I thought *coq au vin* was love in a lorry.

Victoria Wood, *Talent*, 1979

The sex instinct is one of the three or four prime movers of all that we do and are and dream, both individually and collectively.

Philip Wylie, *Generation of Vipers*, 1942

When the prick stands, the brains get buried in the ground.

Yiddish proverb

Shall they *make love*? They may indeed, but what does this love look like when they have made it? It is a pretty phrase, and at least they are making something, but *love*? Is that what they are really making? When they have finished what ontological chorus stands forth to say, here is what they have made, behold, it is love? If they have really made anything it is not so much love as a child.

Wayland Young, Eros Denied, 1965

Semen maketh man . . . sex merely expresses the totality of differences between male and female.

Sir Solly Zuckerman, Chambers Encyclopedia

10. All the Lonely People

If the practice of masturbation be ascertained to exist, steps must be taken to check it. In young infants the habit may be corrected by the ordinary mode of muffling the hand, or applying a sort of strait-waistcoat.

Dr. William Acton, The Function and Disorders of the Reproductive Organs, 1857

Homosexuality is funny, provided it's on the telly; off the telly homosexuals are only fit for being punched up.

Philip Adams, 1968

Bisexuality immediately doubles your chances for a date on Saturday night.

Woody Allen, New York Herald Tribune, 1975

He knew and could name the six or seven kinds of bacilli that inhabited the region [the foot], a special kind for the surface, another for the interstices, another for the nails and so on, redolent with bacilli epidermis et sacrogens

and penicillium glaucus, the same kind exactly that worked on the skin of a Camembert cheese.
Amigo Magazine

WOODY ALLEN: Hey, don't knock masturbation. It's sex with someone I love.
Annie Hall, script: Woody Allen, Marshall Brickman, 1977

MASOCHIST: Beat me!
SADIST: No!
Anonymous

All "abnormal" sex acts are rites of symbolic magic, and one can only properly understand the actual personal relation if one knows the symbolic role each expects the other to play.
W. H. Auden, quoted in C. Osborne, *W. H. Auden: The Life of a Poet*, 1980

Self-abuse is the devil's telephone booth.
Edward Barker, 1981

Most lesbians . . . seek to cultivate the treasures of their femininity.
Simone de Beauvoir, The Second Sex, 1953

Between women love is contemplative . . . there is no struggle, no victory, no defeat; in exact reciprocity each is at once subject and object, sovereign and slave; duality becomes mutuality.
Simone de Beauvoir, The Second Sex, 1953

The dominating woman. She knows what she wants and how to get it. Power is the aphrodisiac; discipline is the key. Her favourite position—on top and in command. If he misbehaves, punish him. He deserves to be punished; he wants to be punished! And he will thank you in the end. They always thank you. And they always come back for more.

Rosetta Brooks, *Brutality Chic*, 1982

If you believe there is a God, a God that made your body, and yet you think you can do anything with that body that's dirty, then the fault lies with the manufacturer.

Lenny Bruce, quoted in J. Cohen, *The Essential Lenny Bruce*, 1967

If homosexuality were the normal way God would have made Adam and Bruce.

Anita Bryant, 1977

S/M is high technology sex.

Pat Califia, *ZG*, 1982

The sexual closet is bigger than you think.

Pat Califia, *ZG*, 1982

The good thing about masturbation is that you don't have to dress up for it.

Truman Capote

I'm a twentieth century failure: a happy, undersexed celibate.

Denise Coffey

I gasped at the sight of the women prisoners stripped naked and bound to whipping posts as grinning Totenkopf perverts lashed them with barbed whips. Paula's beautiful young body had been bound viciously. Her hands had been attached to her feet so that she was misshaped into a taut bow. Her magnificent breasts were thrust outward against her dress. The baron brought a gloved hand up to his opposite shoulder and brought it lashing down against the girl's powdered face. He struck her again, full force. This time she cried out with pain, flung back against the slimy dungeon wall, her wispy black silk peignoir riding up above her milky thighs.

Daring Magazine

Dear La Belle (My God and Master), . . . if you so desired you could torture me in any way you see fit, such as beating me with a whip, chain, rubber hose, sword, cane or shoe while I am strung up by my thumbs or ankles, kneeling and praying to you. You may desire to brand me as yours, kick me and stomp on my face and chest in heels or bare feet, stick me with pins and above all sit on my head and bounce it in the mud. I hereby present my body and above all my soul. You are my God. I crave to pray to you, to your feet and especially to your derriere. You see, I am also a derriere worshipper and would love to have yours on my head while you beat me or burn me with your cigarettes. Your devoted slave who craves to eat the dirt beneath your shoes. I await your decision as to if I qualify.

La Belle Kay [reply]: Oh shut up! You're so cravingly servile you annoy me. Don't pester me. I've got enough to do reading junk like your letters, you filthy pig.

Dominate Magazine, letters to the editor, "La Belle Kay"

The proliferation of massage establishments in London in the last few years appears to indicate a dramatic increase in muscular disorders amongst the male population.

Environmental health officer, New Statesman, 1980

Dear Editor, I would like to tell you about my landlady, her fourteen-year-old daughter and their dog . . .

Fiesta Magazine, 1973

It'll be a sad day for sexual liberation when the pornography addict has to settle for the real thing.
Brendan Francis

Masturbation . . . vitiates the character through *indulgence.* . . . In the first place it teaches people to achieve important aims without taking trouble and by easy paths instead of an energetic exertion of force. . . , secondly, in the fantasies that accompany satisfaction the sexual object is raised to a degree of excellence which is not easily found again in reality.
Sigmund Freud

Be Yourself: Learn to be yourself around women. . . . If you read *Hustler* don't hide the latest issue in the breadbox just because a woman is on the way. This approach can be overdone, however. There is no reason to leave heavy leather-bound volumes of *Enema Island* on display just to show you have nothing to conceal.
Bruce Jay Friedman, Esquire, 1977

Rare, very rare are the hard cocks at the Mineshaft [a New York S/M gay bar]: drugs and alcohol have destroyed simple "sexual energy." But nobody cares: fist replaces cock, piss replaces sperm, showing and looking replace doing. Have slaves or masters instead of lovers; submit instead of being fucked. . . . Be a man, a real one, without being afraid of any possible treason by your unreliable penis. Just buy a whip and a jockstrap.
Guy Hocquenheim, Christopher Street Magazine, 1982

All women are Lesbians, except those who don't know it yet.
Jill Johnston, A Dialogue on Women's Liberation, 1971

However young children may be, they become thin, pale and irritable and their features assume a haggard appearance. We notice the sunken eye, the long cadaverous-looking countenance, the downcast look which seems to arise from a consciousness in the boy that his habits are suspected and, at a later period, from the ascertained fact that his virility is lost. . . . Habitual masturbators have a dank, moist, cold hand, very characteristic of vital exhaustion . . . they may gradually waste away if the evil passion is not got the better of, nervous exhaustion sets in, such as spasmodic contraction, or partial or entire convulsive movements, together with epilepsy, eclampsy and a species of paralysis accompanied with contraction of the limbs.

Claude-François Lallemand, *Les Pertes Seminales Involuntères,* 1835–1842

Recall the old story of the rather refined young man who preferred sex dreams to visiting brothels because he met a much nicer type of girl that way.

Vivian Mercier, *Perspectives on Pornography*

Voyeurism is a healthy, non-participatory sexual activity— the world *should* look at the world.

Desmond Morris, *Playboy,* 1974

Smashing Seeks Dashing Beautiful businesswoman, Ivy educated, 32. Warm, witty, sophisticated, soft-spoken. Diverse interests. Seeks man similar background, attributes for fun, friendship, romance.

The New York Review of Books, personal ad, 1982

The only abnormality is the incapacity to love.

Anaïs Nin

Perversion is a word that has no final meaning. What might be a perversion in one century can be normal in the following. It helps to consider it as a subjective term, denude it of its ethical overtones, and ask of a specific perversion: What physical harm does it do? Then ask a subsequent question: What psychological harm does it do *beyond satisfying the wishes of the protagonists?*
   Ronald Pearsall, The Worm in the Bud, 1969

ESTELLE WINWOOD: Now I'll be the innocent little milkmaid, and you'll be the naughty stableboy.
   The Producers, script: Mel Brooks, 1968

I am sure if wives only knew the hold they could exercise on their husbands by wearing rubber, more would do so: after all what is the difference in wearing rubber or silk panties if they please you. I think that a gentle approach is all that is needed to win over most wives. My husband first told me of his love for rubber when I bought a rubber apron for housework. . . . He may look at other girls in macs, or even photographs of them, but we have a mutual secret which we share and nothing can make up for that. Our ambition now is to save up for a rubber dress and nightie. . . .
   Rubber News Magazine, letters page

It has, moreover, been proved that horror, nastiness and the frightful are what give pleasure when one fornicates. Beauty is a simple thing, ugliness is the exceptional thing. And fiery imaginations, no doubt, always prefer the extraordinary thing to the simple thing.
   Marquis de Sade, The 120 Days of Sodom, 1785

Certainly nothing is unnatural that is not physically impossible.
   Richard Brinsley Sheridan, The Critic, 1779

... The main thing is that the act male homosexuals commit is ugly and repugnant and afterwards they are disgusted with themselves. They drink and take drugs to palliate this ... and they are always changing partners and cannot be really happy. ... In women, it is the opposite. They do nothing they are disgusted by and nothing that is repulsive and afterwards they are happy and they can lead happy lives together.

> *Gertrude Stein, quoted in L. Simon, Gertrude Stein, 1974*

Masturbation: the primary sexual activity of mankind. In the nineteenth century it was a disease, in the twentieth it is a cure.

> *Thomas Szasz, The Second Sin*

Affectionate, intelligent, attractive, healthy, middle-aged, sensitive, solvent male (literate, musical, travelled) seeks gentle, witty, charismatic damsel, no ties (perhaps 24–42), for possible catharsis and contributive fulfillment.

> *Time Out, lonely hearts ad, 1982*

Just as old habits die hard, old hards die habits.

> *Kenneth Tynan, Esquire, 1968*

When a man and woman of unorthodox tastes make love the man could be said to be introducing his foible into her quirk.

> *Kenneth Tynan, The Guardian, 1975*

I was too polite to ask.

> *Gore Vidal, asked whether his first sexual experience had been hetero- or homosexual*

I'm all for bringing back the birch, but only between consenting adults.

> *Gore Vidal, on David Frost's TV show*

Sexual fantasy is as old as civilization (as opposed to as old as the race) and one of its outward and visible signs is pornographic literature, an entirely middle-class phenomenon since we are assured by many investigators . . . that the lower orders seldom rely on sexual fantasy for extra-stimulus. As soon as possible the uneducated man goes for the real thing. This must be the last meaningful class distinction in the West.

 Gore Vidal, The New York Review of Books, 1966

I am married, obviously, have been for eight or nine years. I always say I married too early. We both lacked sexual experience, but then I suppose that's what I was looking for—I mean innocence. The only girl I knew in those days who had sexual experience was Ruth, a very mature girl indeed. . . . Mary is the opposite. She is undersexed. I don't blame her. I blame her parents. But it makes it very difficult. I have to sublimate. I collect old boys' magazines, O.B.B.'s we call them, that's one activity. *The Magnet, The Gem* . . . some very rare issues have passed through my hands. And then fire I'm very fond of. I like to set fire to things. . . . You don't have to tell me what that is, of course. It's a love substitute.

 Keith Waterhouse, Jubb, 1963

I've got plenty of nothing, and nothing's plenty for me/I got my hand, I got my dick, I got my fantasy.

 Ken Weaver, Nothing

I never loved another person the way I love myself.

 Mae West

All pornography, high and low, hard and soft, innocent and morbid, inhabits a world of fantasy. . . . Pornography is meant to remedy the deficiencies of reality.

 Michael Wood, The New York Review of Books, 1979

The middle-age of buggers is not to be contemplated without horror.

Virginia Woolf

11. Body Language

In itself [the vagina] had an erotic appearanc̶ ̶ ̶ ̶ the inside of a giraffe's ear or a tropical fruit not mu̶ ̶ ̶ ̶ ̶ even by the locals.

Kingsley Amis, Jake's Thing, 1978

Most plain girls are virtuous because of the scarcity of opportunity to be otherwise.

Maya Angelou, I Know Why the Caged Bird Sings, 1969

A nice luscious prick!/A stiff standing prick!/For any young maiden it can do the trick./Oh, joys there are plenty, but nothing like a prick!

Anonymous, quoted in Alan Bold, Making Love, 1978

It's only human nature after all/For a boy to get a girl against a wall/And slip his abomination into her accommodation/To increase the population of the coming generation.

Anonymous (20th century), quoted in Alan Bold, Making Love, 1978

Then here's to the female who yields to a man/And here's to the man who'll fuck when he can,/For fucking creates all our joy upon earth,/and from fucking, you know, we all date our birth.

> Anonymous (19th century) quoted in Alan Bold, *Making Love*, 1978

Q. The abbess woke up frantic after she/Had dreamt all night of eating gooseberry fool,/To find her mouth full of the abbot's tool. How had she sinned, though? Greed? Or lechery?
A. She didn't sin, as far as we make out,/In either way. It was an accident—/Although if she had found it in her cunt/Or up her arse, there might have been some doubt.

> Pietro Aretino, *Some More Cases of Love, with Solutions*

... moments . . . twenty, count them, diary, twenty . . . I don't know how he does it. He is perfect.

> Mary Astor (of her lover, George S. Kaufman), *Diary*, 1936

A beautiful face is a silent commendation.

> Francis Bacon, *Apothegems*, 1624

That is the best part of beauty, which a picture cannot express.

> Francis Bacon, *Of Beauty*, 1597

There is no excellent beauty that hath not some strangeness in the proportion.

> Francis Bacon, *Of Beauty*, 1597

If a man cannot distinguish the difference between the pleasures of two consecutive nights, he has married too early.

> Honoré de Balzac, *The Physiology of Marriage*, 1828

Rugged the breast that beauty cannot tame.

> John Codrington Bampfylde, *Sonnet in Praise of Delia*, 1778

I don't know what I am, darling. I've tried several varieties of sex. The conventional position makes me claustrophobic. And the others either give me a stiff neck or lockjaw.

> *Tallulah Bankhead, quoted in Lee Israel, Miss Tallulah Bankhead, 1972*

One hour of right-down love/Is worth an age of dully living on.

> *Aphra Behn, The Rover, 1681*

Let him kiss me with the kisses of his mouth: for thy love is better than wine.

> *The Bible, Song of Solomon*

Stay me with flagons, comfort me with apples: for I am sick of love. His left hand is under my head, his right hand doth embrace me.

> *The Bible, Song of Solomon*

Behold, thou art fair, my love: behold, thou art fair; thou hast doves' eyes within thy locks: thy hair is as a flock of goats, that appear from Mount Gilead. Thy teeth are like a flock of sheep that are even shorn, which come up from the washing; whereof every one bear twins, and none is barren among them. Thy lips are like a thread of scarlet, and thy speech is comely: thy temples are like a piece of pomegranate within thy locks. Thy neck is like the tower of David builded for an armoury, whereon there hang a thousand bucklers all shields of mighty men. Thy breasts are like two young roes that are twins, which feed among the lilies.

> *The Bible, Song of Solomon*

Bait, n: A preparation that makes the hook more palatable.
The best kind of beauty.
Ambrose Bierce, The Devil's Dictionary, 1911

Beauty, n: The power by which a woman charms a lover
and terrifies a husband.
Ambrose Bierce, The Devil's Dictionary, 1911

Ugliness, n: A gift of the gods to certain women, entailing
virtue without humility.
Ambrose Bierce, The Devil's Dictionary, 1911

Now Ravell raised an arm enjoining silence. "It is our privilege and our duty to do honour to this man, my friends.
This god whose slaves we have all become. With your ap-
proval we shall call this massive weapon displayed to us
by a name I myself coined when I first beheld it. Gentlemen—this is *King Prick*."
*The Biggest Ever, quoted in Gillian Freeman, The Undergrowth of
Literature, 1967*

Since copulation is the most important act in the lives of
living creatures because it perpetuates the species, it
seems odd that nature should not have arranged for it to
happen more simply.
Gerald Brenan, Thoughts in a Dry Season, 1979

I could wish that we might procreate like trees, without
conjunction; or that there were any way to perpetuate the
world without this trivial and vulgar way of coition; it is
the foolishest act a wise man commits in his whole life,
nor is there anything that will deject his cold imagination
more, when he shall consider what an odd and unworthy
piece of folly he has committed.
Sir Thomas Browne

The moth's kiss, first!/Kill me as if you made be-
lieve/You were not sure, this eve,/How my face, your
flower, had pursed/Its petals up . . ./The bee's kiss
now!/Kiss me as if you entered gay/My heart at some
noonday.
    Robert Browning, In a Gondola, in Poetical Works, 1863

God's best of beauteous and magnificent/Revealed to
earth—the naked female form.
    Robert Browning, Parleyings with Certain People, 1887

But love's too eager to admit delay/And hurries us along so
smooth a way./Now wanton with delight we nimbly
move/Our pliant limbs in all the shapes of love,/Our motions not like those of gamesome fools/Whose active
bodies show their heavy souls,/But sports of love, in which
a willing mind/Makes us as able as our hearts are kind./At
length all languishing and out of breath/Panting as in the
agonies of death/We lie entranced, till one provoking
kiss/Transports our ravished souls to paradise.
    2nd Duke of Buckingham (George Villiers), The Perfect Enjoy-
    ment, in The Works of George Villiers, 1715

Sexual intercourse is kicking death in the ass while singing.
    Charles Bukowski, Notes of a Dirty Old Man, 1969

Her eyes had langorously opened, and then the lids had
fallen, about halfway, just as the eyelids of a woman ought
to do when she is being kissed properly.
    James Branch Cabell, Jurgen, 1919

If you want to be happy for the rest of your life/Never
make a pretty woman your wife/Just from my personal
point of view/Get an ugly girl to marry you.
    Calypso song

I love not for those eyes, nor hair/Nor cheeks, nor lips, nor teeth so rare;/Nor for thy speech, thy neck, nor breast/Nor for thy belly, nor the rest;/Nor for thy hand, nor foot so small/But wouldst thou know (dear sweet) for all.
    Thomas Carew, The Compliment, in Collected Poems, 1870

JONATHAN: You know it. When you think of what he's got to dip into, any guy with a conscience has a right to turn soft. Am I right, Louise?
    Carnal Knowledge, script: Jules Feiffer, 1971

When the red flower shows its beauty/And exhales its steady perfume/While she stays with you in the night/ And you play and take your pleasure with her/Pointing at the pictures, you follow their sequence/While she blushes and looks abashed/And coyly protests. . . .
    Chang Heng, Ch'i-pien (Chinese sex manual)

In love, a man may lose his heart with dignity; but if he loses his nose, he loses his character into the bargain.
    Lord Chesterfield, Letters, 1750

He makes love like a footballer. He dribbles before he shoots.
    John Cooper Clarke, 1978

Male sexual response is far brisker and more automatic. It is triggered easily by things—like putting a quarter in a vending machine.
    Alex Comfort

An erection at will is the moral equivalent of a valid credit card.
    Alex Comfort, The New York Times, 1978

The human comedy begins with a vertical smile.
> Richard Condon, *The Vertical Smile*, 1971

Beauty is the lover's gift.
> William Congreve, *The Way of the World*, 1700

No-one was ever made wretched in a brothel.
> Cyril Connolly

The working classes have a reputation for potency and being good in bed—a myth probably started by middle-class novelists and by graphologists who claim that anyone with loopy writing must be highly sexed.
> Jilly Cooper, *Class*, 1979

A woman is truly beautiful only when she is naked and she knows it.
> André Courreges, *Metropolitan Museum of Art* (N.Y.C.) *Bulletin*, 1967

The life of the universe depends on the pudendum. As soon as the Word was made flesh, man was unable to be quiet, or work, or think, until he had dropped his seed.
> Edward Dahlberg

Coition is a slight attack of apoplexy.
> Democritus of Abdera

Love built on beauty, soon as beauty, dies.
> John Donne, *Elegies*, in *Collected Works*, 1633

The sexual embrace can only be compared with music and with prayer.
> Havelock Ellis, *On Life and Sex*, 1937

No woman can be a beauty without a fortune.
  George Farquhar, *The Beaux' Strategem*, 1707

The kiss originated when the first male reptile licked the first female reptile, implying in a subtle, complimentary way that she was as succulent as the small reptile he had for dinner the night before.
  F. Scott Fitzgerald, *The Crack-Up*, 1945

You can always tell a virgin by the length of her ear-lobes.
  Errol Flynn

. . . So come on you middle-aged gals who feel life is passing you by. Your cunts aren't dead, they're just asleep. All of you may not be lucky enough to find a neighbour or a bridge club like mine, but certainly each of you has a close friend who is as bored, and sexually frustrated as you are. Open up! Confide your secret desires to her and you may be surprised at how quickly she accepts your invitation. You'll find life has just begun.
  Forum Magazine, The Best of Forum, 1978

What a man most enjoys about a woman's clothes are his fantasies of how she would look without them.
  Brendan Francis

A beautiful woman should break her mirror early.
  Baltasar Gracián

A man of any age can persuade himself that a woman's thighs are altar rails, and that her passion is the hosanna of virtuous love rather than the wanton tumult of nerve endings.
  Ben Hecht, *Gaily Gaily*, 1963

I still have a diary entry ... asking myself whether talk about the size of the male organ isn't a homosexual pre-occupation: if things aren't too bad in other ways I doubt if any woman cares very much.

Lillian Hellman, Pentimento, 1973

Trying to be fascinating is an asinine position to be in.

Katharine Hepburn, ABC-TV, 1975

Only the really plain people know about love. The very fascinating ones try so hard to create an impression that they soon exhaust their talents.

Katharine Hepburn, Look, 1958

What is a kiss? why this, as some approve;/The sure sweet-cement, glue and lime of love.

Robert Herrick, A Kiss, 1648

Fain would I kiss my Julia's dainty leg/Which is as white and hairless as an egg.

Robert Herrick, On Julia's Legs, 1648

I am happy now that Charles calls on my bedchamber less frequently than of old. As it is I now endure but two calls a week, and when I hear his steps outside my door I lie down on my bed, close my eyes, open my legs and think of England.

Lady Alice Hillingdon

Beauty is in the eye of the beholder.

Margaret Hungerford

People will insist ... on treating the *mons Veneris* as though it were Mt. Everest.

Aldous Huxley, Eyeless in Gaza, 1936

Sir, it is a very foolish resolution not to marry a pretty woman. Beauty is of itself very estimable.

Samuel Johnson, quoted in James Boswell, The Life of Samuel Johnson, 1791

Many women have the gut feeling that their genitals are ugly. One reason women are gratified by oral-genital relations is that it is a way of a man's saying "I like your cunt. I can eat it."

Erica Jong, Playboy, 1975

. . . and I thought as well him as another and then I asked him with my eyes to ask again yes and then he asked me would I yes to say yes my mountain flower and first I put my arms around him yes and drew him down to me so he could feel my breasts all perfume yes and his heart was going like mad and yes I said yes I will Yes.

James Joyce, Ulysses, 1922

That gentlemen prefer blondes is due to the fact that, apparently, pale hair, delicate skin and an infantile expression represent the very apex of a frailty which every man longs to violate.

Alexander King, Rich Man, Poor Man, Freud and Fruit

The average girl would rather have beauty than brains because she knows that the average man can see much better than he can think.

Ladies' Home Journal, 1947

Any girl can be glamorous; all you have to do is stand still and look stupid.

Hedy Lamarr

A skirt is no obstacle to extemporaneous sex, but it is physically impossible to make love to a girl while she is wearing trousers.

Helen Lawrenson, Esquire, 1968

Many a man in love with a dimple makes the mistake of marrying the whole girl.

Stephen Leacock

All women's dresses, in every age and country, are merely variations on the eternal struggle between the admitted desire to dress and the unadmitted desire to undress.

Lin Yutang, Ladies' Home Journal, 1945

If this is really so, I'm glad I do not have long to live.

Liverpool stipendiary magistrate, on being told oral sex is widely practiced in Britain, 1978

Glamour is when a man knows a woman is a woman.

Gina Lollobrigida, The Observer, 1956

We can lie in the language of dress, or try to tell the truth; but unless we are naked and bald, it is impossible to be silent.

Alison Lurie, The New York Review of Books, 1981

Lacy and revealing black lingerie . . . is sophisticated, daring, and occasionally wicked in its implications. Women who prefer it are more likely to become bored with partners and places, sexual positions and they are less likely to sit up in bed exclaiming tearfully "Oh, this is awful! What am I doing?"

Alison Lurie, The New York Review of Books, 1981

The reproduction of mankind is a great marvel and mystery. Had God consulted me in the matter, I should have advised him to continue the generation of the species by fashioning them of clay.

    Martin Luther, *Table Talk*

The truly erotic sensibility, in evoking the image of woman, never omits to clothe it. The robing and disrobing, that is the true traffic of love.

    Antonio Machado, *Juan de Mairena*, 1943

Now my hair is nappy and I don't wear no clothes of silk/But the cow that's black and ugly, has often got the sweetest milk.

    Sara Martin, *Mean Tight Mama*

Whoever named it "necking" was a poor judge of anatomy.

    Groucho Marx

The first girl you go to bed with is *always* pretty.

    Walter Matthau, *Esquire*, 1968

There was a little girl/Who had a little curl/Right in the middle of her forehead/When she was good she was very very good/And when she was bad she was very very popular.

    Max Miller, *The Max Miller Blue Book*, c. 1950

A kiss can be a comma, a question mark or an exclamation point. That's basic spelling that every woman ought to know.

    Mistinguett, *Theatre Arts Magazine*, 1955

The orgasm has replaced the Cross as the focus of longing and the image of fulfillment.

> *Malcolm Muggeridge, The Most of Malcolm Muggeridge, 1966*

My arms I'd round her taper waist/Her lovely form I pressed/Her beauteous face reclining/Upon my manly chest/I kissed her twice upon the lips/I wish I'd done it thrice/I whispered, oh it's naughty/She said, it is so nice.

> *Music hall song (19th century), quoted in R. Pearsall, The Worm in the Bud, 1969*

There are other positions . . . in use among the peoples of India. . . . Among those manners are the following, called: 1. the stopperage, 2. frog-fashion, 3. with toes cramped, 4. with legs in the air, 5. he-goat fashion, 6. the screw of Archimedes, 7. the summersault, 8. the tail of the ostrich, 9. fitting on of the sock, 10. reciprocal sight of the posteriors, 11. the rainbow arch, 12. alternative piercing, 13. pounding on the spot, 14. coition from the back, 15. belly to belly, 16. ram-fashion, 17. driving the peg home, 18. love's fusion, 19. sheep-fashion, 20. interchange in coition, 21. the race of the member, 22. the fitter-in, 23. the one who stops in the house, 24. the smith's coition, 25. the seducer.

> *Nefzawi, The Perfumed Garden, 1886*

Who, without agonies of desire, could see breasts round and hard as an apple; a skin whiter than the driven snow, suffused with a glowing warmth, that brightened the colour and heightened the temptation, softer than the down of swans and sweeter than all the balmy spices of Arabia?

> *The New Metamorphosis, c. 1843*

Sexual intercourse . . . a joyous, joyous, joyous, joyous impaling of woman on man's sensual mast.
> Anaïs Nin, *A Spy in the House of Love*

He who has taken kisses, if takes not the rest beside, will deserve to lose even what was granted.
> Ovid, *The Art of Love*

Blemishes are hid by night and every fault forgiven; darkness makes any woman fair.
> Ovid, *The Art of Love*

If Cleopatra's nose had been shorter, the whole face of the earth would have changed.
> Blaise Pascal, *Pensées*, 1670

The pleasure of the act of love is gross and brief, and brings loathing after it.
> Petronius, *Fragments*, c. 50

I lay, rapt and naked, on Irwin's ruffled blanket, waiting for the miraculous change to make itself felt. But all I felt was a sharp, startlingly bad pain.
> Sylvia Plath, *The Bell Jar*, 1963

Fair tresses man's imperial race insnare/And beauty draws us with a single hair.
> Alexander Pope, *The Rape of the Lock*, 1714

Cupid is naked and does not like artifices contrived by beauty.
> Propertius, *Elegies*, 1st century B.C.

All women are sitting on a fortune, if only they recognized it.
> Prostitute, quoted in W. Young, *Eros Denied*, 1965

Fair hasty nymph, be clean and kind/And all my joys restore/By using paper still behind/And sponges for before.

Earl of Rochester (John Wilmot), c. 1670

A kiss, when all is said, what is it?/An oath that's given closer than before/A promise more precise the sealing of/Confessions that till then were barely breathed/A rosy dot placed on the i in loving.

Edmond Rostand, Cyrano de Bergerac, 1897

Amazing! Astonishing! Still can't get over the fantastic idea that when you are looking at a girl, you are looking at somebody who is guaranteed to have on her—a cunt! *They all have cunts!* Right under their dresses! Cunts—for fucking!

Philip Roth, Portnoy's Complaint, 1969

Whatever makes an impression on the heart seems lovely in the eye.

Sa'di, Gulistan, 1258

It is best to have a face which neither dazzles nor frightens, and with mine I get on well with friends of both sexes.

George Sand, My Life, 1854–1855

A thousand times he kissed her/Laying her on the green/But as he farther pressed her/A pretty leg was seen/And something else, but what I dare not name.

Sir Charles Sedley, On the Happy Corydon and Phyllis, 1702

Most women would rather have someone whisper their name at optimum moments than rocket with contractions to the moon.

Merle Shain, Some Men Are More Perfect Than Others, 1973

Love is an appetite of generation by the mediation of beauty.
Socrates

Blue eyes say "Love me or I die"; black eyes say "Love me or I kill thee."
Spanish proverb

Orgasm is the most obvious lie yet devised to thwart man. It can so thoroughly convince him of something which is unreal when he believes that the power of his excitement lies somewhere other than in his own physical apparatus.
William Talisman, The Gaudy Image

GEORGE SEGAL: Well, "very nice" is hardly the phrase to describe two bodies locked in heavenly transport. . . . "Very nice" is when you receive a get-well card from the butcher or the television repairman. That's "very nice." But for what we just did, the operational comments range from "lousy" to "sensational" to "rockets went off" or "the earth moved."
A Touch of Class, script: Melvin Frank, Jack Rose, 1973

It is far easier to love a woman in picturesque rags than in the commonplace garments of respectability.
Lady Troubridge, The Millionaire, 1907

Let's take coitus out of the closet and off the altar and put it in the continuum of human behaviour.
John Updike, Writers at Work, 1977

Never do with your hands what you could do better with your mouth.
Cherry Vanilla

The signs of the enjoyment and satisfaction of the woman are as follows: her body relaxes, she closes her eyes, she puts aside all bashfulness, and shows increased willingness to unite the two organs as closely together as possible. On the other hand, the signs of her want of enjoyment or of failing to be satisfied are as follows: she shakes her hands, she does not let the man get up, feels dejected, bites the man, kicks him and continues to go on moving after he has finished.

> *Vatsyayana, Kama Sutra,* c. 200

O woman's arse/Roundly defeating man's in every class/O arse of arses: Glory! Worship! Praise!

> *Paul Verlaine, A Brief Moral, in Selected Poems,* 1948

So Albert goes with the Queen to Windsor after the ceremony.
He'll go further before morning.
How so?
Why, he'll go in at Bushy, pass Virginia Water, on through Maidenhead, and leave Staines behind.

> *Victorian joke, quoted in R. Pearsall, The Worm in the Bud,* 1969

Two people kissing always look like fish.

> *Andy Warhol, From A to B and Back Again,* 1975

Is that a pistol in your pocket or are you just happy to see me?

> *Mae West*

Give a man a free hand and he'll run it all over you.

> *Mae West*

When choosing between two evils I always like to take the one I've never tried before.

> *Mae West, Klondike Annie,* 1936

My dear young lady, there was a great deal of truth, I dare say, in what you said, and you looked very pretty while you said it, which is much more important.
   Oscar Wilde, A Woman of No Importance, 1894

Life can little else supply/But a few good fucks and then we die.
   John Wilkes, 1763

He who follows Beauty/Breaks his foolish heart.
   Bertye Young Williams, Song Against Beauty

I think pop music has done more for oral intercourse than anything else that ever happened and vice versa.
   Frank Zappa

12. Puppy Love

I'd rather have two girls at seventeen than one at thirty-four.
   Fred Allen, Much Ado About Me, 1956

Nobody loves me; I'm going into the garden and eat worms.
   Anonymous, a Valentine greeting

Why don't the men propose, mamma/why don't the men propose?
   Thomas Haynes Bayly, Why Don't the Men Propose?

Maiden, n: A young person of the unfair sex addicted to clewless conduct and views that madden to crime.
Ambrose Bierce, The Devil's Dictionary, 1911

First love, with its frantic haughty imagination, swings its object clear of the everyday, over the rut of living, making him all looks, silences, gestures, attitudes, a burning phrase with no context.
Elizabeth Bowen, The House in Paris, 1935

And I shall find some girl perhaps/And a better one than you/With eyes as wise, but kindlier/And lips as soft, but true/And I daresay she will do.
Rupert Brooke, The Chilterns, 1918

Who loves, raves—'tis youth's frenzy; but the cure/Is bitterer still.
Lord Byron, Childe Harold's Pilgrimage, 1812–1818

Oh Love! young love! bound in they rosy band./Let sage or cynic prattle as he will,/These hours, and only these, redeem Life's years of ill.
Lord Byron, Childe Harold's Pilgrimage, 1812–1818

To my mind, a lovesick man who pities a rational man resembles a man who reads fairy tales and scoffs at those who read history.
Nicholas-Sébastien Chamfort, Maximes et Pensées, 1796

None ever loved, but at first sight they loved.
George Chapman, The Blind Beggar of Alexandria, 1596

Love, with very young people, is a heartless business. We drink at that age from thirst, or to get drunk; it is only later in life that we occupy ourselves with the individuality of our wine.

Isak Dinesen, Seven Gothic Tales, 1934

The magic of first love is our ignorance that it can ever end.

Benjamin Disraeli, Henrietta Temple, 1837

The bashful virgin's sidelong looks of love/The matron's glance that would those looks reprove.

Oliver Goldsmith, The Deserted Village

Tell me pretty maiden, are there any more at home like you?

Owen Hall, Floradora

What is first love worth, except to prepare for a second?/What does second love bring? Only regret for the first.

John Hay, Distichs

Maidens! Why should you worry in choosing who you will marry?/Choose whom you may, you will find you have got somebody else.

John Hay, Distichs

Blush: a weakness of youth and an accomplishment of experience. The pink of impropriety.

Oliver Herford, John Clay, Cupid's Cyclopedia, 1910

Bet your mama don't know you can scratch like that/I bet she never saw you scratch my back.
  Mick Jagger, Keith Richards, *Stray Cat Blues*

Young men make great mistakes in life; for one thing, they idealize love too much.
  Benjamin Jowett, *letters*

Well, she was just seventeen, you know what I mean . . .
  John Lennon, Paul McCartney, *I Saw Her Standing There*

A youth with his first cigar makes himself sick; a youth with his first girl makes other people sick.
  Mary Wilson Little

There's nothing half so sweet in life/As love's young dream.
  Thomas Moore, *Irish Melodies*, 1807–1835

When once the young heart of a maiden is stolen/The maiden herself will steal after it soon.
  Thomas Moore, *Omens*, 1807–1835

Lolita, light of my life, fire of my loins. My sin, my soul. Lo-lee-ta: the tap of the tongue taking a trip of three steps down the palate to tap, at three, on the teeth. Lo. Lee. Ta.
  Vladimir Nabokov, *Lolita*, 1955

Perhaps at 14 every boy should be in love with some ideal woman to put on a pedestal and worship. As he grows up, of course, he will put her on a pedestal the better to view her legs.
  Barry Norman, *The Listener*, 1978

I'm going to be so happy for the rest of my life/When my brand new baby is my brand new wife.

    Roy Orbison, Claudette

Love is certain to be known/Where a woman's to be found/When one has the first attack/It's like raspberry jam running down one's back.

    The Outsiders of Society, East End Verses, c. 1980

In the merry hay-time we raked side by side/In the harvest he whispered Wilt thou be my bride?/And my girl-heart bounded—Forgive, God the crime/If I loved him more than thee in the merry hay-time.

    C. K. Paul

"No, no; for my virginity/When I lose that," says Rose, "I'll die";/"Behind the elms last night," cried Dick,/"Rose, were you not extremely sick?"

    Matthew Prior, A True Maid, in Poetical Works, 1892

That's the thing about girls. Every time they do something pretty, even if they're not much to look at, or even if they're sort of stupid, you fall half in love with them, and then you never know *where* the hell you are.

    J. D. Salinger, The Catcher in the Rye, 1951

First love is only a little foolishness and a lot of curiosity. No really self-respecting woman would take advantage of it.

    George Bernard Shaw, John Bull's Other Island, 1907

The mass cult of songs, soaps, poems, pulps, flicks, scents, ads, art and miscellaneous hype extols LOVE as all a girl needs. This has a far broader impact than the most exquisite thinking of any social scientist.

    Gail Sheehy, Passages, 1976

The Hero: eight to twelve years older than the heroine . . .
self-assured, masterful, hot-tempered, capable of violence,
passion and tenderness . . . often mysteriously moody . . .
He is always tall, muscular (but not muscle-bound). He is
not necessarily handsome but is above all, virile . . . he
may be divorced, provided that it is made clear that his
ex-wife sought the divorce.
> *Silhouette Books—Contemporary Romances, style sheet, 1980*

Just because he doesn't do/What everybody else does/
That's no reason why/We can't share a love.
> *Phil Spector, He's a Rebel*

DORA BRYAN: Look Jo, one night—well, actually it was afternoon—I loved him. I'd never really been with a man before. It was the first time. You can remember the second
and the third and the fourth time, but there's no time like
the first. It's always there.
> *A Taste of Honey, script: Shelagh Delaney, Tony Richardson,
> 1961*

I can see from your utter misery, from your eagerness to
misunderstand each other, and from your thoroughly bad
temper, that this is the real thing.
> *Peter Ustinov, Romanoff and Juliet, 1961*

One pulse of passion—youth's first fiery glow,—/Is worth
the hoarded proverbs of the sage: /Vex not thy soul with
dead philosophy;/Have we not lips to kiss with, hearts to
love,/and eyes to see?
> *Oscar Wilde, Panthea*

Men always want to be a woman's first love. That is their
clumsy vanity. We women have a more subtle instinct
about things. What we like is to be a man's last romance.
> *Oscar Wilde, A Woman of No Importance, 1893*

In a field by the river my love and I did stand/And on my leaning shoulder she laid her snow-white hand/She bid me take life easy, as the grass grows on the weirs/But I was young and foolish, and now am full of tears.

William Butler Yeats, Down by the Salley Gardens, in Collected Poems, 1950

The only true love is love at first sight; second sight dispels it.

Israel Zangwill

13. Bachelor Boys

Nowadays two can live as cheaply as one large family used to.

Joey Adams, Cindy and I, 1959

WOODY ALLEN: A relationship, I think, is—is like a shark,/ You know? It has to constantly move forward or it dies.

Annie Hall, script: Woody Allen, Marshall Brickman, 1977

A bachelor is one who enjoys the chase but does not eat the game.

Anonymous

Almost all of our relationships begin and most of them continue as forms of mutual exploitation, a mental or physical barter, to be terminated when one or both parties run out of goods.

W. H. Auden, The Dyer's Hand, 1962

He sleeps fastest who sleeps alone.
> Richard Avedon, *Playboy*, 1975

In Paris, when God provides a beautiful woman, the devil at once retorts with a fool to keep her.
> Jules Barbey d'Aurevilly

The trouble with life is that there is so many beautiful women—and so little time.
> John Barrymore

If a mistaken marriage can be purgatory, mistaken celibacy is hell.
> R. H. Benson, *Conventionalists*, 1908

I would be married, but I'd have no wife/I would be married to a single life.
> Richard Crashaw, *On Marriage*, 1646

It is explained that all relationships require a little give and take. This is untrue. Any partnership demands that we give and give and give and at the last, as we flop into our graves exhausted, we are told that we didn't give enough.
> Quentin Crisp, *How to Become a Virgin*, 1981

When you're married to someone, they take you for granted, you're there, you're there to come home to, you're tied to the kitchen sink and when you go out, even if you look nice, they never say "Oh you do look nice" or anything like that, and you sit in a corner all night and that's it. And he'll fuck off and talk to his mates. When you're living with someone it's fantastic. Everything that he does you do. They're so frightened of losing you they've got to keep you satisfied all the time.
> Nell Dunn, *Poor Cow*

Praise a wife, but stay a bachelor.
   Italian proverb

Marriage has many pains, but celibacy has no pleasures.
   Samuel Johnson, Rasselas, 1759

There is simply no dignified way for a woman to live
alone. Oh, she can get along financially, perhaps (though
not nearly as well as a man) but emotionally she is never
left in peace.
   Erica Jong, Fear of Flying, 1973

The advantage of being celibate is that when one sees a
pretty girl one need not grieve over having an ugly one
back home.
   Paul Leautaud, Propos d'un Jour, 1900

A good relationship has a pattern like a dance. . . . To
touch heavily would be to arrest the pattern and freeze
the movement, to check the endlessly changing beauty of
its unfolding. There is no place here for the possessive
clutch, the clinging arm, the heavy hand; only the barest
touch in passing.
   Anne Morrow Lindbergh, Gift from the Sea, 1955

Friendships, like marriages, are dependent on avoiding
the unforgivable.
   John D. MacDonald

Bachelors know more about women than married men. If
they didn't they would be married too.
   H. L. Mencken, A Mencken Chrestomathy, 1949

I have had sympathy enough with my married griefs, but when it came to the perplexing torments of my single life—not a fellow mourner could I find.
> Donald G. Mitchell, quoted in Frederick W. Morton, *Epigram*, 1903

The bachelor's admired freedom is often a yoke, for the freer a man is to himself, the greater slave he often is to the whims of society.
> George Jean Nathan, *The Bachelor Life*, 1941

You can be married many times, but a bachelor only once.
> *Reflections of a Bachelor*, 1903

Never trust a husband too far, nor a bachelor too near.
> Helen Rowland

A bachelor has to have inspiration for making love to a woman—a married man needs only an excuse.
> Helen Rowland

. . . If you wish the pick of men and women, take a good bachelor and a good wife.
> Robert Louis Stevenson, *Virginibus Puerisque*, 1881

Relationship is a pervading and changing mystery.
> Eudora Welty, *The Eye of the Storm*, 1979

One should always be in love. That is the reason why one should never marry.
> Oscar Wilde

Rich bachelors should be heavily taxed. It is not fair that some men should be happier than others.
> Oscar Wilde

Ultimately the bond of all companionship, whether in marriage or friendship, is conversation.

Oscar Wilde, De Profundis, 1905

By persistently remaining single, a man converts himself into a permanent public temptation. Men should be more careful: this very celibacy leads weaker vessels astray.

Oscar Wilde, The Importance of Being Earnest, 1899

Relationships are things that have their good times and their bad times. I try to cope with the bad times by projecting myself into the character of the other person—to consider how that person feels and try to imagine myself in that person's position. It's not a painful process—it helps you. I think if you can manage to do that, at least you don't run into terrible trouble with people.

Tennessee Williams, quoted in John Gruen, Close-up, 1968

The snag in this business of falling in love is that the parties of the first part so often get mixed up with the wrong parties of the second part, robbed of their cooler judgment by the parties of the second part's glamour. Put it like this. The male sex is divided into rabbits and non-rabbits and the female sex into dashers and dormice, and the trouble is that the male rabbit has a way of getting attracted by a female dasher (who would be fine for the male non-rabbit) and realising too late that he ought to have been concentrating on some mild, gentle dormouse with whom he could settle down peacefully and nibble lettuce.

P. G. Wodehouse, Jeeves in the Offing, 1949

A bachelor is a man who never makes the same mistake once.

Ed Wynn, Ladies' Home Journal, 1942

14. A Young Man's Fancy

Life is not long enough for a coquette to play all her tricks in.

Joseph Addison, *The Spectator*, 1711

Those marriages generally abound most with love and constancy that are preceded by a long courtship. The passion should strike root and gather strength before marriage should be grafted on it.

Joseph Addison, *The Spectator*, 1711

Oh Sir Henry do not *touch* me!/Oh Sir Henry do not touch,/Oh Sir Henry do not!/Oh Sir Henry . . . *do*!/Oh!

Anonymous

She was poor but she was honest/And her parents was the same/Till she met a city feller/And she lost her honest name.

Anonymous, 1914–1918

Come, pretty nymph, fain would I know/What thing it is that breeds delight,/That strives to stand, and cannot go,/And feeds the mouth that cannot bite.

Anonymous, *A Riddle*

A stranger loses half his charm the day he is no longer a stranger.

Genevieve Antoine-Dariaux, *The Men in Your Life*, 1968

An engaged woman is always more agreeable than a disengaged. She is satisfied with herself. Her cares are over, and she feels she may exert all her powers of pleasing without suspicion. All is safe with a lady engaged; no harm can be done.
Jane Austen, Mansfield Park, 1814

To speak of love is to make love.
Honoré de Balzac, The Physiology of Marriage, 1828

It's the good girls who keep the diaries; the bad girls never have the time.
Tallulah Bankhead

In love-making, as in the other arts, those do it best who cannot tell how it is done.
J. M. Barrie, Tommy and Grizel, 1900

To obtain a woman who loves you, you must treat her as if she didn't.
Pierre de Beaumarchais

All stratagems/In love, and that the sharpest war, are lawful.
Francis Beaumont, John Fletcher, The Lovers' Progress

All a writer has to do to get a woman is to say he's a writer. It's an aphrodisiac.
Saul Bellow

Make love to every woman you meet; if you get five per cent on your outlay, it's a good investment.
Arnold Bennett

If you want to win her hand/Let the maiden under-stand/That she's not the only pebble on the beach.
  Harry Braisted, You're Not the Only Pebble on the Beach

"I'll be comfortable on the couch." Famous last words.
  Lenny Bruce, quoted in J. Cohen, The Essential Lenny Bruce,
  1967

The caird prevailed—th'unblushing fair/In his embraces sunk/Partly w'love o'ercome sae sair/An' partly she was drunk.
  Robert Burns, The Jolly Beggars, 1785

Blessed is the wooing that is not long a-doing.
  Robert Burton, Anatomy of Melancholy, 1621

Brisk Confidence still best with woman copes/Pique her and soothe in turn—soon passion crowns thy hopes.
  Lord Byron, Childe Harold's Pilgrimage, 1812–1818

A little still she strove, and much repented/And whispering "I will ne'er consent"—consented.
  Lord Byron, Don Juan, 1819–1824

A woman's honour is concerned with one thing only, and it is a thing with which the honour of a man is not con-cerned at all.
  James Branch Cabell, Jurgen, 1919

No young man ever suggested anything to me but a wed-ding ring. They were emotional, violent in their protesta-tions of love, and three men swore they would kill themselves if I wouldn't marry them. But I was un-touched, adored, worshipped and wooed.
  Barbara Cartland

Many a man has fallen in love with a girl in a light so dim he would not have chosen a suit by it.
Maurice Chevalier, 1955

Where does the family start? It starts with a young man falling in love with a girl—no superior alternative has yet been found.
Winston Churchill, quoted in C. Coote, A Churchill Reader, 1947

Love and a cottage! Eh, Fanny! Ah, give me indifference and a coach and six!
George Colman, The Clandestine Marriage, 1766

Words are the weak support of cold indifference; love has no language to be heard.
William Congreve, The Double Dealer, 1694

Courtship to marriage, as a very witty prologue to a very dull play.
William Congreve, The Old Bachelor, 1693

Him, who loves always one, why should they call/More constant than the man who loves always all.
Abraham Cowley, The Inconstant, 1663

Every maiden's weak and willin'/When she meets the proper villain.
Clarence Day, Thoughts Without Words, 1928

GROUCHO MARX: Send two dozen roses to Room 424 and put "Emily I love you" on the back of the bill.
A Day at the Races, script: Robert Pirosh, George Seaton, George Oppenheimer, 1937

"When a man says he's willin'" said Mr. Barkis, "it's as much to say, that a man's waitin' for an answer."
Charles Dickens, David Copperfield, 1849–1850

Without outward declarations, who can conclude an inward love?
John Donne, Sermons, 1623

Ladies and Gentlemen, I give you a toast. It is "Absinthe makes the tart grow fonder."
Hugh Drummond, quoted in S. Hicks, The Vintage Years, 1943

Had a love affair with Nina in the back of my Cortina/A seasoned-up hyena could not have been more obscener/ She took me to the cleaners, and other misdemeanours/ But I got right up between her rum and her ribena.
Ian Dury, Billericay Dickie, 1979

Lay, lady, lay, lay across my big brass bed/Stay, lady stay, stay while the night is still ahead.
Bob Dylan, Lay, Lady, Lay, 1969

A maid that laughs is half taken.
English proverb

His designs were strictly honourable, as the phrase is: that is, to rob a lady of her fortune by way of marriage.
Henry Fielding, Tom Jones, 1749

There are only the pursued, the pursuing, the busy and the tired.
F. Scott Fitzgerald, The Great Gatsby, 1925

Dirty Talk: Women now freely conceded that dirty talk is stimulating. Take this hint and start whispering a lot of it in your partner's ear. But make sure it's dirty. Halfway measures will not do. For example, the line "I've always had great admiration for your labia minora" might well backfire, with chilling consequences.

Bruce Jay Friedman, Esquire, 1977

Just because you don't feel particularly horny on a given occasion, there is no reason to stay home and sulk. On the contrary, go out of your way to schedule dates on Nights When You Are Not Horny. Women will appreciate this. "What a pleasure," your date will say, "not to have to be mauled and pawed at for a change." This relaxed atmosphere will tend to make her horny after a bit. And there is no rule that you can't become Suddenly Horny too.

Bruce Jay Friedman, Esquire, 1977

In the religion of love the courtesan is a heretic, but the nun is an atheist.

Richard Garnett

Would you gain the tender creature?/Softly, gently, kindly treat her/Suff'ring is the lover's part/Beauty by constraint possessing/You enjoy but half the blessing/Lifeless charms, without the heart.

John Gay, Acis and Galatea, 1732

An inconstant woman, tho' she has no chance to be very happy, can never be very unhappy.

John Gay, Polly, 1728

ISABEL JEANS: Love, my dear Gigi, is a thing of beauty like a work of art. And, like a work of art, it is created by artists. The greater the artist, the greater the art.

Gigi, script: Alan Jay Lerner, 1958

Mrs. Miffins on "Ow to Git Yore Man"
The first thing to remember is to git interested in yore man's work. If it's pigs get interested in pigs and if it's leaky taps and cisterns like mr bumbling's get interested in leaky taps and cisterns. As I 'ave said before most gentlemen prefer the larky sporty tipe, but there are also those wot prefers the quiet moony tipe so you will 'ave to be larky and sporty or quiet and moony accordin' to the man you are chasin'.
Nathaniel Gubbins, Daily Express

Diffidence and awkwardness are the two antidotes to love.
William Hazlitt, Sketches and Essays, 1830

Courtship: a picturesque gateway to a commonplace estate.
Oliver Herford, John Clay, Cupid's Cyclopedia, 1910

Flirtation: a way for two people, who are not married, to pass the time . . . a natural attribute to a woman, an easily acquired accomplishment in men.
Oliver Herford, John Clay, Cupid's Cyclopedia, 1910

Oh! a man's love is strong/When fain he comes a-mating./But a woman's love is long/And grows when it is waiting.
Laurence Housman, The Two Loves, in Collected Poems, 1937

He who wins a thousand common hearts is entitled to some renown but he who keeps undisputed sway over the heart of a coquette is indeed a hero.
Washington Irving, The Sketch Book, 1820

She was common, flirty/She looked about thirty/I would have run away but I was on my own/She told me later, she's a machine operator/She said she liked the way I held the microphone.

    Mick Jagger, Keith Richards, The Spider and the Fly

Men are brought up to command, women to seduce. To admit the necessity of seduction is to admit that one has not the strength to command.

    Sally Kempton, Esquire, 1970

Never confuse "I love you" with "I want to marry you."

    Le Roy King, quoted in Cleveland Amory, The Last Resorts, 1952

She delighted in hearing men talk of their own work, and that is the most fatal way of bringing a man to your feet.

    Rudyard Kipling, The New York Times, 1952

Love's greatest miracle is the curing of coquetry.

    Le Rochefoucauld, Maxims, 1665

If a woman hasn't got a tiny streak of the harlot in her, she's a dry stick as a rule.

    D. H. Lawrence, Pornography and Obscenity, 1929

Truth is a great flirt.

    Franz Liszt, The Letters of F. Liszt to Olga V. Meyendorff, 1981

On a plane you can pick up more and better people than on any other public conveyance since the stagecoach.

    Anita Loos, International Herald Tribune, 1973

We might knit that knot with our tongues, that we shall never undo with our teeth.

    John Lyly, Euphues, 1580

You made me love you/I didn't want to do it.
  Joseph McCarthy, *You Made Me Love You*

Flirtation is merely an expression of considered desire coupled with an admission of its impracticability.
  Marya Mannes, *But Will It Sell*, 1955–1964

All really great lovers are articulate, and verbal seduction is the surest road to actual seduction.
  Marya Mannes, *More in Anger*, 1958

Coquetry is an art of the intellect; flirtation is a function of the senses.
  Don Marquis, *The New York Herald*

Had we but world enough, and time/This coyness, lady, were no crime.
  Andrew Marvell, *To His Coy Mistress*, 1681

When from time to time I have seen the persons with whom the great lovers satisfied their desires, I have often been more astonished by the robustness of their appetites than envious of their successes. It is obvious that you need not often go hungry if you are willing to dine off mutton hash and turnip tops.
  W. Somerset Maugham, *The Summing Up*, 1938

She whom I love is hard to catch and conquer/Hard, but O the glory of the winning were she won.
  George Meredith, *Love in the Valley*, 1912

I like the girls who do/I like the girls who don't/I hate the girl who says she will/And then she says she won't./But the girl I like the best of all/And I think you'll say I'm right/—Is the girl who says she never has/but looks as though she . . ./'Ere, listen!
  Max Miller, *The Max Miller Blue Book*, c. 1950

ANON.: Goodness, what beautiful diamonds!
MAE WEST: Goodness had nothing to do with it, dearie.
> *Night After Night, script: Vincent Lawrence, Mae West, 1932*

The male has been taught that he is superior to women in nearly every way, and that is reinforced by the submissive tactics of many women in their desperate antics of flirtation and hunting; it would be a wonder if the average male did not come to believe that he was superior.
> *Joyce Carol Oates, quoted in Barbralee Diamonstein, Open Secrets, 1972*

Permissiveness is simply removing the dust sheets from our follies.
> *Edna O'Brien, quoted in D. Bailey, Goodbye Baby and Amen, 1969*

When a man talks of love, with caution trust him;/But if he swears, he'll certainly deceive thee.
> *Thomas Otway, The Orphan, 1680*

I flee who chases me and chase who flees me.
> *Ovid, Loves*

Why, having won her, do I woo?/Because her spirit's vestal grace/Provokes me always to pursue/But, spirit-like, eludes embrace.
> *Coventry Patmore, The Married Lover, 1860*

WALTER MATTHAU: How about coming up to my place for a spot of heavy breathing?
> *Pete 'n Tillie, script: Julius J. Epstein, 1972*

DORIS DAY (to Rock Hudson): Mr. Allen, this may come as a shock to you, but there are some men who don't end every sentence with a proposition.

Pillow Talk, script: Stanley Shapiro, Maurice Richlin, based on a story by Russell Rouse, Clarence Greene, 1959

For when success a lover's toil attends,/Few ask if fraud or force attain'd his ends.

Alexander Pope, The Rape of the Lock, 1712

As I walked out one morning I met a buxom lass/Belonging to a dairy man, she had a field of grass/It grew between two mountains at the foot of a rising hill/She bir'd me to cut it down while the birds did sweetly sing.

William Pratt

There is nothing like desire for preventing the things we say from having any resemblance to the things in our minds.

Marcel Proust

He that woes a maid must come seldom in her sight/But he that woes a widow must woe her day and night/He that woes a maid must fain, lie and flatter/But he that woes a widow must down with his breeches and at her.

John Ray, A Collection of English Proverbs, 1670

He that would the daughter win/Must with the mother first begin.

John Ray, A Collection of English Proverbs, 1670

There are a great many ways of proposing. All of them are good. In fact, experience teaches that unless you are very careless in the way you propose, you are in positive danger of being accepted.

Frank Richardson, Love and All About It, 1907

Have you not in a chimney seen/A sullen faggot, wet and green/How coyly it receives the heat/And at both ends does fume and sweat?/So fares it with the harmless maid/When first upon her back she's laid;/But the kind, experienced dame/Cracks and rejoices in the flame.
  Earl of Rochester (John Wilmot)

It is easier to keep half a dozen lovers guessing than to keep one lover after he has stopped guessing.
  Helen Rowland

The hardest task in a girl's life is to prove to a man that his intentions are serious.
  Helen Rowland

Of all forms of caution, caution in love is perhaps most fatal to true happiness.
  Bertrand Russell, Conquest of Happiness, 1950

Credit me, friend, it hath been ever thus,/Since the ark rested on Mount Ararat:/False man hath sworn, and woman hath believed—/Repented and reproached, and then believed once more.
  Sir Walter Scott, The Fortunes of Nigel, 1822

I made no advances to her, but she accepted them.
  Louis Scutenaire

Men's vows are women's traitors! . . . A bait for ladies.
  William Shakespeare, Cymbeline, 1609

Sigh no more ladies, sigh no more,/Men were deceivers ever;/One foot in sea, and one on shore,/To one thing constant never.
  William Shakespeare, Much Ado About Nothing, 1598–1600

Do not give dalliance too much the rein.
  William Shakespeare, The Tempest, 1611

Love sought is good, but giv'n unsought is better.
  William Shakespeare, Twelfth Night, 1598–1600

MARLENE DIETRICH: It took more than one man to change my name to Shanghai Lily.
  Shanghai Express, script: Jules Furthman, 1932

The fickleness of the women I love is only equalled by the infernal constancy of the women who love me.
  George Bernard Shaw, The Philanderer, 1908

MAE WEST: Why don't you come up sometime and see me. I'm home every evening.
  She Done Him Wrong, script: Harvey Thew, John Bright, 1933

MAE WEST: When women go wrong, men go right after them.
  She Done Him Wrong, script: Harvey Thew, John Bright, 1933

All's fair in love and war.
  F. E. Smedley, Frank Fairlegh, 1850

No oath too binding for a lover.
  Sophocles, Phoedra, 5th century B.C.

A wise woman never yields by appointment.
  Stendhal

Out upon it, I have loved/Three whole days together/ And am like to love three more/If it prove fair weather.
  Sir John Suckling, Fragmenta Aurea, 1646

Women sometimes forgive those who force an opportunity, never those who miss it.

Charles Maurice de Talleyrand (attrib.)

The less my hope the hotter my love.

Terence, Eunuchus, 2nd century B.C.

A gentleman is a patient wolf.

Henrietta Tiarks, 1957

LAUREN BACALL: You know you don't have to act with me Steve. You don't have to say anything and you don't have to do anything. Not a thing. Oh, maybe just whistle. You know how to whistle, don't you, Steve? You just put your lips together and blow.

To Have and Have Not, script: Jules Furthman, William Faulkner, 1944

ALBERT FINNEY: If you take my heart by surprise, the rest of my body has the right to follow.

Tom Jones, script: John Osborne, 1963

. . . If by the expression of his countenance you perceive he recognises you, if his company has been agreeable, his connections are respectable and you have no objection to his acquaintance, it is your province to salute him; for if he be decidedly a well-bred man and believe you equally a gentlewoman, he will not salute you first.

Victorian etiquette manual, quoted in R. Pearsall, The Worm in the Bud, 1969

Cunegonde . . . saw Dr. Pangloss behind some bushes giving a lesson in experimental philosophy to her mother's waiting woman, a little brunette who seemed eminently teachable.

Voltaire, Candide, 1759

A fox is a wolf who sends flowers.
    Ruth Weston, *New York Post*, 1955

The amount of women in London who flirt with their own husbands is simply scandalous. It looks so bad. It is simply washing one's clean linen in public.
    Oscar Wilde, *The Importance of Being Earnest*, 1899

A woman will flirt with anybody in the world as long as other people are looking on.
    Oscar Wilde, *The Picture of Dorian Gray*, 1891

A bad woman is the sort of woman a man never gets tired of.
    Oscar Wilde, *A Woman of No Importance*, 1894

They may talk of love in a cottage,/And bowers of trellised vine—/Of nature bewitchingly simple,/And milkmaids half divine . . ./But give me a sly flirtation,/By the light of a chandelier—/With music to play in the pauses,/And nobody very near.
    N. P. Willis, *Love in a Cottage*, in *Complete Works*, 1846

Today women give up too easily. I think they should play harder to get.
    Duchess of Windsor

To talk about honour in the mysteries of love, is like talking of Heaven or the Deity in an operation of witchcraft, just when you are employing the devil: it maketh the charm impotent.
    William Wycherley, *The Country Wife*, 1673

15. *I Do*

Marriage, in life, is like a duel in the midst of battle.
Edmond About

Accident counts for as much in companionship as in marriage.
Henry Adams, The Education of Henry Adams, 1907

Marriage is give and take. You'd better give it to her, or she'll take it anyway.
Joey Adams, Cindy and I, 1959

Married love between/man and woman is bigger than oaths guarded by right of nature.
Aeschylus, Eumenides, 458 B.C.

We declare and affirm, by the tenair of these presents, that love cannot extend its rights over two married persons. For indeed lovers grant one another all things mutually and freely . . . whereas husband and wife are held by their duty to submit their wills to each other.
Andrew, chaplain of Queen Eleanor of Aquitaine, Judgment of Eleanor's Court of Love, 1174

Marriage is the price men pay for sex; sex is the price women pay for marriage.
Anonymous

Marriage is a romance in which the hero dies in the first chapter.
Anonymous

Mr. BENNET: An unhappy alternative is before you, Elizabeth. From this day you must be a stranger to one of your parents. Your mother will never see you again if you do *not* marry Mr. Collins, and I will never see you again if you *do*.
Jane Austen, Pride and Prejudice, 1813

A man ought not to marry without having studied anatomy and dissected at least one woman.
Honoré de Balzac, The Physiology of Marriage, 1828

In marriage you are chained, it is an obligation; living with someone is a mutual agreement that is renegotiated and reendorsed every day.
Brigitte Bardot, News of the World, 1974

Marriage is traditionally the destiny offered to women by society. Most women are married or have been, or plan to be or suffer from not being.
Simone de Beauvoir

Well-married a man is winged—ill-matched he is shackled.
Henry Ward Beecher, Proverbs from Plymouth Pulpit, 1887

Affianced, pp: Fitted with ankle-ring for the ball and chain.
Ambrose Bierce, The Devil's Dictionary, 1911

Altar, n: The place whereon the priest formerly raveled out the small intestine of the sacrificial victim for purposes of divination and cooked its flesh for the gods. The word is now seldom used except with reference to the sacrifice of their liberty and peace by a male and a female fool.

Ambrose Bierce, The Devil's Dictionary, 1911

Marriage, n: The state or condition of a community consisting of a master, a mistress and two slaves, making in all, two.

Ambrose Bierce, The Devil's Dictionary, 1911

The great thing about marriage is that it enables one to be alone without feeling loneliness.

Gerald Brenan, Thoughts in a Dry Season, 1978

Marriage is not just spiritual communion and passionate embraces; marriage is also three meals a day and remembering to carry out the trash.

Dr. Joyce Brothers, Good Housekeeping, 1972

The only real argument for Marriage is that it remains the best method for getting acquainted.

Heywood Broun

In matrimony to hesitate is sometimes to be saved.

Samuel Butler, Notebooks, 1912

Marriage from Love, like vinegar from wine/—A sad, sour, sober beverage—by Time/Is sharpened from its high celestial flavour/Down to a very homely household savour.

Lord Byron, Don Juan, 1819–1824

Marriage is the result of the longing for the deep, deep bliss of the double bed after the hurly burly of the chaise-longue.
    Mrs. Patrick Campbell

Bourgeois marriage has put our country into slippers and will soon lead it to the gates of death.
    Albert Camus, The Fall, 1957

Two dollars will buy all the happiness or all the misery in the world. At least that used to be the price of the marriage license.
    Eddie Cantor, The Way I See It, 1959

There are but two objects in marriage: love or money. If you marry for love, you will certainly have some very happy days, and probably many very uneasy ones; if for money, you will have no happy days and probably *no* uneasy ones.
    Lord Chesterfield, Letters to His Son, 1750

Marriage is a feast where the grace is sometimes better than the dinner.
    Charles Caleb Colton, Lacon, 1825

Marriage is a wonderful invention; then again, so is a bicycle repair kit.
    Billy Connolly

The dread of loneliness is greater than the fear of bondage, so we get married.
    Cyril Connolly, The Unquiet Grave, 1945

Marriage is not all bed and breakfast.
    R. Coulson

The consuming desire of most human beings is deliberately to plant their whole life in the hands of some other person. For this purpose they frequently choose someone who doesn't even want the beastly thing. I would describe this method of searching for happiness as immature ... development of character consists solely in moving towards self-sufficiency.

    Quentin Crisp, The Naked Civil Servant, 1968

Wedlock indeed hath often compared been/To public feasts, where meet a public rout/Where they that are without would fain go in/And they that are within would fain go out.

    Sir John Davies, Contention Betwixt a Wife, a Widow and a Maid

How else do you get on in this world except by marrying well.

    Nigel Dempster, The Observer, 1977

The reason that husbands and wives do not understand each other is because they belong to different sexes.

    Dorothy Dix

Sometimes people commit bigamy to please the landlady.

    Sir Gerald Dodson, The Observer, 1942

And sure all marriage in repentance ends.

    John Dryden, Don Sebastian, 1691

Falsely your Church seven sacraments does frame/ Penance and Matrimony are the same.

    Richard Duke, To a Roman Catholic Friend on Marriage, in Poetical Works, 1793

One should not think about it too much when marrying
or taking pills.
> Dutch proverb

. . . An intense one-to-one involvement is as socially con-
ditioned as a hamburger and malt.
> Marie Edwards, *The Challenge of Being Single*, 1975

Having once embarked on your marital voyage, it is impossible not to be aware that you make no way and that the
sea is not within sight, that in fact you are exploring an
enclosed basin.
> George Eliot, *Middlemarch*, 1871–1872

Marriage must be a relation either of sympathy or of conquest.
> George Eliot, *Romola*, 1862–1863

Marriage is the perfection which love aimed at, ignorant of
what it sought.
> Ralph Waldo Emerson, *Journals*, 1850

It is one of the boldest actions of a man's life to marry.
Whoever passes that rubicon has need of the fortune of
Caesar to make him happy.
> Sir George Etherege

Marry, and with luck/it may go well/But when a marriage fails/then those who marry live at home in hell.
> Euripides, *Orestes*, 408 B.C.

When widows exclaim loudly against second marriages, I
would always lay a wager that the man, if not the wedding
day, is absolutely fixed on.
> Henry Fielding, *Amelia*, 1751

Keep your eyes wide open before marriage, half shut afterwards.
> Benjamin Franklin, *Poor Richard's Almanack*, 1732–1757

More belongs to marriage than four legs in a bed.
> Thomas Fuller, *Gnomologia*, 1732

Be not hasty to marry. It's better to have one plow going than two cradles, and more profit to have a barn filled than a bed.
> Thomas Fuller

A man in love is incomplete until he is married. Then he is finished.
> Zsa Zsa Gabor, *Newsweek*, 1960

Marriage is a lot like the army: everyone complains, but you'd be surprised at the large number that re-enlist.
> James Garner, 1980

Nearly all marriages are mysterious, and the two-thirds of marriages that are stable are, usually, the most mysterious.
> Jonathan Gathorne-Hardy, *Love, Sex, Marriage and Divorce*, 1981

Do you think your mother and I should have lived so comfortably so long together, if ever we had been married?
> John Gay, *The Beggar's Opera*, 1728

ISABEL JEANS: Bad table manners, my dear Gigi, have broken up more households than infidelity.
> *Gigi*, screenplay: Alan Jay Lerner, 1958

One should celebrate only a happy *ending*; celebrations at the outset exhaust the joy and energy needed to urge us forward and sustain us in the long struggle. And of all celebrations a wedding is the worst; no day should be kept more quietly and humbly.

Johann Wolfgang von Goethe

The sum which two married people owe to one another defies calculation. It is an infinite debt, which can only be discharged through all eternity.

Johann Wolfgang von Goethe, Elective Affinities, 1809

Marriage is the only evil that men pray for.

Greek proverb

Care: the Mother of Thrift and the Child of Extravagance. If you do not take it before marriage, it will overtake you after.

Oliver Herford, John Clay, Cupid's Cyclopedia, 1910

Loneliness . . . the married man's meat, the single man's poison.

Oliver Herford, John Clay, Cupid's Cyclopedia, 1910

Marriage: the conventional ending of a love affair. A lonesome state.

Oliver Herford, John Clay, Cupid's Cyclopedia, 1910

Wedding: a necessary formality before securing a divorce.

Oliver Herford, John Clay, Cupid's Cyclopedia, 1910

The silken texture of the marriage tie bears a daily strain of right and wrong and insult to which no other human relation can be subjected without lesion.

William Dean Howells, The Rise of Silas Lapham, 1885

I guess walking slow getting married is because it gives you time to maybe change your mind.

Virginia Hudson, O Ye Jigs and Juleps, 1962

Marriage is a mistake every man should make.

George Jessel

Marriages would in general be as happy, and often more so, if they were all made by the Lord Chancellor, upon due consideration of the characters and circumstances without the parties having any choice in the matter.

Samuel Johnson

If you marry, you will regret it; if you do not marry, you will also regret it.

Søren Kierkegaard, Either/Or, 1843

Marriage is a lottery, but you can't tear up your ticket if you lose.

F. M. Knowles, A Cheerful Year Book, 1907

Of course a platonic relationship is possible—but only between husband and wife.

Ladies' Home Journal

Advice to Married Couples—both parties should try and talk about subjects that the other is interested in. There ain't no husband cares a damn if the washerwoman that is coming next week goes into a different church than the one that was here last week, and there's very few wives that cares the same amt. whether Max Baer is going to be the next heavyweight champion.

Ring Lardner, The Lardner Reader, 1963

Intellectually of course, we didn't believe in getting married. But you don't love someone intellectually.
John Lennon

Marriage is a triumph of habit over hate.
Oscar Levant, *Memoirs of an Amnesiac*, 1965

Kate Smith & Harvey Holroyd request your presence at a Spring Festival—a celebration of Open Commitment and Feeling Exchange where you can just *Be*. Come reaffirm with us our belief that in Life, it's the Journey that counts, not the Goal.
Cyra McFadden, *The Serial*, 1978

I have been called a monster. But I am not. No bigamist is. Nor yet a woman hater. The man who marries just once proves only his ignorance of women. The man who marries many times proves, in spite of his disillusionments, his faith in women.
Don Marquis, *Reveries of a Bigamist*

A marriage without conflicts is almost as inconceivable as a nation without crises.
André Maurois, *The Art of Living*, 1939

Marriage is three parts love and seven parts forgiveness of sins.
Langdon Mitchell, *The New York Idea*, 1907

I see no marriages which sooner fail than those contracted on account of beauty and amorous desire.
Michel de Montaigne, *Essays*, 1588

In almost every marriage there is a selfish and an unselfish partner. A pattern is set up and soon becomes inflexible, of one person always making the demands and one person always giving way.

Iris Murdoch, *A Severed Head*, 1961

Marriage is based on the theory that when a man discovers a particular brand of beer exactly to his taste, he should at once throw up his job and go to work in the brewery.

George Jean Nathan

Marriage is the meal where the soup is better than the dessert.

Austin O'Malley

But if they cannot contain, let them marry; for it is better to marry than to burn.

Saint Paul

Marriages peter out or pan out.

Anthony Pietropinto, *Husbands and Wives*, 1979

Marriage is a lottery in which men stake their liberty and women their happiness.

Virginie des Rieux

Marriage is nothing but a civil contract.

John Selden, *Table Talk*, 1689

What is wedlock forced but a hell/An age of discord and continual strife? Whereas the contrary bringeth bliss/ And is a pattern of celestial peace.

William Shakespeare, *Henry IV, Part I*, 1597

What God hath joined together, no man shall ever put asunder: God will take care of that.
George Bernard Shaw, Getting Married, 1911

Those who talk most about the blessings of marriage and the constancy of its vows are the very people who declare that if the chain were broken and the prisoners left free to choose, the whole social fabric would fly asunder. You cannot have the argument both ways. If the prisoner is happy, why lock him in? If he is not, why pretend he is?
George Bernard Shaw, Man and Superman, 1903

'Tis safest in matrimony to begin with a little aversion.
Richard Brinsley Sheridan, The Rivals, 1775

It is a matter of life and death for married people to interrupt each other's stories, for if they did not, they would burst.
Logan Pearsall Smith, Afterthoughts

Marriage resembles a pair of shears, so joined that they cannot be separated; often moving in opposite directions, yet always punishing anyone who comes between them.
Sydney Smith, quoted in Lady Holland, Memoir, 1855

Sexuality is something, like nuclear energy, which may prove amenable to domestication, through scruple, but then again may not.
Susan Sontag, Styles of Radical Will, 1969

Marriage: a ceremony in which rings are put on the finger of a lady and through the nose of the gentleman.
Herbert Spencer

The married state, with and without the affection suitable to it, is the compleatest image of heaven and hell we are capable of receiving in this life.
    Richard Steele, The Spectator, 1711

The Lion is the King of the Beasts, but he is scarcely suitable for a domestic pet. In the same way, I suspect love is rather too violent a passion to make, in all cases, a good domestic sentiment.
    Robert Louis Stevenson, Virginibus Puerisque, 1881

Even if we take matrimony at its lowest, even if we regard it as no more than a sort of friendship recognised by the police.
    Robert Louis Stevenson, Virginibus Puerisque, 1881

We study ourselves three weeks, we love each other three months, we squabble three years, we tolerate each other thirty years, and then the children start all over again.
    Hippolyte Taine, Vie et Opinions de Thomas Graingorge, 1867

Remember, it is as easy to marry a rich woman as a poor woman.
    William Thackeray, Pendennis, 1848

WILLIAM GARGAN: Getting married is serious business. It's kinda formal, like funerals or playing stud poker.
    They Knew What They Wanted, script: Robert Ardrey, 1940

Both marriage and death ought to be welcome: the one promises happiness, doubtless the other assures it.
    Mark Twain, letter, 1888

Marriage is the only adventure open to the cowardly.
    Voltaire, Thoughts of a Philosopher, 1734

Marriage is hardly a thing that one can do now and then—
except in America.
    Oscar Wilde, *The Picture of Dorian Gray*, 1891

16. Happy Families

Honey, a swinging signorina to a happily married man is
like a plate of ravioli to a guy who has just eaten. Sure it's
tasty, but who needs it?
    Joey Adams, *Cindy and I*, 1959

The joys of parents are secret and so are their griefs and
fears.
    Francis Bacon, *Of Parents and Children*, 1597

In order to be happy in wedlock, you must either be a
man of genius married to an affectionate and intellectual
woman, or by a chance which is not as common as might
be supposed, you must both of you be exceedingly stupid.
    Honoré de Balzac, *Petty Troubles of Married Life*

It is as absurd to say that a man cannot love one woman
all the time as it is to say that a violinist needs several
violins to play the same piece of music.
    Honoré de Balzac, *The Physiology of Marriage*, 1828

Two souls with but a single thought,/Two hearts that
beat as one.
    Von Munch Bellinghausen, *Ingomar the Barbarian*

'Tis sweet to know there is an eye will mark/Our coming and look brighter when we come.

> *Lord Byron, Don Juan, 1819–1824*

Let us live, my Lesbia, and love, and value at a penny all the talk of crabbed old men.

> *Catullus, Odes, 1st century B.C.*

We've been together now for forty years/An' it don't seem a day too much/There ain't a lady livin' in the land/As I'd swop for my dear old Dutch.

> *Albert Chevalier, My Old Dutch*

Oh Finger with the circlet slight/That keeps it warm and cosy/Wee winsome third left-handed doight/So white and warm and rosy—/More taper digits there may be/More lips may kiss and cling on/This tiny finger's best to me/The one I put the ring on.

> *H. Cholmondeley-Pennell, From Grave to Gay, 1884*

In a perfect union the man and the woman are like a strung bow. Who is to say whether the string bends the bow or the bow tightens the string? Yet male bow and female string are in harmony with each other, and their arrow can be aimed. Unstrung the bow hangs aimless, the cord flaps idly.

> *Cyril Connolly, The Unquiet Grave, 1945*

Love is not enough. It must be the foundation, the cornerstone, but not the complete structure. It is much too pliable. Too yielding.

> *Bette Davis, The Lonely Life, 1962*

The value of marriage is not that adults produce children, but that children produce adults.

> *Peter De Vries*

Love is funny and I am funny. It needs wife's little breast-
ies every two hours like a baby and if they seem far off—it
do shriek.

> Havelock Ellis, letter to his wife in P. Grosskurth, *Havelock Ellis:
> A Biography*, 1980

There are six requisites in every happy marriage: the first
is Faith and the other five are Confidence.

> Elbert Hubbard, *The Note Book*, 1927

Nothing is more distasteful to me than that entire compla-
cency and satisfaction which beam in the countenances
of a new-married couple.

> Charles Lamb, *Essays of Elia*, 1820–1823

There are some good marriages, but no delightful ones.

> Le Rochefoucauld, *Maxims*, 1665

Only the strong of heart can be well married, since they
do not turn to marriage to supply what no other human
being can ever get from another—a sure sense of the fortress within himself.

> Max Lerner, *The Unfinished Country*, 1959

A simple enough pleasure, surely, to have breakfast alone
with one's husband, but how seldom married people in
the midst of life achieve it.

> Anne Morrow Lindbergh, *Gift from the Sea*, 1955

Ideally, both members of a couple in love free each other
to new and different worlds.

> Anne Morrow Lindbergh, *Hour of Gold, Hour of Lead*, 1973

As unto the bow the cord is,/So unto the man is woman;/Though she bends him, she obeys him,/ Though she draws him, yet she follows;/Useless each without the other!
    Henry Wadsworth Longfellow, Hiawatha, 1858

There is no more lovely, friendly and charming relationship, communion or company than a good marriage.
    Martin Luther, Table Talk, 1569

In a successful marriage there's no such thing as one's way. There is only the way of both, only the bumpy, dusty, difficult but always mutual path.
    Phyllis McGinley, The Province of the Heart, 1959

Marriage was all a woman's idea, and for man's acceptance of the pretty yoke it becomes us to be grateful.
    Phyllis McGinley, The Province of the Heart, 1959

After a few years of marriage a man and his wife are apt to be, if nothing else, at least the sort of enemies who respect each other.
    Don Marquis, The New York Herald

A happy marriage is a long conversation which always seems too short.
    André Maurois, Memories, 1970

Who are happy in marriage? Those with so little imagination that they cannot picture a better state, and those so shrewd that they prefer quiet slavery to a hopeless rebellion.
    H. L. Mencken, Prejudices, 1920

. . . the apt and cheerful conversation of man with woman, to comfort and refresh him against the solitary life.

John Milton, *On the Aims of Marriage*

A real marriage bears no resemblance to . . . marriages of interest or ambition. It is two lovers who live together.

Lady Mary Wortley Montagu, *Works*, 1803

The great secret of successful marriage is to treat all disasters as incidents and none of the incidents as disasters.

Harold Nicolson

If married couples did not live together, happy marriages would be more frequent.

Friedrich Nietzsche, *Human, All Too Human*, 1878

Nuptial love bears the clearest marks of being nothing other than the rehearsal of a communion of a higher nature.

Coventry Patmore, *Religio Poetae*, 1893

A happy marriage is still the greatest treasure within the gift of fortune.

Eden Phillpotts, *A Year with Bisshea-Bantam*, 1934

It's a mistake to suppose that it is absolutely necessary to give up being in love directly you are married.

Frank Richardson, *Love and All About It*, 1907

A good marriage is that in which each appoints the other guardian of his solitude.

Rainer Maria Rilke, *Letters*

It takes patience to appreciate domestic bliss, volatile spirits prefer unhappiness.

George Santayana, The Life of Reason, 1905–1906

A lifetime of happiness! No man alive could bear it: it would be hell on earth.

George Bernard Shaw, Man and Superman, 1903

Some pray to marry the man they love/My prayer will somewhat vary/I humbly pray to Heaven above/That I love the man I marry.

Rose Pastor Stokes, My Prayer

The reasons why so few marriages are happy, is, because young ladies spend their time in making nets, not in making cages.

Jonathan Swift, Thoughts on Various Subjects, 1714

How I do hate those words "an excellent marriage." In them is contained more wicked worldliness than any other words one ever hears spoken.

Anthony Trollope

The proper basis for marriage is mutual misunderstanding.

Oscar Wilde, Lord Arthur Savile's Crime, 1891

Of course married life is merely a habit, a bad habit. But then one regrets the loss of even one's worst habits. Perhaps one regrets them the most. They are such an essential part of one's personality.

Oscar Wilde, The Picture of Dorian Gray, 1891

How can a woman be expected to be happy with a man who insists on treating her as if she were a perfectly normal human being.
    Oscar Wilde, A Woman of No Importance, 1894

In Hollywood all marriages are happy. It's trying to live together afterwards that causes the problems.
    Shelley Winters

The world is a wedding.
    Yiddish proverb

17. Trouble and Strife

If it were not for the presents, an elopement would be preferable.
    George Ade, Forty Modern Fables, 1901

Don't assume that every sad-eyed woman has loved and lost—she may have got him.
    Anonymous

The loves of some people are but the result of good suppers.
    Anonymous

A man has no business to marry a woman who can't make him miserable. It means she can't make him happy.
    Anonymous

These panting damsels, dancing for their lives/Are only maidens waltzing into wives./Those smiling matrons are appraisers sly/Who regulate the dance, the squeeze, the sigh/And, each base cheapening buyer having chid/ Knock down their daughters to the highest bid.
    Anonymous

The glances over cocktails/That seemed to be so sweet/ Don't seem quite so amorous/Over Shredded Wheat.
    Anonymous, quoted in Frank Muir Goes Into . . ., 1978

Bigamy is having one husband too many. Monogamy is the same.
    Anonymous woman, quoted in Erica Jong, Fear of Flying, 1975

Habit . . . is the chloroform of love/is the cement that unites married couples/is getting stuck in the mud of daily routine/is the fog that masks the most beautiful scenery/is the end of everything.
    Genevieve Antoine-Dariaux, The Men In Your Life, 1968

Marriage always demands the greatest understanding of the art of insincerity possible between two human beings.
    Vicki Baum, And Life Goes On, 1931

Women, deceived by men, want to marry them; it is a kind of revenge as good as any other.
    Philip de Remi Beaumanoir

Romances paint at full length people's wooings/But only give a bust of marriages/For no-one cares for matrimonial cooings/There's nothing wrong in a connubial kiss;/Think you, if Laura had been Petrarch's wife/He would have written sonnets all his life?
    Lord Byron, Don Juan, 1819–1824

To marry a woman you love and who loves you is to lay a wager with her as to who will stop loving the other first.
    Alfred Capus, *Notes et Pensées*, 1926

If you are afraid of loneliness, don't marry.
    Anton Chekhov

Oh, how many torments lie in the small circle of a wedding-ring!
    Colly Cibber, *The Double Gallant*, 1707

SHARPER: Thus grief still treads upon the heels of pleasure/Marry'd in haste, we may repent at leisure.
SETTER: Some by experience find these words misplac'd/At leisure marry'd, they repent in haste.
    William Congreve, *The Old Bachelor*, 1693

The complaints which anyone voices against his mate indicate exactly the qualities which stimulated attraction before marriage.
    Dr. Rudolf Dreikurs, *The Challenge of Marriage*, 1946

Marriage is two people agreeing to tell the same lie.
    Karen Durbin

That monstrous animal a husband and wife.
    Henry Fielding, *Tom Jones*, 1749

God, for two people to be able to live together for the rest of their lives is almost unnatural.
    Jane Fonda

It is not marriage that fails, it is people that fail. All that marriage does is show people up.
    Harry Emerson Fosdick

The spiritual disillusionment and bodily deprivation to which most marriages are . . . doomed puts both partners back in the state they were in before their marriage, except for being the poorer by the loss of an illusion.

Sigmund Freud, Complete Works, 1955

Love is an ideal thing, marriage is a real thing; a confusion of the real with the ideal never goes unpunished.

Johann Wolfgang von Goethe

There's one consolation about matrimony. When you look around you can always see somebody who did worse.

Warren H. Goldsmith, Ladies' Home Journal, 1948

Loneliness is never more cruel than when it is felt in close propinquity with someone who has ceased to communicate.

Germaine Greer, The Female Eunuch, 1970

How to Be Happy Though Married

Rev. E. J. Hardy, book title, 1910

Marriage is a ghastly public confession of a strictly private intention.

Ian Hay

Holy Deadlock

A. P. Herbert, book title

The critical period in matrimony is breakfast-time.

A. P. Herbert, Uncommon Law

When you're away, I'm restless, Lonely/Wretched, bored, dejected, only/Here's the rub, my darling dear/I feel the same when you are here.

Samuel Hoffenstein, Poems in Praise of Practically Nothing, 1929

Marriage is a good deal like a circus: there is not as much in it as represented in the advertising.
 Edgar Watson Howe, Country Town Sayings, 1911

Domesticity is death.
 Mick Jagger

'Tis said that marriages are made above/It may be so, some few, perhaps, for love./But from the smell of sulphur I should say/They must be making *matches* here all day.
 Benjamin Jowett, quoted in Margot Asquith, Autobiography, 1936

At length he stretches out his foolish head to the conjugal halter.
 Juvenal, Satires, c. 100

Weddings make a lot of people sad/But if you're not the groom, they're not so bad.
 Gus Kahn, Makin' Whoopee, 1928

He gave way to the queer, savage feeling that sometimes takes by the throat a husband twenty years married, where he sees, across the table, the same face of his wedded wife, and knows that, as he has sat facing it, so must he continue to sit until the day of its death or his own.
 Rudyard Kipling, Plain Tales from the Hills, 1888

The honeymoon is over when he phones to say he'll be late for supper and she's already left a note that it's in the refrigerator.
 Bill Lawrence

I do not think marriage is the product of love.
 John Lennon, 1968

She had become so dully habituated to married life that in her full matronliness she was as sexless as an anaemic nun.
   Sinclair Lewis, Babbitt, 1920

You're so alike, you're matched for life/A nitwit man, his nitwit wife/(I wonder why then it should be/That such a pair cannot agree?)
   Martial, Epigrams, 1st century B.C.

Marriage, to tell the truth, is an evil, but a necessary evil.
   Menander, 4th century B.C.

JOSÉ FERRER: Marriage is like a dull meal, with the dessert at the beginning.
   Moulin Rouge, script: Anthony Veiller, John Huston, 1952

I can think of nothing marriage could give me, but I can think of many things it could take away from me.
   George Jean Nathan, Man Against Woman

Marriage: a book of which the first chapter is written in poetry and the remaining chapters in prose.
   Beverley Nichols

EDDIE ALBERT: I wanted to marry her when I saw the moonlight shining on the barrel of her father's shotgun.
   Oklahoma!, script: Sonya Levien, William Ludwig, 1955

Strange to say what delight we married people have to see these poor fools decoyed into our condition.
   Samuel Pepys, Diary, 1665

ROCK HUDSON: Jonathan, before a man gets married, he's a—he's like a tree in the forest. He—he stands there independent, an entity unto himself. And then he's chopped down. His branches are cut off, and he's stripped of his bark, and he's thrown into the river with the rest of the logs. Then this tree is taken to the mill. Now, when it comes out, it's no longer a tree. It's a vanity table, a breakfast nook, a baby crib and the newspaper that lines the family garbage can.
Pillow Talk, script: *Stanley Shapiro, Maurice Richlin, 1959*

They dream in courtship, but in wedlock wake.
Alexander Pope, The Wife of Bath

Marriage is like paying an endless visit in your worst clothes.
J. B. Priestley

When you're bored with yourself marry, and be bored with someone else.
David Pryce-Jones, Owls and Satyrs

Better be half hang'd than ill-wed.
John Ray, A Collection of English Proverbs, 1670

Marriage . . . the log of pleasure, the luggage of life.
Earl of Rochester (John Wilmot)

It doesn't much signify whom one marries, for one is sure to find out next morning that it was someone else.
Samuel Rogers

In olden times sacrifices were made at the altar—a practice which is still continued.
Helen Rowland

When two people are under the influence of the most violent, most insane, most delusive, and most transient of passions, they are required to swear that they will remain in that excited, abnormal and exhausting condition continuously until death do them part.
　George Bernard Shaw

Even the God of Calvin never judged anyone as harshly as married couples judged each other.
　Wilfred Sheed, Max Jamison

In marriage, a man becomes slack and selfish, and undergoes a fatty degeneration of his moral being.
　Robert Louis Stevenson, Virginibus Puerisque, 1881

Marriage is a step so grave and decisive that it attracts light-headed, variable men by its very awfulness.
　Robert Louis Stevenson, Virginibus Puerisque, 1881

Marriage is a covered dish.
　Swiss proverb

Marriage! That feeble institution! Child, it will pass away with priestcraft from the pulpit into the crypt, into the abyss. For does not Nature herself teach us that marriage is against nature. Look at the birds—they pair for the season and part, but how merrily they sing! While marrying is like chaining two dogs by the collar. They snarl and bite each other because there is no hope of parting.
　Alfred, Lord Tennyson, The Promise of May, 1882

The fact that one is married by no means proves that one is a mature person.
　Clara Thompson, quoted in P. Mullahy, New Contributions to Psychiatry, 1949

What cloying meat is love, when matrimony's the sauce to it!
    Sir John Vanbrugh, *The Provok'd Wife*, 1697

Marriage is a most delightful thing, in the beginning so very sweet, all love, sugar and honey, but in a short time after, the matter changes amazingly and there is a great deal of mustard, pepper and vinegar.
    Wedlock's Joys, Victorian music hall monologue

Marriage is a great institution—but I'm not ready for an institution yet.
    Mae West

There is one thing worse than an absolutely loveless marriage. A marriage in which there is love, but on one side only.
    Oscar Wilde, *An Ideal Husband*, 1899

I have often noticed that in married households the champagne is rarely of first-rate brand.
    Oscar Wilde, *The Importance of Being Earnest*, 1899

How marriage ruins a man. It's as demoralising as cigarettes, and far more expensive.
    Oscar Wilde, *Lady Windermere's Fan*, 1892

The real drawback to marriage is that it makes one unselfish. And unselfish people are colourless.
    Oscar Wilde, *The Picture of Dorian Gray*, 1891

It was so cold I almost got married.
    Shelley Winters, *The New York Times*, 1956

MARJORIE MAIN: But ma'am, you know how them big, strong, red-headed men are: they just got to get to the point. So we got married, ma'am. Natcherly, I ain't had no chance to think about love since.
The Women, script: Anita Loos, Jane Murfin, 1939

Marrying to increase love is like gaming to become rich: alas! you only lose what little stock you had before.
William Wycherley, The Country Wife, 1672

In how many lives does Love really play a dominant part? The average tax payer is no more capable of a "grand passion" than of a grand opera.
Israel Zangwill, Romeo and Juliet and Other Love Stories

ANTHONY QUINN: Am I not a man? And is not a man stupid? I'm a man, so I married. Wife, children, house, everything—the full catastrophe.
Zorba the Greek, script: Michael Cacoyannis, 1964

18. Man About the House

The most popular labour-saving device today is still a husband with money.
Joey Adams, Cindy and I, 1959

A husband is simply a lover with a two days' growth of beard, his collar off and a bad cold in the head.
Anonymous

All husbands are alike, but they have different faces so you can tell them apart.
    Anonymous

It is often seen that bad husbands have very good wives: whether it be, that it raiseth the price of their husbands' kindness when it comes, or that the wives take a pride in their patience.
    Francis Bacon, Essays, 1597

The majority of husbands remind me of an orangutan trying to play the violin.
    Honoré de Balzac, The Physiology of Marriage, 1828

The man who enters his wife's dressing room is either a philosopher or a fool.
    Honoré de Balzac, The Physiology of Marriage, 1828

Brute, n: see Husband
    Ambrose Bierce, The Devil's Dictionary, 1911

Husband, n: One who, having dined, is charged with the care of the plate.
    Ambrose Bierce, The Devil's Dictionary, 1911

"Adam knew Eve his wife and she conceived." It is a pity that this still is the only knowledge of their wives at which some men seem to arrive.
    Francis Herbert Bradley

An archaeologist is the best husband any woman can have—the older she gets the more he is interested in her.
    Agatha Christie, The Observer, 1955

Married men make very poor husbands.
    Frank Crowninshield

I fell in love with my husband simply because he was so different from every other boy I had ever met. He did not like love-making and neither do I. He has never actually told me he loves me. . . . He never actually proposed, but we saw a three-piece suite we liked and that clinched the idea.

Daily Herald letter, quoted in Frank Muir Goes Into . . . , 1978

This man, she reasons, as she looks at her husband, is a poor fish. But he is the nearest I can get to the big one that got away.

Nigel Dennis, Cards of Identity, 1960

When you're a married man, Samivel, you'll understand a good many things as you don't understand now; but vether it's worth while goin' through so much to learn so little, as the charity boy said ven he got to the end of the alphabet, is a matter o' taste.

Charles Dickens, Pickwick Papers, 1837

Manny a man that cud rule a hundred millyon shtrangers with an ir'n hand is careful to take off his shoes in th' front hallway whin he comes home late at night.

Finley Peter Dunne, Mr. Dooley on Making a Will, 1919

. . . the superiority of your husband simply as a man . . . In the character of a noble, enlightened and truly good man, there is a power and a sublimity so nearly approaching what we believe to be the nature and capacity of angels, that . . . no language can describe the degree of admiration and respect which the contemplation of such a character must excite . . . to be admitted to his heart—to share his counsels and to be the chosen companion of his joys and sorrows!—it is difficult to say whether humility or gratitude should preponderate in the feelings of the woman thus distinguished and thus blest.

Sarah Ellis, 1842

Husbands are like fires—they go out when unattended.
    Zsa Zsa Gabor, Newsweek, *1960*

A wife is to thank God her husband hath faults . . . a husband without faults is a dangerous observer.
    Marquis of Halifax

I should like to see any kind of man, distinguishable from a gorilla, that some good and even pretty woman could not shape a husband out of.
    Oliver Wendell Holmes, Sr., The Professor at the Breakfast Table, *1860*

A man should be taller, older, heavier, uglier and hoarser than his wife.
    Edgar Watson Howe, Country Town Sayings, *1911*

Romantic love can be very well represented in the moment, but conjugal love cannot, because an ideal husband is not one who is such once in his life, but one who every day is such.
    Søren Kierkegaard

. . . She always managed a smile for me, until I came in one day to find her in a doorway, gripping the molding on both sides of the wall and crying as she smashed her head repeatedly against the doorframe. . . . Although one of the reasons I had chosen Frances to be the mother of my children was her size and strength, which should have enabled her to bear half a dozen high-performance children, I certainly had not intended to risk damage by pushing her to design limit.
    G. Gordon Liddy, Will, *1980*

You think we should be in total darkness when we're screwing:/I prefer a light, I like to see what I am doing./Women should co-operate, caressing, squirming, squealing:/You lie back and think of Rome, or contemplate the ceiling.
 Martial, Epigram 104

The wise husband never becomes indignant. Like a sailor in a storm he slackens the sails, waits, hopes, and the passing storms do not prevent his loving the sea.
 André Maurois

Marriage, as everyone knows, is chiefly an economic matter. But too often it is assumed that its economy concerns only the wife's hats; it also concerns, and perhaps more importantly, the husband's cigars. No man is genuinely happy, married, who has to drink worse whiskey than he used to drink when he was single.
 H. L. Mencken, Prejudices, 1924

Woman's vanity demands that a man be more than a happy husband.
 Friedrich Nietzsche

RAFAELLA: As for husbands, it's enough to pretend to love them. And that's good enough for them.
MARGARITA: Do you mean to tell me that a gentlewoman should cheat her own husband?
RAFAELLA: Cheat, indeed? Straight as a die! The cheating's what you do with your husband.
 Allesandro Piccolomini, Good Form for Women, c. 1540

No louder shrieks to pitying heav'n are cast/When husbands, or when lapdogs breathe their last.
  Alexander Pope, The Rape of the Lock, 1714

It is nothing—they are only thrashing my husband.
  Portuguese proverb

When you see what some girls marry, you realize how they must hate to work for a living.
  Helen Rowland

A husband is what's left of a man after the nerve is extracted.
  Helen Rowland

Before marriage, a man declares that he would lay down his life to serve you; after marriage, he won't even lay down his newspaper to talk to you.
  Helen Rowland, A Guide to Men, 1925

I think every woman is entitled to a middle husband she can forget.
  Adela Rogers St. Johns, Los Angeles Times, 1974

A woman who takes her husband about with her everywhere is like a cat that goes on playing with a mouse long after she's killed it.
  Saki

. . . A woman should never use her husband as her confessor; it demands more virtue of him than his situation allows.
  George Sand, Valentine, 1833

There you are you see, quite simply, if you cannot have your dear husband for a comfort and a delight, for a breadwinner and a crosspatch, for a sofa, chair, or a hot-water bottle, one can use him as a Cross to be borne.
Stevie Smith

. . . a little in drink, but at all times your faithful husband . . .
Sir Richard Steele, letter to his wife

Lastly (and this, perhaps, the golden rule) no woman should marry a teetotaller, or a man that does not smoke.
Robert Louis Stevenson, Virginibus Puerisque, 1881

It's most dangerous nowadays for a husband to pay any attention to his wife in public. It always makes people think that he beats her when they're alone.
Oscar Wilde, Lady Windermere's Fan, 1892

The husbands of very beautiful women belong to the criminal classes.
Oscar Wilde, The Picture of Dorian Gray, 1891

The Ideal Husband? There couldn't be such a thing. The institution is wrong.
Oscar Wilde, A Woman of No Importance, 1893

That slight sheepishness which comes to married men when the names of those whom they themselves esteem highly, but of whom they are aware that their wives disapprove, crop up in the course of conversation.
P. G. Wodehouse, Lord Emsworth and Others, 1937

19. A Woman's Work

The best mothers, wives and managers of households know little or nothing of sexual indulgences. Love of home, children and domestic duties are the only passions they feel ... she submits to her husband, but only to please him; and, but for the desire of maternity, would far rather be relieved from his attentions.

Dr. *William Acton, Function and Disorders of the Reproductive Organs*, 1857

The wife of Willis Anderson came again to petition for his pardon. She hinted that her husband did not wish to be discharged from prison himself, and that it would be no relaxation of his punishment to turn him over to her.

John Quincy Adams, Diary, 1828

If you want peace in the house, do what your wife wants.

African proverb

I have a wife, you have a wife, we all have wives. We've had a taste of paradise, we know what it means to be married.

Sholem Aleichem, On Account of a Hat

Basically my wife was immature. I'd be at home in the bath and she'd come in and sink my boats.

Woody Allen

A wife is one who stands by a man in all the trouble he wouldn't have had if he hadn't married her.

Anonymous

A sad barnyard where the hen crows louder than the cock.

G. L. Apperson, *English Proverbs*, 1929

Wives are young men's mistresses, companions for middle age and old men's nurses.

Francis Bacon, *On Marriage and Single Life*, 1597

In a husband, there is only a man; in a married woman there is a man, a father, a mother, and a woman.

Honoré de Balzac, *Petty Troubles of Married Life*

Putting yourself in the wrong with your lawful wife is solving the problem of Perpetual Motion.

Honoré de Balzac, *Petty Troubles of Married Life*

Your wife will defend you like the bear in La Fontaine's fable; she will throw paving stones at your head to drive away the flies that settle on it.

Honoré de Balzac, *The Physiology of Marriage*, 1828

If a man strike his mistress it is a self-inflicted wound, but if he strike his wife it is suicide.

Honoré de Balzac, *The Physiology of Marriage*, 1828

A loving wife is better than making 50 at cricket, or even 99. Beyond that I will not go.

J. M. Barrie, *The Observer*, 1925

Every man who is high up loves to think that he has done it all himself; and the wife smiles, and lets it go at that. It's our only joke. Every woman knows that.

J. M. Barrie, *What Every Woman Knows*, 1908

Whoso findeth a wife findeth a good thing.

The Bible, *Proverbs*

Bride, n: A woman with a fine prospect of happiness behind her.

Ambrose Bierce, *The Devil's Dictionary*, 1911

By marriage, the very being or legal existence of a woman is suspended, or at least it is incorporated or consolidated into that of the husband, under whose wing, protection or cover she performs everything, and she is therefore called in our law a feme covert.

Sir William Blackstone, *Commentaries on the Laws of England*, 1765

In a wife I would desire/What in whores is always found—/The lineaments of gratified desire.

William Blake, *In a Wife*

When a man has married a wife, he finds out whether/Her knees and elbows are only glued together.

William Blake, *Miscellaneous Epigrams*

Reader, I married him.

Charlotte Brontë, *Jane Eyre*, 1847

The bitterest creature under heaven is the wife who discovers that her husband's bravery is only bravado, that his strength is only a uniform, that his power is but a gun in the hands of a fool.

Pearl S. Buck, *To My Daughters, With Love*, 1967

The wife carries the husband on her face; the husband carries the wife on his linen.
> *Bulgarian proverb*

Ah gentle dames, it gars me greet/To think how mony counsels sweet/How mony lengthen'd sage advices/The husband frae the wife despises!
> *Robert Burns, Tam O'Shanter, 1787*

Wives in their husband's absences grow subtler/And daughters sometimes run off with the butler.
> *Lord Byron, Don Juan, 1819–1824*

If you are human you love and doubt. The only thing there shouldn't be any doubt about is your wife. If there is, it's finished.
> *Marc Chagall, The Observer, 1977*

Variability is one of the virtues of a woman. It obviates the crude requirements of polygamy. If you have one good wife, you are sure to have a spiritual harem.
> *G. K. Chesterton*

Oh! born to bless me with thy love/My dear, my joy, my life—/Soon will those tender names unite/In that dear name of wife.
> *Clergyman, quoted in The Lovers' Dictionary, 1867*

In my conscience I believe the baggage loves me, for she never speaks well of me her self, nor suffers any body else to rail at me.
> *William Congreve, The Old Bachelor, 1693*

The true index of a man's character is the health of his wife.
> *Cyril Connolly, The Unquiet Grave, 1945*

WILLIAM HOLDEN: [Wives . . .] they all start out as Juliets and end up as Lady Macbeths.
The Country Girl, script: George Seaton, 1954

We have hetairai (prostitutes) for our pleasure, concubines for our daily needs, and wives to give us legitimate children and look after the housekeeping.
Demosthenes, In Neaeram, 4th century B.C.

Once a woman has forgiven her man, she must not reheat his sins for breakfast.
Marlene Dietrich, Marlene Dietrich's ABC, 1961

John Donne, Anne Donne, Un-Done.
John Donne, letter to his wife

Here lies my wife: here let her lie!/Now she's at rest, and so am I.
John Dryden, epitaph intended for his wife

Whooo-eee! Ride me high/Tomorrow's the day/My bride's gonna come/Oh, oh, are we gonna fly/Down in the easy chair!
Bob Dylan, You Ain't Goin' Nowhere, 1967

A man's wife has more power over him than the state.
Ralph Waldo Emerson, Journals, 1836

He that loses a wife and a farthing hath a great loss of a farthing.
English proverb

Man's best possession is a sympathetic wife.
Euripides, Antigone, 5th century B.C.

He who gets a dowry with his wife, sells himself for it.
Euripides, *Phaeton*, 5th century B.C.

A man does not have to be a bigamist to have one wife too many.
Farmer's Almanac, 1966

A woman seldom comes out of a sullen spell until she's sure her husband has suffered as much as she thinks he should.
William Feather, *The Business of Life*, 1949

In a society which really supported marriage the wife would be encouraged to go to the office and make love to her husband on the company's time and with its blessing.
Brendan Francis

You can bear your own faults, and why not a fault in your wife?
Benjamin Franklin, *Poor Richard's Almanack*, 1732–1757

The torch of love is lit in the kitchen.
French proverb

Choose a wife rather by your ear than your eye.
Thomas Fuller, *Gnomologia*, 1732

A fair wife without fortune is a fine house without furniture.
Thomas Fuller, *Gnomologia*, 1732

The comfortable estate of widowhood is the only hope that keeps up a wife's spirits.
John Gay, *The Beggar's Opera*, 1728

A wife loves out of duty, and duty leads to constraint, and constraint kills desire.
　　Jean Giraudoux, Amphitryon 38, 1929

I have one case record of a man who claims *he* thought he was taking his wife to see the psychiatrist, not realising until too late that his wife had made the arrangements.
　　Erving Goffman, Asylums, 1961

I chose my wife, as she did her wedding gown, not for a fine glossy surface, but such qualities as would wear well.
　　Oliver Goldsmith, The Vicar of Wakefield, 1766

Women are not gamblers even to the small extent men are. Wives tend to limit their husband's enterprise, especially if it involves risks, and consequently the opportunities for achievement, delight and surprise are limited.
　　Germaine Greer, The Female Eunuch, 1970

This is the unspoken contract of a wife and her works. In the long run, wives are to be paid in a peculiar coin—consideration for their feelings. And it usually turns out this is an enormous, unthinkable inflation few men will remit, or if they will, only with a sense of being over-charged.
　　Elizabeth Hardwick, Seduction and Betrayal, 1974

There are only about twenty murders a year in London and not all are serious—some are just husbands killing their wives.
　　Police Commander G. H. Hatherill, The Observer, 1954

Holy is the wife, revered the mother; galliptious is the summer girl—but the bride is the certified check among the wedding presents that the gods send in when man is married to mortality.
　　O. Henry, The Four Million, 1906

Wife: a darning attachment for the domestic machine.
   Oliver Herford, John Clay, Cupid's Cyclopedia, 1910

A man does not buy his wife a fur coat to keep her warm, but to keep her pleasant.
   Sir Seymour Hicks, The Observer, 1946

Two days are the best of a man's wedded life/The days when he marries and buries his wife.
   Hipponax, c. 540 B.C.

A sharp tongue is the only edged tool that grows keener with constant use.
   Washington Irving, The Sketch Book, 1820

I have learned that only two things are necessary to keep one's wife happy. First, let her think she's having her way. And second, let her have it.
   Lyndon Baines Johnson

Always see a fellow's weak point in his wife.
   James Joyce, Ulysses, 1922

There are few wives so perfect as not to give their husbands at least once a day good reason to repent of ever having married, or at least of envying those who are unmarried.
   Jean de La Bruyère, Les Caractères, 1688

If ever I marry a wife/I'll marry a landlord's daughter/For then I may sit in the bar/And drink cold brandy and water.
   Charles Lamb, Coeleb in Search of a Wife, in Works, 1818

Wives . . . are people that think when the telephone bell rings it is against the law not to answer it.

Ring Lardner, *Say It with Oil*, 1923

Wives . . . are people whose watch is always off a quarter hour either one way or the other. But they wouldn't have no idear what time it was anyway as this daylint savings gets them all balled up.

Ring Lardner, *Say It with Oil*, 1923

Wives, don't love your husbands nor your children nor anybody. Sit still and say Hush! . . . And when your husband comes in and says he's got a cold and is going to have double pneumonia say quietly "Surely not." And if he wants the ammoniated quinine, give it him if he can't get it for himself. But don't let him drive you out of your solitude, your singleness within yourself.

D. H. Lawrence, *Fantasia of the Unconscious*, 1922

Not all women give most of their waking thoughts to the problem of pleasing men. Some are married.

Emma Lee

I would find the woman I wanted to bear my children: a highly intelligent, tall, fair, powerfully built Teuton, whose mind worked like the latest scientific wonder, the electronic computer. . . . I believed I had earned the right to seek my mate from amongst the finest genetic material available. . . . When I learned that she did calculus problems for recreation the way I did crossword puzzles, I knew she was the woman I wanted to bear my children. A Teuton/Celt of high intelligence. She had it all.

G. Gordon Liddy, *Will*, 1980

Ten years ago, wives were wives, rather than women, and "affirmative action" was popping them right in the orthodontia when they stopped baking chocolate chip cookies in their spare time and started screwing around.
    Cyra McFadden, *The Serial*, 1978

The wives who are not deserted, but who have to feed and clothe and comfort and scold and advise, are the true objects of commiseration; wives whose existence is given over to a ceaseless vigil of cantankerous affection.
    William McFee, *Harbours of Memory*, 1921

Marriage is a lot of things—an alliance, a sacrament, a comedy or a mistake, but it is definitely not a partnership because that implies equal gain. And every right-thinking woman knows the profit in matrimony is by all odds hers.
    Phyllis McGinley, *The Province of the Heart*, 1959

The wife should be inferior to the husband—that is the only way to ensure equality between the two.
    Martial

I know a woman's portion when she loves,/It's hers to give, my darling, not to take;/It isn't lockets, dear, nor pairs of gloves,/It isn't marriage bells nor wedding cake,/It's up and cook, although the belly ache;/And bear the child, and up and work again,/And count a sick man's grumble worth the pain.
    John Masefield, *The Widow in the Bye Street*, 1912

One can, to an almost laughable degree, infer what a man's wife is like from his opinions about women in general.
    John Stuart Mill

For nothing lovelier can be found/In woman, than to study household good/And good works in her husband to promote.
John Milton, *Paradise Lost*, 1667

Who was that lady I saw you with last night?
That was no lady, that was my wife!
Music hall/vaudeville standby

The dowry of a wife is quarrelling.
Ovid, *Ars Amatoria*, c. A.D. 8

She who ne'er answers till a husband cools/Or, if she rules him, never shows she rules/Charms by accepting, by submitting, sways/Yet has her humour most, when she obeys.
Alexander Pope, *Moral Essays*, 1731–1735

A man without a wife is like a man in winter without a fur hat.
Russian proverb

Man has found remedies against all poisonous creatures, but none was yet found against a bad wife.
François Rabelais

All any woman asks of her husband is that he love her and obey her commandments.
John W. Raper, *What This World Wants*, 1945

The cunning wife makes her husband her apron.
John Ray, *English Proverbs*, 1670

Men are April when they woo, December when they wed;
maids are May when they are maids, but the sky changes
when they are wives.
   William Shakespeare, As You Like It, 1598–1600

A man may pass through a barrage with less damage to
his character than through a squabble with a nagging
wife. Many domestic and commercial experiences leave
blacker and more permanent marks on the soul than
thrusting a bayonet through an enemy in a trench fight.
   George Bernard Shaw

Having created a technological and sociological jugger-
naut by which they are daily buffeted, men tend to use
their wives as opiates against the impact of the forces they
have set in motion against themselves.
   Philip Slater, The Pursuit of Loneliness, 1970

Married women are kept women and they are beginning
to find out.
   Logan Pearsall Smith, Afterthoughts, 1931

By all means marry; if you get a good wife, you'll become
happy; if you get a bad one, you'll become a philosopher.
   Socrates

JUDY GARLAND: Hello everybody. This is Mrs. Norman
Maine.
   *A Star Is Born, script: Moss Hart, based on an earlier script by
   Dorothy Parker, Alan Campbell, Robert Carson, 1954*

The family: home of all social evils, a charitable institution
for indolent women, a prison workshop for the slaving
breadwinner, and a hell for children.
   August Strindberg

An ideal wife is a woman who has an ideal husband.
> Booth Tarkington, *Looking Forward to the Great Adventure*, 1926

An exquisite slave is what we want for the most part; a humble, flattering, smiling, tea-making, pianoforte playing being, who laughs at our jokes however old they may be, coaxes us and wheedles us in all our humours and fondly lies to us through life.
> William Thackeray, *Letters to a Young Man About Town*, 1853

Why do you always, when you mention my name in your diaries, speak so ill of me? Why do you want all future generations and our descendants to hold my name in contempt, as that of a *frivolous*, ill-tempered wife who caused you unhappiness? . . . [Are you] afraid that your glory after death will be diminished unless you show me to have been your torment and yourself, as a martyr, bearing a cross in the form of your wife?
> Sonya Tolstoy, *letter to her husband, Leo*, 1895

Rest in peace—until we meet again.
> Widow's epitaph for her husband, quoted in Jessica Mitford, *The American Way of Death*

No man should have a secret from his wife—she invariably finds it out.
> Oscar Wilde

Marriage is a bribe to make the housekeeper think she's a householder.
> Thornton Wilder, *The Matchmaker*, 1955

Too many homes are built on the foundations of crushed women.
> Clough Williams-Ellis, *The Observer*, 1946

I once stayed at the residence of a newly married pal of mine, and his bride had carved in large letters over the fireplace in the drawing room the legend: "Two Lovers Built This Nest," and I can still recall the look of dumb anguish in the other half of the sketch's eyes, every time he came in and saw it.

P. G. *Wodehouse*, *The Code of the Woosters*, 1938

20. O Mistress Mine

The way to a man's heart is through his wife's belly, and don't you forget it.

Edward Albee, *Who's Afraid of Virginia Woolf?*, 1964

Absence makes the heart grow fonder—of somebody else.

Anonymous

The eternal triangle.

Anonymous, *Daily Chronicle*, 1907

Love interferes with fidelities.

Sylvia Ashton-Warner, *Teacher*, 1963

A lover teaches a wife all that her husband has concealed from her.

Honoré de Balzac, *The Physiology of Marriage*, 1828

Adultery . . . it takes so little time and it causes so much trouble.

John Barrymore

Vows! dost think the gods regard the vows of lovers? They are things made in necessity and ought not to be kept, nor punished when broken.
Aphra Behn, *The Dutch Lover*, 1673

Fidelity, n: A virtue peculiar to those about to be betrayed.
Ambrose Bierce, *The Devil's Dictionary*, 1911

Incompatibility, n: In matrimony, a similarity of tastes, particularly the taste for domination. Incompatibility may, however, consist of a meek eyed matron living just around the corner. It has even been known to wear a moustache.
Ambrose Bierce, *The Devil's Dictionary*, 1911

A tap at the pane, the quick sharp scratch/And blue spurt of a lighted match,/And a voice less loud, thro' its joys and fears/Than the two hearts beating each to each!
Robert Browning, *Meeting at Night*

Never tell. Not if you love your wife. . . . In fact, if your old lady walks in on you, deny it. Yeah. Just flat out, and she'll believe it: "I'm tellin' ya. This chick came downstairs with a sign around her neck "Lay on Top of Me or I'll Die." I didn't know what I was gonna do. . . ."
Lenny Bruce, quoted in J. Cohen, *The Essential Lenny Bruce*, 1967

The husband who doesn't tell his wife everything probably reasons that what she doesn't know won't hurt him.
Leo J. Burke

For glances beget ogles, ogles sighs,/Sighs wishes, wishes words, and words a letter . . . /And then, God knows what mischief may arise,/When love links two young people in one fetter,/Vile assignations and adulterous beds,/Elopements, broken vows and hearts and heads.
Lord Byron, *Beppo*, 1818

What men call gallantry, and gods adultery/Is much more common where the climate's sultry.
   Lord Byron, *Don Juan*, 1819–1824

Merely innocent flirtation/Not quite adultery, but adulteration.
   Lord Byron, *Don Juan*, 1819–1824

Great is their love who love in sin and fear.
   Lord Byron, *Heaven and Earth*, 1822

I've looked on a lot of women with lust. I've committed adultery in my heart many times. This is something God recognizes I will do—and I have done it—and God forgives me for it.
   Jimmy Carter, *Playboy*, 1976

But a woman's sayings to her lover/Should be in wind and running water writ.
   Catullus, *Carmina*, 1st century B.C.

A woman must never let a man get accustomed to her absence.
   Lucas Cleeve, *The Rose Geranium*, 1907

Do not adultery commit/Advantage rarely comes of it.
   Arthur Clough, *The Latest Decalogue*, in *Poems*, 1951

There can only be one end in marriage without love, and that is love without marriage.
   John Churton Collins

Love Laughs at Locksmiths
   George Colman the younger, play title, 1808

There is sanctuary in reading, sanctuary in formal society, in the company of old friends, and in the giving of officious help to strangers, but there is no sanctuary in one bed from the memory of another.
  Cyril Connolly

It is the fear of middle-age in the young, of old age in the middle-aged, which is the prime cause of infidelity, that infallible rejuvenator.
  Cyril Connolly, The Unquiet Grave, 1945

As we all know from witnessing the consuming jealousy of husbands who are never faithful, people do not confine themselves to the emotions to which they are entitled.
  Quentin Crisp, The Naked Civil Servant, 1968

DIRK BOGARDE: Your idea of fidelity is not having more than one man in the bed at the same time.
  Darling, script: *Frederic Raphael,* 1965

A husband should tell his wife everything he is sure she will find out, and before anyone else does.
  Thomas Dewar

Love's sweetest part, Variety . . .
  John Donne, The Indifferent

I have been faithful to thee, Cynara, in my fashion.
  Ernest Dowson, Non Sum Qualis Eram, 1896

A wife is only to have the ripe fruit, that falls of itself; but a wise man will always preserve a shaking for his mistress.
  John Dryden, Marriage a la Mode, 1672

Fool, not to know that love endures no tie/And Jove but laughs at lovers' perjury.
John Dryden, *Palamon and Arcite*, 1699

So heavy is the chain of wedlock that it needs two to carry it, and sometimes three.
Alexandre Dumas

When lovely woman stoops to folly and/Paces about her room again, alone,/She smoothes her hair with automatic hand,/And puts a record upon the gramophone.
T. S. Eliot, *The Waste Land*, 1922

Adultery can be a more "healthy" recreation than for example the game of Mah Jongg or watching television.
Dr. Albert Ellis, 1967

A sound marriage is not based on complete frankness—it is based on sensible reticence.
Morris L. Ernst

When cheated, wife or husband feels the same.
Euripides, *Andromache*, c. 426 B.C.

Love and scandal are the best sweeteners of tea.
Henry Fielding, *Love in Several Masques*, 1728

Love is like linen often chang'd, the sweeter.
Phineas Fletcher, *Sicelides*, 1631

Religion has done love a great service by making it a sin.
Anatole France

Frankie and Johnny were lovers, my gawd how they could love,/Swore to be true to each other, true as the stars above;/He was her man, but he done her wrong.
    Frankie and Johnny

A Code of Honor: Never approach a friend's girlfriend or wife with mischief as your goal. There are too many women in the world to justify that sort of dishonorable behaviour. Unless she's *really* attractive.
    Bruce Jay Friedman, *Esquire*, 1977

He knows little who will tell his wife all he knows.
    Thomas Fuller, *The Holy State and the Profane State*, 1642

A miss for pleasure and a wife for breed.
    John Gay, *The Toilette*

Doubtless love's worst affliction is not being deceived by the woman one loves, but rather in deceiving her oneself.
    André Gide, *Characters*, 1925

A faithful woman looks to the spring, a good book, perfume, earth quakes and divine revelation for the experience others find in a lover. They deceive their husbands, so to speak, with the entire world, men excluded.
    Jean Giraudoux, *Amphitryon 38*, 1929

The blush is beautiful, but it is sometimes inconvenient.
    Carlo Goldoni, *Pamela*, 1756

When lovely woman stoops to folly/And finds too late that men betray/What charm can soothe her melancholy/What art can wash her guilt away?
    Oliver Goldsmith, *The Vicar of Wakefield*, 1766

Never sleep three in a bed—or you'll wake up three in a bed.
   Günter Grass, Dog Years, 1966

For a woman to have a liaison is almost always pardonable, and occasionally, when the lover is sufficiently distinguished, even admirable; but in love as sport, the amateur status must be strictly adhered to.
   Robert Graves, Occupation: Writer, 1951

When a man steals your wife, there is no better revenge than to let him keep her.
   Sacha Guitry, Elles et Toi, 1948

Honesty: a bunker in the game of love.
   Oliver Herford, John Clay, Cupid's Cyclopedia, 1910

The world wants to be cheated: So cheat.
   Xaviera Hollander, The Happy Hooker, 1972

... that melancholy sexual perversion known as continence.
   Aldous Huxley, Mortal Coils, 1925

The woman whose behaviour indicates that she will make a scene if she is told the truth asks to be deceived.
   Elizabeth Jenkins

Adultery is in your heart not only when you look with excessive sexual desire at a woman who is not your wife, but also if you look in the same manner at your wife.
   Pope John Paul II, 1980

It is as foolish to make experiments upon the constancy of a friend, as upon the chastity of a wife.

> Samuel Johnson, quoted in James Boswell, *The Life of Samuel Johnson*, 1791

To set your neighbor's bed a-shaking is now an ancient and long-established custom. It was the silver age that saw the first adulterers.

> Juvenal, *Satires*

Marriage is not harmed by seducers but by cowardly husbands.

> Søren Kierkegaard, *Either/Or*, 1843

The truth has been staring us in the face for some twenty thousand years: Men are forever on the lookout to have Affairs . . . while the majority of women . . . even the most debauched of them . . . are . . . eternally . . . seemingly in search of love.

> Alexander King, *Rich Man, Poor Man, Freud and Fruit*, 1965

Adultery is extravagance.

> Maxine Hong Kingston, *The Woman Warrior*, 1976

The violence we do to ourselves in order to remain faithful to the one we love is hardly better than an act of infidelity.

> La Rochefoucauld, *Maxims*, 1665

In love deceit nearly always goes further than mistrust.

> La Rochefoucauld, *Maxims*, 1665

Monogamy is for those who are whole and clear, all in one stroke. But for those whose stroke is broken into two different directions, then there must be two fulfillments.

> D. H. Lawrence, *Selected Letters*

The first man who can think of how he's going to stay in love with his wife and another woman is going to get that prize they're always talking about in Sweden.

Clare Boothe Luce, The Women, 1937

The head never rules the heart, but just becomes its partner in crime.

Mignon McLaughlin, The Neurotic's Notebook, 1963

When a woman who admits she is unhappily yoked holds long conversations about "the soul" with a man not her husband, it isn't the soul either of them is thinking about.

Don Marquis, The New York Herald

I submit to my fellow-dramatists that the unfaithfulness of a wife is no longer a subject for drama, but only for comedy.

W. Somerset Maugham, Collected Plays

When a man's in love, he at once makes a pedestal of the Ten Commandments and stands on the top of them with his arms akimbo. When a woman's in love she doesn't care two stars for Thou Shalt and Thou Shalt Not.

W. Somerset Maugham, Lady Frederick, 1907

A legal kiss is never as good as a stolen one.

Guy de Maupassant, A Wife's Confession

A woman does not want her love affairs talked about. Yet she wants everybody to know that someone loves her.

André Maurois, Ladies' Home Journal, 1942

Adultery is the application of democracy to love.

H. L. Mencken, A Book of Burlesques, 1920

Constancy is suitable only for ridicule.
> Molière, *Don Juan*, 1665

It is a public scandal that offends; to sin in secret is no sin at all.
> Molière, *Tartuffe*, 1664

'Tis sweet to think that, where'er we rove/We are sure to find something blissful and dear/And that, when we're far from the lips we love/We've but to make love to the lips we are near.
> Thomas Moore, *Irish Melodies*, 1807–1835

Consider the story of a lover, a husband and an unfaithful wife. The wife confesses all to her husband. He sends for her lover. They are closeted in the living room together. The wife stands outside the door, trembling with fear. She strains her ears to discover what's going on in the room. Some terrible quarrel? A duel or fight to the death perhaps? At last she can stand the suspense no longer. She flings open the door and what does she see? Blood? Broken furniture? One of them stretched out on the carpet? Not at all. The two men are sitting by the fire drinking bottled ale and discussing the best method of pruning apple trees. Naturally the woman's furious. She packs and leaves for her mother's.
> Clifford Mortimer, quoted in John Mortimer, *Clinging to the Wreckage*, 1982

I know many married men, I even know a few happily married men; but I don't know one who wouldn't fall down the first open coal-hole running after the first pretty girl who gave him a wink.
> George Jean Nathan, quoted in *Men Against Women*, ed. Charles Neider

WILLIAM HOLDEN: And it's a happy ending. Wayward husband comes to his senses, returns to his wife with whom he's established a long and sustaining love. Heartless young woman left alone in her arctic desolation. Music up with a swell. Final commercial. And here are a few scenes from next week's show.
  Network, script: *Paddy Chayefsky,* 1976

As stolen love is pleasant to a man, so is it also to a woman; the man dissembles badly: she conceals desire more cleverly.
  Ovid, *The Art of Love*

To deceive a trusting maid is glory but cheaply won.
  Ovid, *Heroines*

One doesn't die from love. Sometimes one dies from another's love when he buys a revolver.
  Marcel Pagnol

Every love's the love before/In a duller dress.
  Dorothy Parker, *Death and Taxes,* 1931

A secret love affair is much more enjoyable than an open one.
  Paulus Silentiarius, epigram

A mistress kept at first is sweet/And joys to do the merry feat/But bastards come and hundreds gone/You'll wish you'd left her charms alone/Such breeding hussies are a pest/A neighbour's wife is far the best.
  The Pearl, c. 1879

I by water to Westminster Hall and there did see Mrs. Lane and de la, elle and I to the cabaret at the Cloche in the street du Roy; and there, after some caresses, je l'ay foutee sous de la chaise deux times, and the last to my great pleasure; mais j'ai grand peur que je l'ay fait faire aussi elle meme. Mais after I had done, elle commencait parler as before and I did perceive that je n'avais fait rien de danger a elle. Et avec ca, I came away. . . .

> *Samuel Pepys, Diary, 1664*

JOHN HALLIDAY: What most wives fail to realize is that their husband's philandering has nothing whatever to do with them.

> *The Philadelphia Story, script: Donald Ogden Stewart, 1940*

Love finds an altar for forbidden fires.

> *Alexander Pope, Eloisa to Abelard, 1717*

A woman we love rarely satisfies all our needs, and we deceive her with a woman whom we do not love.

> *Marcel Proust*

The joy of promiscuity. And the pain. Ecstatic freedom and release. Loneliness, desolation. A glorious adventure that, always at the brink, stops even time. Panic, frenzy, fear. Ambivalences and contradictions. The outlaw faces the saboteur.

> *John Rechy, The Sexual Outlaw, 1977*

One man's folly is another man's wife.

> *Helen Rowland*

Papa loved Mamma/Mamma loved men/Mamma's in the graveyard/Papa's in the pen.

> *Carl Sandburg*

Mistresses tend to get a steady diet of whipped cream, but no meat and potatoes; and wives get the reverse, when both would like a bit of each.

> *Merle Shain, Some Men Are More Perfect Than Others, 1973*

Friendship is constant in all other things/Save in the office and affairs of love.
William Shakespeare, Much Ado About Nothing, 1598–1600

What is virtue but the Trade Unionism of the married?
George Bernard Shaw, Man and Superman, 1903

Those who run around with women don't walk tight ropes. They find it hard enough to crawl on the ground.
Isaac Bashevis Singer, The Magician of Lublin, 1960

It is not impossible to become bored in the presence of a mistress.
Stendhal

ALEX: I can't see why having an affair with someone on and off is any worse than being married for a course or two at meal-times.
Sunday, Bloody Sunday, script: Penelope Gilliatt, 1971

There is nothing in this world constant but inconstancy.
Jonathan Swift, A Critical Essay upon the Faculties of Mind, 1707

The lover thinks oftener of reaching his mistress than does the husband of guarding his wife. The prisoner thinks oftener of escaping than the jailer of shutting the door.
Stendhal

The way of the adulterer is hedged with thorns; full of fears and jealousies, burning desires and impatient waitings, tediousness of delay, and sufferance of affronts, and amazements of discovery.
Jeremy Taylor, Holy Living, 1650

To our sweethearts and wives. May they never meet.
  Toasts for All Occasions

There is trouble with a wife, but it's even worse with a woman who is not a wife.
  Leo Tolstoy, *Anna Karenina*, 1873–1876

. . . In France there is something refined about sin. A halo of sentimentality shines around the head of a breaker of the seventh commandment, and the faithless wife always has an air about her of dying pathetically to slow, soft, and solemn music.
  The Tomahawk, 1870

. . . Women hardly ever love those who are their most faithful lovers. . . . I find it painful to see a knave get as much or more by his tricks as the faithful lover.
  Bernard de Ventadour

Adultery is an evil only inasmuch as it is a theft; but we do not steal that which is given to us.
  Voltaire, *The Philosophical Dictionary*, 1764

They do not sin at all/Who sin for love.
  Oscar Wilde, *The Duchess of Padua*, 1907

In married life three is company and two is none.
  Oscar Wilde, *The Importance of Being Earnest*, 1899

Those who are faithful know only the trivial side of love; it is the faithless who know love's tragedies.
  Oscar Wilde, *The Picture of Dorian Gray*, 1891

Faithfulness is to the emotional life what consistency is to the life of the intellect—simply a confession of failures.
  Oscar Wilde, *The Picture of Dorian Gray*, 1891

The happiness of a married man depends on the women he has not married.

Oscar Wilde, *A Woman of No Importance*, 1894

I don't remember any love affairs. One must keep love affairs quiet.

Duchess of Windsor, *Los Angeles Times*, 1974

Women are divided broadly into two classes—those who, when jilted, merely drop a silent tear and those who take a niblick from their bag and chase the faithless swain across country with it.

P. G. Wodehouse, quoted in R. Usborne, *Wodehouse at Work*, 1961

LUCILE WATSON: We women are so much more sensible! When *we* tire of ourselves, we change the way we do our hair, or hire a new cook. Or redecorate the house. I suppose a man could do over his office but he never thinks of anything so simple. No dear, a man has only one escape from his old self—to see a different self in the mirror of some woman's eyes.

The Women, script: Anita Loos, Jane Murfin, 1939

No, mistresses are like books. If you pore upon them too much, they doze you and make you unfit for company; but if used discreetly, you are the fitter for conversation by 'em.

William Wycherley, *The Country Wife*, 1672

21. The Party's Over

I loved thee once. I'll love no more,/Thine be the grief, as is the blame;/Thou art not what thou wast before,/What reason I should be the same?
> Sir Robert Aytoun, *To an Inconstant Mistress*, 1637

Alimony is like buying oats for a dead horse.
> Arthur Baer, *New York American*

Many a man owes his success to his first wife, and his second wife to his success.
> Jim Backus

I leave before being left. *I* decide.
> Brigitte Bardot, *Newsweek*, 1973

The night has a thousand eyes,/And the day but one;/Yet the light of the bright world dies/With the dying sun./The mind has a thousand eyes,/And the heart but one:/Yet the light of a whole life dies/When love is done.
> Francis William Bourdillon, *Light*, c. 1900

The best proof that experience is useless is that the end of one love does not disgust us from beginning another.
> Paul Bourget

Love is also like a coconut which is good while it's fresh, but you have to spit it out when the juice is gone, what's left tastes bitter.

Bertolt Brecht, *Baal*, 1926

I thought when love for you died, I should die. It's dead. Alone, most strangely, I live on.

Rupert Brooke, *The Life Beyond*, 1918

If you're going to break up with your old lady and you live in a small town, make sure you don't break up at three in the morning. Because you're screwed—there's nothing to do. You sit in the car all night, parked somewhere. Yeah. So make it about nine in the morning, so you can go to the five and ten, bullshit around, worry her a little, then come back at seven in the night, y'know.

Lenny Bruce, *quoted in* J. Cohen, *The Essential Lenny Bruce*, 1967

The bad break-up is a long-time break-up. If you're married seven years, you got to kick for two.

Lenny Bruce, *quoted in* J. Cohen, *The Essential Lenny Bruce*, 1967

And if you broke up and you go anywhere alone, there's always *momsers* that ask about your wife . . . Chinese restaurant . . . "Where's maw-maw? How come you don't bring maw-maw in? Maw-maw sicka? Ah so, maw-maw velly sick. You better bring maw-maw home some cookies. Tell maw-maw say hello . . ." "I'm divorced." *"Ohhh, you bettuh awf!!"*

Lenny Bruce, *quoted in* J. Cohen, *The Essential Lenny Bruce*, 1967

Had we never loved sae kindly/Had we never loved sae blindly/Never met—or never parted/We had ne'er been broken hearted.
Robert Burns, *Ae Fond Kiss*

'Tis better to have loved and lost than never to have lost at all.
Samuel Butler, *The Way of All Flesh*, 1903

Absence is to love what wind is to fire: it extinguishes the small, it enkindles the great.
Bussy-Rabutin, *Maximes d'Amour*, 1665

The worst reconciliation is better than the best divorce.
Miguel de Cervantes

The only solid and lasting peace between a man and his wife is, doubtless, a separation.
Lord Chesterfield, *Letters to His Son*, 1763

There are two great moments in a woman's life: when she first finds herself to be deeply in love with her man and when she leaves him. . . . Women are different from men, and to break with the past and to mangle their mate in the process fulfills a dark need of theirs.
Cyril Connolly, *The Unquiet Grave*, 1945

The *vie de bohème* is a way of life that has two formidable enemies—time and marriage. Even hooligans marry, though they know that marriage is but for a little while. It is alimony that is for ever. . . .
Quentin Crisp, *The Naked Civil Servant*, 1968

Marriage to many people appears to be nothing but a necessary preliminary step towards being divorced.
> Mr. Justice Darling, *quoted in* The Observer, 1920

Parting is all we know of heaven/And all we need of hell.
> Emily Dickinson, *Parting*

"I'm sorry." "I know you're sorry. I'm sorry." "We could try," one or the other would say after a while. "We've already tried," the other would say.
> Joan Didion, *Play It As It Lays*, 1970

The day breaks not: it is my heart/Because that you and I must part.
> John Donne

Love reckons hours for months, and days for years/And every little absence is an age.
> John Dryden, *Amphitryon*, 1690

Most Likely You Go Your Way and I'll Go Mine
> Bob Dylan, *song title*

I ain't sayin' you treated me unkind/You coulda done better but I don't mind/You just kinda wasted my precious time/But don't think twice, it's all right.
> Bob Dylan, *Don't Think Twice, It's All Right*, 1964

You say you're looking for someone/Who'll pick you up each time you fall/To gather flowers constantly/An' to come each time you call/A lover for your life an' nothing more/But it ain't me, babe/No, no, no it ain't me, babe/It ain't me you're lookin' for, babe.
> Bob Dylan, *It Ain't Me, Babe*, 1964

Everything passes,/Everything changes,/Just do what you think you should do./And some day, maybe,/Who knows, baby,/I'll come and be cryin' to you.
    Bob Dylan, To Ramona, 1964

Madame, I was told that you took the trouble to come here to see me three times last evening. I was not in. And, fearing lest persistence expose you to humiliation, I am bound by the rules of politeness to warn you that *I shall never be in.*
    Gustave Flaubert, to his former lover, Louise Colet

Better a tooth out than always aching.
    Thomas Fuller, Gnomologia, 1732

It's a toss-up between marriage and divorce. They're both right and wrong now and then, but mostly right.
    Nat Goodwin

"Do you know why/we di-/vorced? . . ./We would go to the movies/your father and I"/I nodded at her/"And I'd come out/being Carole Lombard/only he refused/to be Humphrey Bogart."
    Susan Griffin, Dear Sky, 1973

Divorce is the sacrament of adultery.
    Jean François Guichard, Maxims, 1802

Well, if I send you over I'll be sorry as hell—I'll have some rotten nights—but that'll pass.
    Dashiell Hammett, The Maltest Falcon, 1930

You Called Me Baby Doll a Year Ago
    Clifford Harris, song title

Only a marriage with partners strong enough to risk divorce is strong enough to avoid it.
  Carolyn Heilbrun, *Ms.*, 1974

A sharp knife cuts the quickest and hurts the least.
  Katharine Hepburn

Alimony: the fine for speeding in the joy-ride of Matrimony.
  Oliver Herford, John Clay, *Cupid's Cyclopedia*, 1910

Who wants yesterday's papers?/Who wants yesterday's girl?
  Mick Jagger, Keith Richards, *Yesterday's Papers*, 1966

Well, being divorced is like being hit by a Mack truck. If you live through it you start looking very carefully to the right and to the left.
  Jean Kerr, *Mary, Mary*, 1960

No disguise can long conceal love where it exists, or long feign it where it is lacking.
  La Rochefoucauld, *Maxims*, 1665

There are scarcely any who are not ashamed of being beloved, when they love no more themselves.
  La Rochefoucauld, *Maxims*, 1665

Why, tell me why, did you not treat me right?/Love has a nasty habit of disappearing over night.
  John Lennon, Paul McCartney, *I'm Looking Through You*

She always believed in the old adage—leave them while you're looking good.
  Anita Loos, *Gentlemen Prefer Blondes*, 1925

Wives invariably flourish when deserted . . . it is the deserting male, the reckless idealist rushing about the world seeking a non-existent felicity, who often ends in disaster.
William McFee, Harbours of Memory, 1921

The pain of leaving those you grow to love is only the prelude to understanding yourself and others.
Shirley MacLaine, Don't Fall Off the Mountain, 1970

Alimony is the curse of the writing classes.
Norman Mailer (who has had four wives, two mistresses, and nine children), 1980

Alimony—the ransom that the happy pay to the devil.
H. L. Mencken, A Book of Burlesques, 1920

After all, my erstwhile dear,/My no longer cherished,/Need we say it was not love,/Just because it perished?
Edna St. Vincent Millay, Second April, 1921

And if I loved you Wednesday,/Well, what is that to you?/I do not love you Thursday—/So much is true.
Edna St. Vincent Millay, Thursday

There is something inexpressibly charming in falling in love and, surely, the whole pleasure lies in the fact that love isn't lasting.
Molière, Don Juan, 1665

Falling out of love is very enlightening, for a short while you see the world with new eyes.
Iris Murdoch, 1968

If there is any realistic deterrent to marriage, it's the fact that you can't afford divorce.
　Jack Nicholson, Playboy, 1972

Changing husbands is only changing troubles.
　Kathleen Norris, Hands Full of Living, 1931

I do not love thee! no! I do not love thee/And yet when thou art absent I am sad.
　Caroline Norton, I Do Not Love Thee

BETTE DAVIS: You cad! You dirty swine! I never cared for you, not once. I was always making a fool of you. You bored me stiff. I hated you. It made me sick when I had to let you kiss me. I only did it because you begged me. You hounded me. You drove me crazy. And, after you kissed me, I always used to wipe my mouth—*wipe my mouth*—but I made up for it. For every kiss, I had to laugh.
　Of Human Bondage, script: Lester Cohen, 1934

You who seek an end to love, be busy, and you will be safe.
　Ovid, Love's Cure

All love is vanquished by a succeeding love.
　Ovid, Love's Cure

Love, free as air at sight of human ties,/Spreads his light wings, and in a moment flies.
　Alexander Pope, Eloisa to Abelard, 1717

I'm Left, You're Right, She's Gone
　Elvis Presley, song title

An absence, the decline of a dinner invitation, an unintentional coldness can accomplish more than all the cosmetics and beautiful dresses in the world.
  Marcel Proust, *Remembrance of Things Past*, 1913–1927

Divorce is marriage carried on by other means, with a bond of hostility replacing the erotic bond.
  Psychiatrist to Brenda Maddox, quoted in *The Half Parent: Living with Other People's Children*, 1975

The hour of parting can sometimes be more vivid than a sweet tryst.
  Aleksandr Sergeyevich Pushkin, *The Last Flowers*

Where love fails we espy all faults.
  John Ray, *English proverbs*, 1670

A reasonable man can get out of most any trouble, except marriage, without going to law.
  Reflections of a Bachelor

The only love letters which are of any use are those of goodbye.
  Etienne Rey

As long as we love, we lend to the beloved object qualities of mind and heart which we deprive him of when the day of misunderstanding arrives.
  Joseph Roux, *Meditations of a Parish Priest*, 1886

Love, the quest; marriage, the conquest; divorce, the inquest.
  Helen Rowland

There is something that never dies if one has cared deeply for a person.
    Bertrand Russell

There is a warning love sends and the cost of it is never written till long afterward.
    Carl Sandburg, *Complete Poems*, 1950

Is there any stab as deep as wondering where and how you failed those you loved?
    Florida Scott-Maxwell, *The Measure of My Days*, 1972

Love is a wonderful thing, but as long as it is blind I will never be out of a job.
    Justice Selby, 1968

You can end love more easily than you can moderate it.
    Seneca the Elder, *Controversiae*

There lives within the very flame of love/A kind of wick or snuff that will abate it.
    William Shakespeare, *Hamlet*, 1600–1601

When love begins to sicken and decay,/It useth an enforced ceremony./There are no tricks in plain and simple faith.
    William Shakespeare, *Julius Caesar*, 1600–1601

This thou perceiv'st, which makes thy love more strong,/To love that well which thou must leave ere long.
    William Shakespeare, *Sonnet 73*

O spirit of love! how quick and fresh art thou,/That, notwithstanding the capacity/Receiveth as the sea, nought enteres there,/Of what validity and pitch soe'er,/But falls into abatement and low price,/Even in a minute!
    William Shakespeare, *Twelfth Night*, 1598–1600

Could I her faults remember,/Forgetting every charm,/
Soon would impartial reason/The tyrant love disarm.
  Richard Brinsley Sheridan, The Duenna, 1775

There Must Be Fifty Ways to Leave Your Lover
  Paul Simon, song title

It is worthwhile falling in love, if only for the parting.
  Julius Słowacki, Beniowski, 1841

They sin who tell us Love can die./With life all other passions fly,/All others are but vanity . . . /But Love is inde-
structible./Its holy flame for ever burneth,/From Heaven
it came, to Heaven returneth . . . /It soweth here with toil
and care,/But the harvest time of Love is there.
  Robert Southey, The Curse of Kehama, 1810

. . . the double way of shame/At first you did not love
enough/And afterwards you loved too much/And you
lacked the confidence to choose/And you have only
yourself to blame.
  Stephen Spender, The Double Shame

And the best and the worst of this is/That neither is
most to blame,/If you have forgotten my kisses/And I
have forgotten your name.
  Algernon Charles Swinburne, Hymn to Proserpine, 1866

Old love, old love/How can I be true?/Shall I be faithless
to myself/Or to you?
  Sara Teasdale, Rivers to the Sea, 1915

'Tis better to have loved and lost/Than never to have
loved at all.
  Alfred, Lord Tennyson, In Memoriam, 1850

There are two deaths: to cease loving and being loved—is unbearable. But to cease to live is of no consequence.
Voltaire, *À Madame du Châtelet,* 1740

There is always something ridiculous about the emotions of people whom one has ceased to love.
Oscar Wilde, *The Picture of Dorian Gray,* 1891

Judges, as a class, display, in the matter of arranging alimony, that reckless generosity which is found only in men who are giving away someone else's cash.
P. G. Wodehouse, *Louder and Funnier,* 1932

D-I-V-O-R-C-E
Tammy Wynette, *song title,* 1975

I think lots of men die of their wives and *thousands* of women die of their husbands. But not an American. Here, if there is a little trouble over a hand glass or a tooth brush, they shake hands and part, unless, of course, there is a lot of money, when the lawyers take a hand.
J. B. Yeats, *Letters to His Son, W. B. Yeats, and Others,* 1944

Desire dies because every touch consumes the myth and yet, a myth that cannot be consumed becomes a spectre.
William Butler Yeats

22. As Time Goes By

You may be certain that age is galloping upon you when
. . . a feminine voice over the telephone says "Do you
know who this is?" And you say "no" and hang up the
receiver.
>   Franklin P. Adams

I cannot love as I have loved,/And yet I know not
why;/It is the one great woe of life/To feel all feeling die.
>   P. J. Bailey, *Festus: A Party*, 1839

Women over thirty are at their best, but men over thirty
are too old to recognize it.
>   Jean-Paul Belmondo

A twenty-five-year-old virgin is like the man who was set
upon by thieves—everyone passes by.
>   Charlotte Bingham, *The Wit of Women*

So sweet love seemed that April morn,/When first we
kissed beside the thorn,/So strangely sweet, it was not
strange/We thought that love could never change./But I
can tell—let truth be told—/That love will change in growing old;/Though day by day is nought to see,/So delicate his motions be.
>   Robert Bridges, *So Sweet Love Seemed*, in *Poetical Works*, 1936

All love, at first, like generous wine,/Ferments and frets until 'tis fine;/But, when 'tis settled on the lee,/And from th'impurer matter free,/Becomes the richer still the older,/And proves the pleasanter the colder.

    Samuel Butler, Miscellaneous Thoughts

He was a lover of the good old school,/Who still become more constant as they cool.

    Lord Byron, Beppo, 1818

Love makes those young whom age doth chill,/And whom he finds young, keeps young still.

    William Cartwright, To Chloe, in Poems, 1810

Love lasteth as long as the money endureth.

    William Caxton, The Game of Chesse, 1474

When the glowing of passion's over, and pinching winter comes, will amorous sighs supply the want of fire, or kind looks and kisses keep off hunger?

    Susannah Centlivre, Artifice, 1724

Filth and old age, I'm sure you will agree,/Are powerful wardens upon chastity.

    Geoffrey Chaucer, Canterbury Tales, 1387–1400

We should measure affection, not like youngsters by the ardor of its passion, but by its strength and constancy.

    Cicero, Da Officiis, 44 B.C.

Show me one couple unhappy merely on account of their limited circumstances and I will show you ten who are wretched from other causes.

    Samuel Taylor Coleridge, Table Talk, 1824

Hunger stops love, or, if not hunger, Time.
> Crates, quoted in Diogenes Laertius, *Lives and Opinions of Eminent Philosophers*

What better proof of love can there be than money? A ten shilling note shows incontrovertibly just how mad about you a man is.
> Quentin Crisp, *The Naked Civil Servant,* 1968

Love is done when Love's begun/Sages say./But have Sages known?
> Emily Dickinson, c. 1880

The richest love is that which submits to the arbitration of time.
> Lawrence Durrell, *Clea,* 1960

Ecstasy cannot last, but it can carve a channel for something lasting.
> E. M. Forster, *Albergo Empedocle and Other Writings,* 1971

Husbands who have the courage to be tender enjoy marriages that mellow through the years.
> Brendan Francis

When poverty comes in at the door, love creeps out at the window.
> Thomas Fuller, *Gnomologia,* 1732

She may very well pass for forty-three/In the dusk with a light behind her.
> W. S. Gilbert, *Trial by Jury,* 1875

Strange difference of sex, that time and circumstance, which enlarge the views of most men, narrow the views of women almost invariably.
> Thomas Hardy, *Jude the Obscure,* 1895

I look into my glass/And view my wasting skin,/And say "Would God it came to pass/My Heart had shrunk as thin!"

> *Thomas Hardy, quoted in B. Faust, Women, Sex and Pornography, 1980*

The voyage of love is all the sweeter for an outside stateroom and a seat at the Captain's table.

> *Henry S. Haskins*

Methinks this birth-day of our married life is like a cape, which we now have doubled, and find a more infinite ocean of love stretching out before us. God bless and keep us, for there is something more awful in happiness than in sorrow—the latter being earthly and finite, the former composed of the texture and substance of eternity, so that spirits still embodied may well tremble at it.

> *Nathaniel Hawthorne, The American Notebooks*

It takes a man a lifetime to find out about one, particular woman. But if he puts in, say, ten years, industrious and curious, he can acquire the general rudiments of the sex.

> *O. Henry, Heart of the West, 1907*

Cash: a sort of window-fastener to keep Love from flying out.

> *Oliver Herford, John Clay, Cupid's Cyclopedia, 1910*

Forever: Love's promissory note (subject to discount).

> *Oliver Herford, John Clay, Cupid's Cyclopedia, 1910*

Love me little, love me long.
  John Heywood, *Proverbs*, 1546

Alas! for the love that's linked with gold.
  Thomas Hood, *Miss Kilmansegg: Her Courtship*, 1843

There is only one thing for a man to do who is married to a woman who enjoys spending money, and that is to enjoy earning.
  Ed Howe

Love is too pure a light to burn long among the noisome gasses that we breathe, but before it is choked out we may use it as a torch to ignite the cozy fire of affection.
  Jerome K. Jerome, *The Idle Thoughts of an Idle Fellow*, 1889

Where's the cheek that does not fade/Too much gaz'd at? Where's the maid/Whose lip mature is ever new?
  John Keats, *Fancy*

A woman's a woman until the day she dies, but a man's only a man as long as he can.
  Moms Mabley

A man is only as old as the woman he feels.
  Groucho Marx

The great tragedy of life is not that men perish, but that they cease to love.
  W. Somerset Maugham, *The Summing Up*, 1938

We are not the same persons this year as last; nor are those we love. It is a happy chance if we, changing, continue to love a changed person.
  W. Somerset Maugham, *The Summing Up*, 1938

Kissing don't last—cookery do.
  George Meredith, The Ordeal of Richard Feverel, 1859

Can one ever remember love? It's like trying to summon up the smell of roses in a cellar. You might see a rose, but never the perfume.
  Arthur Miller, After the Fall, 1964

You study one another for three weeks, you love each other for three months, you fight for three years and you tolerate the situation for thirty.
  André de Misson

GROUCHO MARX: That's what I always say: Love flies out the door when money comes innuendo.
  Monkey Business, script: S. J. Perelman, Will B. Johnstone, 1931

"Tell me, what's Love?" said Youth, one day,/To drooping Age, who crost his way.—/"It is a sunny hour of play,/For which repentance dear doth pay,/Repentance! Repentance!/And this is Love, as wise men say."
  Thomas Moore, Youth and Age

Women, as they grow older, rely more and more on cosmetics. Men, as they grow older, rely more and more on a sense of humor.
  George Jean Nathan, American Mercury, 1925

One must cease letting oneself be eaten when one tastes best: that is known to those who want to be loved long.
  Friedrich Nietzsche, Thus Spake Zarathustra, 1883–1891

Nothing cures like time and love.
  Laura Nyro, Time and Love, 1970

Love fed fat soon turns to boredom.
  Ovid, Love

Love may laugh at locksmiths, but he always has a profound respect for money bags.
  Sidney Paternoster, The Folly of the Wise, 1907

O Death, all-eloquent! you only prove/What dust we dote on, when 'tis man we love.
  Alexander Pope, Eloisa to Abelard, 1717

Some fellows marry poor girls to settle down, and others rich ones to settle up.
  The Pun Book

Who marrieth for love without money hath good nights and sorry days.
  John Ray, Proverbs, 1678

Time and love are both wasted so long as time remains working hours and love without a song.
  Eugen Rosenstock-Huessy

As I grow older and older/And totter towards the tomb/I find that I care less and less/Who goes to bed with whom.
  Dorothy L. Sayers

Is it not strange that desire should so many years outlive performance?
  William Shakespeare, Henry IV, Part II, 1598

Then let thy love be younger than thyself/Or thy affection cannot hold the bent.
  William Shakespeare, Twelfth Night, 1598–1600

Chains do not hold a marriage together. It is threads, hundreds of tiny threads which sew people together through the years. That is what makes a marriage last—more than passion or even sex!

    Simone Signoret, Daily Mail, 1978

Love is not a matter of counting the years—it's making the years count.

    Wolfman Jack Smith

Love is the emblem of eternity: it confounds all notion of time: effaces all memory of a beginning, all fear of an end.

    Mme. de Staël, Corinne, 1807

Times are changed with him who marries; there are no more by-path meadows, where you may innocently linger, but the road lies long and straight and dusty to the grave.

    Robert Louis Stevenson, Virginibus Puerisque, 1881

There will be sex after death, we just won't be able to feel it.

    Lily Tomlin

No man or woman really knows what perfect love is until they have been married a quarter of a century.

    Mark Twain, Notebooks, 1935

"After she was dead, I loved her." That is the story of every life—and death.

    Gore Vidal, The New York Review of Books, 1980

Will you love me in December as you do in May,/Will you love me in the good old fashioned way?/When my hair has all turned gray,/Will you kiss me then and say,/That you love me in December as you do in May?

    James J. Walker, Will You Love Me in December As You Do in May, 1905

Love conquers all things except poverty and toothache.
  Mae West

Apart/Must dwell those angels known as Peace and Love,/For only Death can reconcile the two.
  Ella Wheeler Wilcox, *Peace and Love*, 1912

Twenty years of romance make a woman look like a ruin, but twenty years of marriage make her something like a public building.
  Oscar Wilde

Young men want to be faithful and are not; old men want to be faithless, and cannot.
  Oscar Wilde, *The Picture of Dorian Gray*, 1891

Who, being loved, is poor?
  Oscar Wilde, *A Woman of No Importance*, 1893

Love is sweet, but tastes best with bread.
  Yiddish proverb

23. Fear and Loathing

When I love most Love is disguised/In Hate; and when Hate is surprised/In Love, then I hate most.
  Robert Browning, *Pippa Passes*, 1841

When Love becomes a command, Hatred can become a pleasure.
  Charles Bukowski, *Notes of a Dirty Old Man*, 1969

Now hatred is by far the longest pleasure;/Men love in haste, but they detest at leisure.

Lord Byron, *Don Juan*, 1819–1824

Few (especially young) people know how to love, or how to hate; their love is an unbounded weakness, fatal to the person they love; their hate is a hot, rash, and imprudent violence, always fatal to themselves.

Lord Chesterfield, *Letters*, 1752

When Love is suppressed Hate takes its place.

Havelock Ellis, *On Life and Sex: Essays of Love and Virtue*, 1937

The true opposite of love is not hate but indifference. Hate, bad as it is, at least treats the neighbour as a *thou*, whereas indifference turns the neighbour into an *it*, a thing.

Joseph Fletcher

Love that is ignorant and hatred have almost the same ends.

Ben Jonson, *Timber*, 1640

Hatred paralyzes life; love releases it. Hatred confuses life; love harmonizes it. Hatred darkens life; love illumines it.

Martin Luther King, Jr., *Strength to Love*, 1963

Mourning the loss of someone we love is happiness compared with having to live with someone we hate.

Jean de La Bruyère

Aversion gives love its death wound and forgetfulness buries it.

Jean de La Bruyère

We are nearer loving those who hate us than those who love us more than we wish.
> La Rochefoucauld, *Maxims*, 1665

If one judges love by the majority of its effects, it is more like hatred than friendship.
> La Rochefoucauld, *Maxims*, 1665

As the best wine doth make the sharpest vinegar, so the deepest love turneth to the deadliest hate.
> John Lyly, *Euphues*, 1579

To love you was pleasant enough,/And oh! 'Tis delicious to hate you!
> Thomas Moore

In one sense, the opposite of fear is courage, but in the dynamic sense the opposite of fear is love, whether this be love of man or love of justice.
> Alan Paton, *Saturday Review*, 1967

Years of love have been forgot/In the hatred of a minute.
> Edgar Allan Poe

SAMUEL S. HINDS: We hate the people we love because they're the only ones that can hurt us.
> *Private Worlds*, script: Lyn Starling, 1935

Oh, I have loved him too much to feel no hate for him.
> Jean Racine, *Andromache*, 1667

Hatreds are the cinders of affection.
> Sir Walter Raleigh, letter to Sir Robert Cecil, 1593

We love without reason, and without reason we hate.
> Jean François Régnard, *Les Folies Amoureuses*, 1704

Love is the direct opposite of hate. By *definition* it's something you can't feel for more than a few minutes at a time, so what's all this bullshit about loving somebody for the rest of your life.

> Judith Rossner, *Nine Months in the Life of an Old Maid*, 1969

It is a greater grief/To bear love's wrong than hate's known injury.

> William Shakespeare, *Sonnets*

Hatred which is entirely conquered by love passes into love, and love on that account is greater than if it had not been preceded by hatred.

> Baruch Spinoza, *Ethics*, 1677

ELIZABETH TAYLOR: Is that what love is? Using people? And maybe that's what hate is. Not being able to use people.

> *Suddenly Last Summer*, script: Gore Vidal, Tennessee Williams, 1959

Who cannot hate, can love not.

> Algernon Charles Swinburne, *In the Bay*, in *Collected Works*, 1904

This is the worst of life, that love does not give us common sense, but is a sure way of losing it. We love people, and we say that we were going to do more for them than friendship, but it makes such fools of us that we do far less, indeed sometimes what we do could be mistaken for the work of hatred.

> Rebecca West, quoted in Peter Wolfe *Rebecca West: Artist and Thinker*

Love lights more fire than hate extinguishes,/And men grow better as the world grows old.
    Ella Wheeler Wilcox, Optimism, 1912

24. Sisterhood Is Powerful

Lesbianism is far more than a sexual preference—it is a political stance.
    Sidney Abbott, Sappho Was a Right-On Woman, 1972

A woman needs a man like a fish needs a bicycle.
    Anonymous

The vast majority of women who pretend vaginal orgasms are faking it "to get the job."
    Ti-Grace Atkinson

The division of the sexes is a biological fact, not an event in history.
    Simone de Beauvoir, Esquire, 1971

Masculine desire is as much an offence as it is a compliment; in so far as she feels herself responsible for her charm, or feels she is exerting it of her own accord, she is much pleased with her conquests, but to the extent that her face, her figure, her flesh are facts she must bear with, she wants to hide them from this independent stranger who lusts after them.
    Simone de Beauvoir, The Second Sex, 1953

You may marry or you may not. In today's world that is no longer the question for women. Those who glom onto men so that they can collapse with relief, spend the rest of their days shining up their status symbol and figure they never have to reach, stretch, learn, grow, face dragons or make a living are the ones to be pitied. They, in my opinion, are the unfulfilled ones.

Helen Gurley Brown, *Sex and the Single Girl*, 1963

To love without role, without power plays, is revolution.

Rita Mae Brown, 1970

Rape is . . . nothing more or less than a conscious process of intimidation by which all men keep all women in a state of fear.

Susan Brownmiller, *Against Our Will*, 1975

I do not believe that a beautiful relationship has to always end in carnage. I do not believe that we have to be fraudulent and pretentious, because that is the source of future difficulties and ultimate failure. If we project fraudulent, pretentious images, or if we fantasize each other into distorted caricatures of what we really are, then, when we awake from the trance and see beyond the sham and front, all will dissolve, all will die and transform into bitterness and hate.

Eldridge Cleaver, *Soul on Ice*, 1968

Nothing contrasts more sharply with the masculine image of self-confidence, rationality and control than men's sulky, obtuse and, often virtually, total dependence on their wives to articulate and deal with their own unhappy feelings, and their own insensitivity, fear and passivity, in helping their wives to deal with theirs.

Marc Feigen Fasteau, *The Male Machine*, 1974

When modern woman discovered the orgasm it was (combined with modern birth control) perhaps the biggest single nail in the coffin of male dominance.

Eva Figes, quoted in E. Morgan, *The Descent of Woman*, 1972

We must not think that by saying yes to sex, one says no to power.

Michel Foucault, *History of Sexuality*, 1980

I, like other women, thought there was something wrong with me because I didn't have an orgasm waxing the kitchen floor.

Betty Friedan, *The Feminine Mystique*, 1977

To hell with love, Margaret thought. It's an ache in my stomach, it's a terrible feeling in my head, it's a skin crawling fear that I've done something wrong. I've forgotten the password and the frog isn't going to change into Prince Charming, the secret door isn't going to open. And the world isn't going to end any minute.

Shirley Ann Grau, *The Condor Passes*, 1971

If I had a cock for a day I would get myself pregnant.

Germaine Greer

The penis is obviously going the way of the vermiform appendix.

Jill Johnston

Bisexuality is not so much a copout as a fearful compromise.

Jill Johnston, *Lesbian Nation*, 1973

I'm saving the bass player for Omaha.

Janis Joplin

If men could get pregnant, abortion would be a sacrament.
    Florynce Kennedy, 1976

If a woman's husband gets on her nerves, she should fly at him. If she thinks him too sweet and smarmy with other people, she should let him have it on the nose, straight out. She should lead him a dog's life and never swallow her bile.
    D. H. Lawrence, *Fantasia of the Unconscious*, 1922

Just a few years ago, the husbands in her peer group had stroked her bare spine when she wore her backless black cocktail dress to parties and told her she figured spectacularly in their dream lives. Now that they were liberated, all the men she knew who had propositioned her had long since apologized and told her they really, *really* respected her as a person.
    Cyra McFadden, *The Serial*, 1978

Their first priority, Kate and Harvey agreed, was to work each other through their conflicts, stop laying bad trips on each other; and restructure their marriage. It was a heavy number, for sure; but they could do it.
    Cyra McFadden, *The Serial*, 1978

Don't accept rides from strange men/and remember that all men are strange as hell.
    Robin Morgan, *Sisterhood Is Powerful*, 1970

Women must come down off the pedestal. Men put us up there to get us out of the way.
    Lady Rhondda, *The Observer*, 1920

For there is no more defiant denial of one man's ability to possess one woman exclusively than the prostitute who refuses to be redeemed.

Gail Sheehy, Hustling, 1971

We are becoming the men we wanted to marry.

Gloria Steinem, 1978

The admission of women to complete equality with men would be the most certain mark of civilization: it would double the intellectual forces of the human race and its probabilities of happiness.

Stendhal, Rome, Naples, Florence, 1817

By the age of twelve, at the latest, most women have decided to become prostitutes. Or, to put it another way, they have planned a future for themselves which consists of choosing a man and letting him do all the work. In return for his support, they are prepared to let him make use of their vagina at certain given moments. The minute a woman has taken this decision she ceases to develop her mind.

Esther Vilar, The Manipulated Man, 1971

All that is good and commendable now existing would continue to exist if all marriage laws were repealed tomorrow. . . . I have an inalienable constitutional and natural right to love whom I may, to love as long or as short a period as I can, and to change that love every day if I please!

Victoria Woodhull, quoted in Germaine Greer, The Female Eunuch

25. *In Dreams*

If you want to be understood by anyone outside the University of Rome, speak clearly and say fuck, prick, cunt and arse. You and your thread in the eye, obelisk in the Colosseum, door in the orchard, bolt in the exit, key in the lock, pestle in the mortar, nightingale in the nest, dibble in the ditch, pump in the balloon, sword in the sheath, and then your stake and your crozier, your parsnip, sparrow, "him," "her," apples, leaves of the missal . . . Now why don't you say yes when you mean yes and no when you mean no or else shut up?

    Pietro Aretino, *Ragionamenti,* 1584

"Hold, rash one!" cried the tender Julie. "My dear love . . . oh God . . . I . . . I am dying!" and the words expired upon her rosy lips. The hour has struck in Cythera; love has brandished his torch on high; I fly upon wings; I do battle; the heavens open . . . I have won . . . oh Venus, cover us with the girdle of the Graces. . . .

    Count Mirabeau, *Ma Conversion,* 18th century

Never, oh never, shall I forget the delicious transports that followed the stiff insertion; and then, ah me! by what thrilling degrees did he, by his luxurious movement, fiery kisses, and strange touches of his hand to the most crimson parts of my body, reduce me to a voluptuous state of insensibility.

    The Lustful Turk, 1828

Tales of Twilight: or the Amorous Adventures of a Company of Ladies Before Marriage

The Royal Wedding Jester or All the Fun and Facetiae of the Wedding Night, with all the good things said, sung or done on that joyous occasion (reduced to ⅔)

Onanism Unveiled, or the Private Pleasures and Practices of the Youth of Both Sexes Exposed

The Connubial Guide, or Married People's Best Friend

The Spreeish Spouter or Flash Cove's Slap-Up Reciter

The Voluptuarian Cabinet or Man of Pleasure's Miscellany

The Wedding Night or the Battles of Venus

The Jolly Companion, Woman Disrobed (a most capital tale)

Adventures of a Bedstead

Venus in the Cloisters, or the Jesuit and the Nun

Julia or I Have Saved My Rose.

> *Henry Smith of the Strand, sales list, 1840s*

With what rapture do I view/The soft bosom's glassy hue!/Now my wanton fingers rove/O'er the beauteous mounds of love!/Now my eager lips I close/On each blooming, blushing rose!/Now my eager hand I slip/O'er the glossy marble hip!/And on each round swelling thigh/Cast my charm'd delighted eye.

> *The Exquisite, c. 1843*

My adored one, how lovely you are! What admirable hips! What an adorable—*arse!*

Oh! Alfred! What is that naughty word?

Don't be frightened, darling, lovers can say anything.

Those words, out of place in colder moments, add fresh relish to the sweet mystery of love. You will soon say them too, and understand their charm.

> *Voluptuous Confessions of a French Lady of Fashion, 1860*

Her lovely thighs and heavy mount of love, shaded by the softest golden-haired down, whilst one finger was fairly hidden within the fair lips of the pinkest possible slit below the dewy moisture from which glistened in the light . . . the battering ram of love had to be vigorously applied before a breach was made sufficient to effect a lodgment. What sighs, what murmurs of love and endearment were mixed with her moans of pain.

 The Boudoir: The Three Chums, 1860

. . . He wrapped his arms around her as she stood before him, tighter, tighter, and bent down his head from its stately height to her small uplifted face, nearer, nearer till their lips met, and were joined in a wedlock so fast, so long enduring, that it seemed as if they would never be divorced again.

 Rhoda Broughton, *Not Wisely But Too Well*, 1867

At the touch of her soft mouth, that has been to him hitherto, despite his nominal betrothal, a sealed book, his steadfast heart begins to pulse frantically fast; as if a river of flame instead of blood were pouring through his veins; they could not have throbbed with insaner heat.

 Rhoda Broughton, *Red As a Rose Is She*, 1870

Once, very near to the end, there came a gleam of light. The lips, which had been voiceless for many hours, moved faintly, and Edmund, leaning down to catch the feeble whisper, heard Sylvia's last words: "Kiss me once again before I go—as you kissed me in the churchyard—before I betrayed you. . . ." Living and dying lips met in the last kiss that had been fatal.

 Mary Elizabeth Braddon, *Taken at the Flood*, 1875

They seize her. One by one her garments are taken off, in spite of her struggles, disclosing first her beautiful polished shoulders, her round, firm, swelling virgin breasts, with a valley between them where Cupid himself might nestle his head in rapture. Her beautiful moulded arms, ripe, well formed waist, which, as she moved and writhed in their hands, showed suppleness of a most voluptuous character; and at last she stands before them panting, naked but for drawers, which she tenaciously clung round her, her beautiful eyes flashing with anger.

The Secret Life of Linda Brent, 1882

It was a second's flash of absolute beauty, a beauty expressive of the divinity of first love. To him it was the vision of the first woman in the first garden. They were the first of all cherry-flowers and the first of all wisterias; there had never been any others. Love suddenly flung aside the petals of his prison and stepped forth, dew-blown and laughing, into the first of all possible worlds.

Mrs. *Baillie-Saunders, London Lovers*, 1906

A madness of tender caressing seized her. She purred as a tiger might have done, while she undulated like a snake. She touched him with her fingertips, she kissed his throat, his wrists, the palms of his hands, his eyelids, his hair. Strange subtle kisses, unlike the kisses of women. And often, between her purrings she murmured lovewords in some fierce language of her own, brushing his ears and his eyes with her lips the while. And through it all, Paul slept on, the Eastern perfume in the air drugging his senses.

Elinor Glyn, *Three Weeks*, 1907

His quick breath scorched her face, and in a moment almost before she knew what was happening, his lips were on her own. He kissed her as she had never been kissed before—a single fiery kiss that sent all the blood in tumult to her heart. She shrank and quivered under it, but she was powerless to escape. There was sheer unshackled savagery in the holding of his arms and dismay thrilled her through and through.

Ethel M. Dell, *The Knave of Diamonds*, 1913

Terror, agonising, soul-shaking terror such as she had never imagined, took hold of her. The flaming light of desire burning in his eyes turned her sick and faint. Her body throbbed with the consciousness of a knowledge that appalled her. She understood his purpose with a horror that made each separate nerve in her system shrink against the understanding that had come to her under the consuming fire of his ardent gaze, and in the fierce embrace that was drawing her shaking limbs closer and closer against the man's own pulsating body. She writhed in his arms as he crushed her to him in a sudden access of possessive passion. His head bent slowly down to her, his eyes burned deeper, and, held immovable, she endured the first kiss she had ever received. And the touch of his scorching lips, the clasp of his arms, the close union with his warm strong body robbed her of all strength, of all power of resistance.

E. M. Hull, *The Sheik*, 1919

Her lips were fire on his cheeks. The perfume of her was the fire in his mind. Her arms were chains, chains of fire about his body. He crushed her to him; crushed her mouth under his lips. Her whole body ached for him, ached to surrender itself. A sharp pang as of hatred went through her body; she hated him for the thing he could not do; hated herself for the longings in her body.

Gilbert Frankau, *The Love Story of Aliette Brunton*, 1922

CLARK GABLE: There's one thing I *do* know, and that is that I love you, Scarlett. In spite of you and me and the whole silly world going to pieces around us, I love you. Because we're alike—bad lots both of us, selfish and shrewd, but able to look things in the eyes and call them by their right names.

> *Gone with the Wind,* script: Sidney Howard, 1939

Now she was sealed fast in his arms. She had no resistance left. Her last vestige of control snapped and vanished when she felt his heart beat against her own. She would never forget the magic of those arms, and of those lips which brushed her lashes and strayed to her quivering mouth. He was a wonderful, masterful lover. There could never have been, there could never again be such a lover.

> Denise Robins, *This One Night,* 1942

"Leonie, you will do well to consider. You are not the first woman in my life." She smiled through her tears. "Monseigneur, I would so much rather be the last woman, than the first," she said.

> Georgette Heyer, *These Old Shades,* 1926

Bond . . . put one hand in her hair so that he could hold her mouth where he wanted it. And after a while his other hand went to the zip fastener at the back of her dress and without moving away from him she stepped out of her dress and panted between their kisses. "I want it all, James. Everything you've ever done to a girl. Now. Quickly." And Bond bent down and put an arm round her thighs and picked her up and laid her gently on the floor.

> Ian Fleming, *Diamonds Are Forever,* 1956

Bond's eyes were fierce blue slits. He got up and went down on one knee beside her. He picked up her hand and looked into it. At the base of the thumb the Mount of Venus swelled luxuriously. Bond bent his head down into the warm soft hand and bit softly into the swelling. He felt her other hand in his hair. He bit harder. The hand he was holding curled round his mouth. She was panting. He bit still harder. She gave a little scream and wrenched his head away by the hair. "What are you doing?" Her eyes were wide and dark. She had gone pale. She dropped her eyes and looked at his mouth. Slowly she pulled his head down towards her. Bond put out a hand to her left breast and held it hard. He lifted her captive, wounded hand and put it round his neck. Their mouths met and clung, exploring. Above them, the candles began to dance.

Ian Fleming, *Dr. No*, 1958

There must be nymphomaniacs in the world. They do exist, they're not made up. They don't belong in the world of mythology. Why do you think people write about them? Where do you think they get their information? "I tell you solemnly, Sir Hugh, that the woman is prey to dark, insensate passions—passions that neither you nor I would have suspected in a woman of her breeding." I'm not talking about trash now, I'm talking about well-informed authors. Modern writers. "I'm going to have you Tim" she said quite flatly, as though ordering seedcake. "I don't mind whether it's in the Senior Common Room or in bed . . ." This isn't put in for effect. This is character. They have met these people. Look at detective stories . . . American novels. *The Hot and the Cold.* "They sank slowly to the bathroom floor and it was wrong and dangerous but it was clean and good and the tiles felt cool against her burning shoulder," "Write about what you know," you see—Mr. Arnold Bennet, quoted in *Hobbies Digest* June '59.

"Slowly the rich, musquash coat fell apart. She was completely naked except for wispy suspender belt and sheer black stockings."

Keith Waterhouse, *Jubb*, 1963

Dear Mr. . . . Thank you for your enquiry. We feel confident you are not interested in the Sterile type of Childish Pin-Up Photos which are flooding the market at the moment. The collections listed below are ALL HAND PRINTED POSTCARD ENLARGEMENTS, taken from Negatives which have come into our possession from the Libraries of PRIVATE COLLECTORS POSSESSION. Many originate from FRANCE and other less Orthodox Cities in Europe. They are intended for and CAN ONLY BE SOLD TO RESPONSIBLE PERSONS WHO ARE PREPARED TO USE THE UTMOST DISCRETION WITH THEIR USE. They come to you exactly as the lens of the Camera recorded the INTIMATE DETAIL—COMPLETELY UNMUTILATED. . . . All are calculated to REVEAL MAXIMUM INTIMATE ANATOMICAL DETAIL. . . .
Collection No. 2   A SENSATIONAL AND FRENZIED COLLECTION OF CONTINENTAL LOVELIES IN TEN AMAZING AND THRILLING CONTORTION STUDIES that will have even the Experienced Adult Connoisseur astounded. UNBELIEVABLE POSTURES with VIVID and SUBTLE MIRROR DETAIL. Posed by these RAVISHING GIRLS FOR YOUR BREATHLESS VIEWING!!!!! TERRIFIC!!!!! AND STIMULATING!!!!!   . . .45/-.

Pornographer, quoted in W. Young, *Eros Denied*, 1965

Of course, it's so much easier, let's be frank, to write a romantic book set in an old-fashioned era than today, because then virginity counts. You can write a whole book on somebody protecting their virginity as long as they're in costume—it's very difficult in a permissive society.

Barbara Cartland, quoted in Rachel Anderson, *The Purple Heart Throbs*, 1974

I don't really think that romantic novels should be called "romantic" really. Between you and me, I think they're basically twisted sex stories. I mean, it is a bit sadistic, isn't it, to be reading about a man blowing his top with frustration because he can't get it. And I think women love reading all this stuff because it gives them a bit of a thrill to think about it. . . . Good God, I tell you, honestly, sometimes I get so worked up myself writing the stuff that I don't know what to do.

> *Violet Winspear, quoted in Rachel Anderson, The Purple Heart Throbs, 1974*

I hold that love—using the word in its accepted sense—being the forerunner of birth, cannot possibly be excluded from any novel or any story which attempts to depict life whole.

> *Gilbert Frankau, quoted in Rachel Anderson, The Purple Heart Throbs, 1974*

She fought in her mind to escape him, but her body was swept by sensations against which she had fought for too long. With the rush of a bursting dam, the flood of desire drowned her mind.

> *Charlotte Lamb, Duel of Desire, 1976*

In a short time, the pain receded. His kisses nearly smothered her, and Sarah felt a strange warmth spread throughout her lower body. Not exactly pleasurable, yet not wholly unpleasant either, it puzzled her. And even more strange, her body seemed to have a will of its own, wanting to move, wanting to meet his thrust. . . . Was it possible that a second time would not be unpleasant at all, might even bring her some pleasure?

> *Patricia Matthews, Love's Wildest Promise, 1978*

The Runaway Wife; The Virgin Swappers; Her Sister's Revenge; The Lonely Bride; Brother, Sister and Father; The Young Widow; A Family Affair; His Mother's Girl Friend; The Young Salesgirl; The Wife's Desire; Teacher's Young Boy; The Wife's Punishment; Lesson for the Bride; Intimate Neighbors; Health Spa Wife; The Blackmailed Wife; The Mayor's Wife; The Innocent Actress; The New Teacher; The Farmer's Daughter; Tricked into White Slavery; Black Fashion Model; The New Secretary; The Salesman's Wife.

Monterey Library Press, order form, 1978

The Heroine: always young . . . not beautiful in the high fashion sense, is basically an ingenue and wears modest make-up and clothes . . . she has a good figure and is often petite and slight of build . . . in spite of her fragile appearance, she is independent, high-spirited and not too subservient. She should not be mousy and weepy . . . though she wants to work, and plans to after marriage, her home and children will always come first. She is almost always a virgin. . . .

Silhouette Romances, style sheet, 1980

Love Scenes: . . . descriptions of love-making should be sensuous with some details. They cannot be limited to "he kissed her passionately" . . . nudity is permissible . . . but it should not be too graphic. The only pain permitted is the sweet pain of fulfilled (or unfulfilled) desire.

Silhouette Romances, style sheet, 1980

The Other Woman: usually mean, over-sophisticated, well-groomed. She often catches the heroine in embarrassing situations—in a tender scene with the hero, dressed in old clothes, etc. She *never* gets our hero.

Silhouette Romances, style sheet, 1980

Love is a mystery full of twists and surprises that are not predictable by science or reason. It is natural that its infinite variations should be probed most interestingly by novelists rather than by experts and statisticians: no one has dared set up a Chair of Amorology.

Theodore Zeldin, London Review of Books, 1980

I tried to hustle him on to the floor to get as much time as possible in his arms! And once there, it was Heaven. Tony held me gently—though of course I longed for him to crush me in a passionate embrace—and I rested my head on his shoulder as we moved slowly round the floor. His hand on my waist seemed to be burning right through the thin material of my dress, and I could smell his lovely, tangy after-shave. I had my arms round his neck, and his thick, dark hair brushed against my hands. Suddenly I had an overwhelming urge to twine strands of it round my fingers—but of course, I didn't. Not yet . . . I had to be sure Tony felt the same way about me before I put my cards on the table. . . . So I had to keep working on Ruth..

Love Affair Magazine, 1982

Jenny Browning has become Jenny Miller, married after a whirlwind courtship to a man she hardly knows. Peter has already attacked a man and a woman in the street, only to completely forget the incident later. But when the woman is revealed to be Barbara, his divorced wife, it's Jenny herself who suffers at Peter's hands. Peter seems to forget that incident too, but he's forced to face reality by Barbara and her new husband, intent on getting his signature for legal purposes. Having to accept their existence creates a traumatic shock in Peter's mind—a breakdown from which Jenny fears her husband will never recover. . . .

Photo-Love and Secret Love Magazine, 1980

Index